The Joshua Principle
Leadership Secrets of RSVPselling™
— © 2010 —
Tony J. Hughes: Sydney Australia
All Rights Reserved

First published: March 2010
Second printing: July 2010
Third printing: January 2011
www.RSVPselling.com

Editors: Catherine Bradshaw, Barry Hughes and Matt Wills

Cover and book design: Tim Madden, Louie Creative
www.louiecreative.com

Illustrations and logo design: Laura Barber
www.thesunthemoonandthestars.com.au

Proof reading: Caroline McGrory, Barry Hughes and Richard Bradshaw

ISBN: 978-0-646-51340-9
Dewey Number: 658.85

Cataloguing-in-Publishing (CiP) details available from
National Library of Australia
www.nla.gov.au
Book also deposited with State Library of New South Wales

Narrative typeset: Helvetica Neue LT 9 point
E-mail typeset: Arial Narrow 9 point
Other text: Times New Roman 10 point

Spelling is deliberately an amalgam of UK and USA English.

Praise For RSVPselling™

"I'm very impressed with The Joshua Principle and I hope that the readable format brings it to the attention of the wide audience it deserves."

Professor Neil Rackham
Creator of SPIN Selling™
Author of three New York Times bestsellers

"This is next generation selling, and professional selling for the next generation. Everyone who has read SPIN Selling needs to also read this book."

Adrian Rudman
General Manager, Marketing
Objective Corporation

"The RSVPselling™ concepts enabled me to achieve over 700% of my annual quota, quadruple my income, and become the number one sales person world-wide. RSVPselling™ is a proven winner!"

Brett Shields
Senior Sales Executive
Hummingbird Corporation

"Finally we have a book about professional selling that's also great to read! A fascinating blend of instruction and entertainment with a plot that keeps you guessing right to the end. Buy one for yourself and every salesperson you want to be successful."

Andrew Everingham
Public Relations Director, Asia-Pacific
Salesforce.com

"The principles laid out in this book are used by our solutions selling teams across the region with phenomenal success. As one of the largest SAP system integrators and applications transformation consulting organizations globally, we rely heavily on having tools that are simple to understand, use and deliver immediate benefits. I loved the story based approach and this book is a definite must for every aspiring sales professional"

Brian E. Pereira
Head of Asia-Pacific, Japan, India and the Middle East
HCL - AXON

Presented to

_____

The Joshua Principle
Leadership Secrets of RSVPselling™

— © 2010 —
Tony J. Hughes: Sydney Australia
All Rights Reserved

® Registered International Trade Mark
Tony J. Hughes: Sydney, Australia
All rights reserved

Website: www.RSVPselling.com

Contact: mail@RSVPselling.com

Foreword: By Michael Le Master

This book can unlock the potential that lies within and is ideal for anyone seeking to understand the power and value of positive influence. The concepts and philosophy within these pages can inspire entire sales teams to embrace transformational change that creates genuine value for customers and improved revenue and profit results for sales organizations.

Tony Hughes has taken complexity and made it elegantly simple. He has combined the powerful emotions of life with the science and art of professional selling. In doing so, Tony has successfully married business strategy with the time-proven principles of success. This book reveals a powerful new paradigm for conducting business in today's world and elevates professional selling like never before. This is the best professional selling book I've read in my 30 year sales career.

When I first discovered the RSVPselling.com website I was amazed with how the concepts resonated with my own approach to professional selling. When I subsequently read this book, I was drawn into the professional and personal journey of Joshua Peters and wanted the same transformational experience for the sales people I mentor and coach. The power of the internet had linked me to a like-minded soul on the other side of the world and I immediately established a partnership where I am enthusiastically promoting RSVPselling™ in North America.

Every business leader and sales professional we engage in coaching or training is now exposed to the concepts in this book which can be implemented effectively in the real world. Success today requires a sales person to be adept at managing complexity by creating clarity, focusing on value and navigating organizational politics, personal agendas and competing business priorities. This book will challenge and inspire you to convert your potential into higher levels of success. Enjoy discovering The Joshua Principle for yourself and the transformational power of thinking RSVP in everything you do.

Michael Le Master is a Revenue Advisor®, Revenue Coach®, strategist, speaker, and the President and Founder of Sales Coaches International and Revenue Advisors. The ability to provide structure and consistency to sales processes, systems and selling skills is the hallmark of his disciplined approach to growth.

The Joshua Principle
Leadership Secrets of RSVPselling™

Prelude

Everyone sells. Some do it as their profession. Few become masterful.

I was twenty-seven when my mentorship began. I remember, like it was yesterday, opening the Fed-Ex package from Germany and wondering what was inside the intricate wooden box. It contained an invitation that triggered a sequence of events which changed the course of my life forever. Back then, I was a salesman in the telecommunications industry. It was ironic that I helped people and systems to communicate, yet I was completely disconnected from my father – the man best equipped to assist me in my career.

This is a story about the way our lives are interconnected. Sometimes we clash, sometimes we coalesce, but every now and then we truly connect. For Tony Hughes and me, our lives intersected because of two cancelled flights and time spent waiting in an airport Club Lounge watching the PGA. We initially talked about the golf but as the conversation went progressively deeper, Tony became interested in how I had become Vice President of Worldwide Sales at such a young age in a large corporation. He was a lecturer in business leadership at the University of Sydney and he was fascinated with the role a mentor had played in the redirection of my career and life. We stayed in touch and developed an enduring friendship.

Over time, Tony convinced me to allow him to tell this story. In reconstructing the events, I provided him with access to all of the correspondence between my mentor and me, and introductions to the key people he wanted to interview. Although many of the e-mails are not included in this book, he tells the story as it happened.

Suspend judgment as you read. Maybe learn from my experience and the wisdom of a mentor who made an amazing difference. I hope that through this book you will come to view professional selling differently and that you can find greater success and purpose in your career. I also hope this book provides you with a more strategic approach and a framework for excellence in execution.

I've always been attracted to selling but I used to hope it would lead to something better – I've grown to understand that selling *is* better. My father was promoted to CEO after a spectacular career in sales and I suspect selling is in my genes. Maybe we all have an innate desire and ability to sell, but only a few become masterful in influencing others for the creation of real value.

One day I'll write a book recounting the story of my dad and his father (my grandfather) which precedes the events you're about to read here. That story, and the one within this book, have much in common – never underestimate the importance of influence or the power of a father's love for his son.

The Joshua Principle was named after me by my mentor but my sincere wish is that you also make it your own, as something that guides your career and life.

Yours fully there,

Joshua Peters

Chapter One: Restless Ambition

Every business and every family is dysfunctional in its own special way.

The Peters clan appeared idyllic against a backdrop of material prosperity and good manners, yet nothing is ever truly as it seems. Joshua stood on the veranda of the family home in the early evening drinking a glass of wine. He had not set foot in his parent's house in three years and only returned now for his sister's twenty-first birthday. He had mixed emotions about being there but was glad to see Annie. She had graduated from university and just secured a cadetship with one of the big law firms. *At least one of Mark Peters' children has followed the tried and true pathway to success*, Joshua thought.

Joshua's teenage years had been dominated by a steady deterioration in the relationship with his father. Tensions simmered, occasionally boiling over, but as Joshua grew older the stakes increased and the arguments became more intense. He told his parents he was not going to finish his economics degree but instead move to London with his girlfriend. His father, Mark, had lived by the adage that there are no shortcuts to success. Hardworking, tenacious and resourceful, he had become his corporation's youngest ever CEO. The last thing he wanted was his son to abandon university. Joshua, however, abhorred being lectured by the man he regarded as a judgmental relic from times long past.

On the night it happened, they argued until the inevitable explosion. The yelling reverberated off the kitchen walls as father and son went head to head while mother and daughter clung to the wreckage. Joshua remembered shoving his father, the scuffle, the sounds of his mother screaming, and Mark falling backwards as if in slow motion. He remembered his sister crying, his father's bleeding face, smashed Waterford crystal, and a photo frame lying face-up in shards of broken glass – a picture of a father and son in a small fishing boat. Now they *really were* all at sea.

Three years had passed and now he was back at the scene of the crime. The prodigal had returned to face the father once more and Joshua was not sure what to expect, he certainly wasn't seeking a warm embrace. The only communication with his father in the last few years had been filtered through his mother. He poured himself another glass of wine as fortification against the imminent face-to-face reunion.

He had been back in Australia for five months and was heavily in debt but resurrecting a career that had stalled in London. He comforted himself with the fact that he had landed with job offers from two recruiting agencies. Joshua could feel his mobile phone vibrating in his pocket. He usually had it on silent and preferred to wait for a voicemail or text message. He liked to think it maintained control, but subconsciously he knew it was an avoidance technique. He waited and then looked at the missed call number – it was Mandy, another deal he failed to close. They had divided the possessions accumulated during a five year relationship and he knew she was calling about collecting the big screen television with her brother. It had been the most bitterly disputed item, and Mandy ensured she had won to make a point.

His father had seen the break-up of Joshua and Mandy as inevitable but his mother, Clare, had been particularly upset. She and Mandy had a special relationship and she regarded Mandy as the ideal partner for her son. Before the pair moved to London, Mandy had been the only person to ever give her a run for her money at Scrabble. They had occasionally managed to get her husband and son to join them despite their mutual aversion to the board game; chess had once been their preferred leisure activity, before Joshua felt perpetually in check – now he preferred stalemate.

Joshua met the guests who were starting to arrive but there was no sign of his father. *Typical*, he thought, *never around when needed but when he does arrive, in the nick of time, it will be a grand entrance no doubt*. He went to the kitchen to find a corkscrew after collecting a fresh bottle from the ice buckets on the veranda. His mother joined him.

"I'll say one thing for Dad, he doesn't buy cheap wine."

"Go easy please. Remember what happened the last time we were all together in this house."

Clare had not meant to sound acerbic but she was tired of carrying the grief of her family's disintegration. She wanted to keep the peace for Annie's sake and knew that alcohol was fuel to the fire.

"Don't worry. I'm playing wine waiter for Annie."

Clare re-joined the guests and Joshua moved back to the veranda where he could avoid his mother's judgmental looks. He saw an airport limousine pull into the driveway with his father handing over his credit card. Joshua retreated to the corner, out of sight and waited for the inevitable. Within a minute he heard the familiar, larger than life voice – Mark Peters had arrived.

"Where's my birthday girl?" Annie laughed and embraced her dad. Mark was not yet aware of his son's presence and Joshua was happy to be forgotten in the shadows outside until more guests arrived. The house was soon full of Annie's friends, elderly aunts and a few cousins. Joshua was aware he'd already had too much to drink and considered slipping away. He was scrolling through his phone contacts getting ready to call a cab when his father stepped outside. Mark had retrieved a bottle of champagne from the ice and was busy dispensing with the foil wrapping, unaware he was being observed by his son.

Joshua was taken aback by his father's appearance. This was the first time he had seen him in years, and Mark had aged, he no longer seemed indomitable. Three steps forward would put him into his father's line of vision. Almost involuntarily, he stepped out into the light.

"Hello Dad."

Mark Peters turned his head. "Your mother said you'd come – I'm glad you're here."

Then with a twist of his wrist he released the cork with a muffled pop. He smiled, turned and walked casually back into the house with the bottle of champagne. It was an anti-climax but his father's casual façade had been betrayed by his initial expression the moment he heard his son's voice. Joshua felt both relieved and disappointed.

Minutes later, Joshua circulated politely and did his best not to slur his words. He avoided his father as he mingled, and within an hour the cake was cut. Joshua called his cab and slipped away after hugging Annie and wishing her a happy birthday.

He arrived home to find Mandy had taken the television and left a note with her key. It simply said that she hadn't been able to find the remote and would collect it another time. *It's finally over*, he thought as he collapsed into bed in his rented granny flat. The darkness seemed to torment him. The restless ambition of his youth had been frustrated and battered by the realities of life. His thoughts drifted to the shattered picture of a boy in a fishing boat with his dad, and he was surprised when he felt a tear roll past his ear onto the pillow.

Mark had seen the last relative into a taxi and hugged Annie goodnight as she headed out with friends to continue partying. He sat exhausted on the lounge before speaking with Clare.

"Joshua was drunk."

"When did you speak with him?"

"I went to get more champagne and he stepped out of the shadows. He took me by surprise."

"What did you say?" Clare's question was tentative.

"I didn't know what to say. It's been a long time since I've heard his voice. I said I was glad to see him, but then he avoided me all night."

"You didn't say anything else, like welcome home or I've missed you Son?"

"I didn't want to say the wrong thing or trigger any distractions. This was Annie's night."

Clare rubbed her forehead with exhaustion. "You might get another chance to talk with him tomorrow. He left his car here."

"Thank God he had the sense to call a cab."

"Mark, please – no judgments."

"You know my mother was killed by a drunk. I'm just relieved that he didn't get behind the wheel."

"Your parents are long gone but your son is still here. He needs you – and you need him."

Mark reflected on Clare's words. He was now in his late fifties and more aware of his own mortality. He knew that his children, rather than his success in business, would be the most meaningful measure of his life after he was gone.

"I was so determined to avoid what happened with my own father, yet I allowed Joshua to drift away. He hasn't returned a call in years. It's all so broken with him."

"Reach out when he comes back tomorrow to get his car."

"I'm not sure how to."

"Ask him to play golf. Maybe you should stop behaving like his father and start being his friend. He's a man now and you need to accept that."

They went to bed but Mark lay staring at the ceiling, pondering the relationship with his son – time had not healed the past. He needed to act and slipped quietly out of bed after Clare was asleep. He went to his study downstairs, determined to find a way to repair the relationship before it was too late. Mark stared at the photo on his desk, Joshua and him in a small fishing boat, taken fifteen years earlier. It was his most treasured memory of the good times, yet the chipped frame was a constant reminder of how things had gone awry.

Mark thought back to when he was the same age as Joshua in the photo. His own teenage years had been filled with conflict with his father, and Mark reflected on how generations can repeat the very dysfunction they intend to avoid. He knew Clare was right – he needed to back away from judging and instructing. It was time to say sorry and work on becoming a friend, but he still wanted to help him get his life and career back on track – he sensed that Joshua was lost.

Mark had been mentored though a school program back in his youth and again later in his business life. He considered the possibilities for Joshua and sat making notes, leafing through his business cards and contacts. Mark's network was global, and the more he thought about it, jotting ideas, the more optimistic he became concerning the potential for his son.

Clare appeared in the doorway. "What are you doing? It's after three o'clock!"

Annie knocked on Joshua's door at around 11:00am. "Thanks for at least hanging about until we cut the cake. You look like crap."

"I left early because I didn't want any dramas with Dad on your birthday."

"So are you going to invite me in? I thought you'd want a ride back to get your car."

Annie stepped inside with a look of wry amusement on her face. "Wow! Is this place retro or just bad taste?" Annie wasn't known for her subtlety.

"I'm just here while I get back on my feet. The rent is cheap and the landlady does my washing. Elizabeth is kind of like the grandmother I never had."

"Go and have a shower and I'll make you a coffee."

Annie looked around and sighed. Mandy's departure had left the place looking sparse and she could see Joshua would no doubt become a valuable Ikea customer as he rebuilt his life. *If only families could be reassembled like kit furniture*, she thought while waiting for the water to boil. She pondered the conflicted relationship between her brother and father – *surely we had the same upbringing*. They had both lived with the fact that their father had a job that required incessant travel but Annie had always been more self sufficient. Her childhood and teenage memories were wonderful and her relationship with her father was positive. She knew Mark loved her despite working long hours to provide for their upbringing. Vacations were always fun and she couldn't understand why, for Joshua, his experience was so different. Her father and brother were both restless types, regularly reaching beyond their grasp, and there seemed to be a gravitational field that caused them to collide. For Annie, it was all a troubling mystery.

Joshua finally emerged after his shower and she handed him a coffee.

"Thanks, I need this. I feel a little bit second-hand."

"So where's your television?"

Joshua gave his sister a pointed glare.

"Don't tell me you got the bed and she took the television?"

"Well, yes, but…"

Annie laughed. "I always liked Mandy. She's good. You don't get to watch the thing that constantly annoyed her and if you do manage to lure someone else back here, she knows you'll be thinking of her while you're doing the business!"

Joshua saw nothing funny, and Annie realized that she had unintentionally cut too deeply.

"I'm sorry about everything Josh, you and Mandy made a great couple."

"Yeah, but I guess it's time to move on."

"One broken relationship is enough – you should give Dad another chance. He really does love you."

"I don't want to talk about it. Let's go, so I can collect my car."

"You're so stubborn! Do you know you're part of the problem too?"

They drove in silence. Joshua had no intention of going inside but his father was standing in the driveway watering the garden as they arrived.

"Hi Josh. Sorry we didn't get to talk last night."

I guess we'll all pretend the past never happened, Joshua thought as he hesitantly shook his father's hand.

Annie broke the tension. "Mandy took Joshua's TV. Can he borrow your old one?"

Mark responded before Joshua could protest. "Sure, the picture rolls sometimes but it's better than nothing."

"Why don't you stay for lunch?" Joshua looked up to see his mother smiling down at him from the veranda. He glanced across at his father who nodded warmly.

"Okay, but I can't stay for long."

Clare and Annie worked to create momentum as they all sat eating but Joshua was subdued and Mark was being careful not to say the wrong thing. They all searched for shallow safe ground and the conversation eventually turned to work after they discussed Annie's cadetship.

"Is this job working out son?" Mark instantly regretted his phrasing – an accidental spark cast onto gunpowder.

"What do you mean, *this* job?"

Annie jumped in. "Come on Josh, Dad didn't mean anything by it."

"No, Annie, I think he did. What do you really want to say to me Dad? That I can't seem to get it right? That you told me going to London would be a disaster? That Mandy was too good for me? Come on! Tell us all what the *great* Mark Peters really thinks of his son."

Mark breathed deeply before lifting his eyes to Joshua.

"Son, I don't want this for us anymore. I've made mistakes but can't you forgive me – please? Let's move on."

Mark desperately wanted to say more. He saw so much of himself in Joshua and it frightened him – he didn't want to watch his son replicate his mistakes. He wanted to acknowledge that he had lectured instead of listened, that he had been a critic when he should have been an encourager, that he had been away when he should have been there – but words and explanations were of no use now. Their communication had been at cross purposes for so long that the simpler the message, the better chance it could be received as intended.

There was a long awkward silence. "It's not that simple."

Annie leaned toward Joshua. "Dad just apologized. What's wrong with you?"

"I have to go. Thanks for lunch."

Joshua rose abruptly while his family sat paralyzed, not quite knowing how to respond. The table was silent as the front door slammed shut.

Joshua was about to start his engine when Annie appeared on the front veranda glaring at him and shaking her head. He was taken aback by her angry body language but rationalized it away as collateral damage from the feud with his father. He hit the ignition, shrugged at her, and roared down the road.

A few hours later, Joshua was preparing to go out when there was a knock at the door. He was already running late and hoped it wasn't the landlady, there was no such thing as a short conversation with Elizabeth. He was surprised to see his father standing there.

"I've got the television. Can you give me a hand to carry it inside?"

They slid it out of Clare's four wheel drive and Joshua was forced to face his father as they shuffled up the narrow path. Joshua felt uncomfortable with their proximity and intimidated by his father's eye contact. He felt relieved when they finally set it down. Joshua plugged it in and Mark produced the remote from his back pocket, pressing the button that crackled the box to life.

"If you give it a thump on the side it usually stops the picture from rolling. Keep it for as long as you need it."

Mark handed over the remote and Joshua turned it off.

"Thanks for bringing it over but I can't talk now. I'm running late to meet friends."

"It's okay, we can talk when you're ready."

"No, it's not that I don't want to talk. I really am running late and I'm keeping them waiting."

Mark realized that he had accidentally hit a raw nerve. "I'll be off then."

As Mark walked down the path, Joshua stood contemplating another miscommunication. He felt guilty for not being able to forgive the sins of the past. Deep down he knew he was equally to blame – maybe more so.

"Dad!"

Mark stopped and turned.

Joshua was unsure of what he really wanted to say. "Thanks for coming over with the TV."

Mark smiled and nodded. He turned and continued walking before Joshua could see his real emotions.

Chapter Two: The Invitation

It had been two months since Annie's party and the few subsequent interactions with his father had been cordial and uneventful. Joshua had managed to avoid dealing with the unresolved relationship with his father but he wanted to reconnect with Mandy. He still loved her and had tried to use the television remote as a reason to meet, but to no avail – none of his messages or e-mails had been returned.

Joshua's London experience had proved he had a talent for selling and he knew it paid well and could fast-track him up through an organization. He was performing well in his new job but had just discovered the deal he was counting on to make his numbers for the year was gone. He had told his boss that it would slip into next quarter but, in truth, he knew it had slid off the face of the planet. Three weeks earlier, at a sales meeting, Joshua had confidently forecast the revenue. The client was seeking price clarifications and, in Joshua's mind, the earlier technical hiccups were behind them. He had a good relationship with one of the project team members and he had tested the possibility, with the project manager, of using special pricing to close the deal.

Joshua wondered what had happened in the last three weeks. He thought the deal was 'his to lose' and was careful not to oversell, nor introduce any new information. But when they went quiet and stopped returning his calls, he knew that something was wrong. He worried that his competitor was desperately meddling but he was unable to confirm his suspicions. Unwanted questions began to come from the client and no amount of effort countered the weaknesses that were being systematically exposed. The rules had been changed and Joshua now felt that he was a victim of someone else's agenda.

He fought hard internally to secure a substantial discount if an order was placed in the current month. Price was the final card he would play. *Surely my relationships and a killer offer will get me over the line,* Joshua thought. He was about to discover that false hope intensifies the pain of failure.

He and his boss, Michael Blunt, went together to close the deal, but the Chief Financial Officer (CFO) cancelled at the last minute and they were left meeting with the project manager and Information Technology (IT) manager. The IT manager was polite but non-committal.

"If you can put the offer in writing, we'll take it to the team and get back to you. Thanks for making the effort to come in."

Joshua's attempts to get them to engage meaningfully proved futile and Michael agitated them when he intimated that he would phone the CFO directly. Joshua fumed as they walked to the car.

"How the hell can you work a deal for months building good relationships and then get treated like crap without explanation? They'll just take our revised price and use it as leverage on whom they really want to buy from."

There was no sympathy from his boss. Instead, he received a caustic lecture. "Sell the value of our solution before you go discounting! I went out on a limb to get that pricing and they clearly weren't ready to be closed. We met with the wrong people today. Why didn't you cover the CFO and confirm he was going to be there?"

Joshua knew Michael was venting. The questions were rhetorical and there was nothing to be gained by defending himself. The twenty minute trip back to the office was filled with stilted lectures and pointed questions. The tension was palpable and Joshua was relieved when they finally reached the office car park. He told Michael that he had another appointment to go to. Joshua was lying.

At home, Joshua sat stewing, staring blankly at a dating game show on the dilapidated television on loan from his father. *Desperate and dateless.* He missed Mandy. At twenty-seven, he had not anticipated living alone in a granny flat eating frozen meals thawed in the microwave. *Ironic,* he thought, as he reflected on the day's events. He realized there was much more at stake in this deal than he wished to acknowledge. He was drawn out of his brooding by a knock at the door. It was Elizabeth, the landlady. *Just what I need – a twenty minute chat about nothing.*

"Hi Elizabeth, it's a bad time right now. I need to make some phone calls for work."

Elizabeth was holding the courier package like a Christmas gift. "They insisted I sign for it, so it must be important."

Joshua focused on the package and could see it had been sent from Germany. "Thanks. I really appreciate you bringing it over."

The package was weighty and he was curious to see what was inside. He struggled to tear open the plastic satchel and resorted to using scissors. He pulled out a wooden box cocooned in bubble wrap. As he removed the wrapping he was astonished to see his name skillfully burned into the lid. *They're spending a lot of money on direct marketing these days*, he thought.

The box was a work of impeccable craftsmanship. It was bigger than a cigar box but smaller than what would be required to package a bottle of wine. Nautical in appearance, the lid was recessed and held shut with a dozen fine brass countersunk screws. He went to the garage to find a small screwdriver. After carefully removing the recessed lid, he discovered an envelope and what appeared to be an antique pocket-watch. He opened the thick hinged cover, revealing a simple yet elegant compass with an inscription inside: TRUE NORTH – OD DAS VEILS. He turned his attention to the envelope which had his name hand written on the front and on the back the letters RSVP were embossed on a red wax seal.

He studied the sender's details on the satchel: Damien Drost, Executive Apartment 7, Strand Beach Hotel, Westerland. Sylt. 25980. Deutschland. He took a kitchen knife and broke the sealing wax. The letter inside was printed on expensive personalized stationery. The top right corner was embossed with a name and e-mail address but bore no postal address or phone number – his eyes were drawn to the contents.

Hello Joshua,

I am writing to you following an application lodged on your behalf by your father. I feel that I may be able to help you, and without wishing to be overly dramatic, my offer has the potential to change your life. I will simply state the facts and ask you to participate in an initial assessment phase before I make any decision concerning your possible mentorship.

Years ago, I was mentored by a generous and amazing person. She passed a great gift on to me and I went from being moderately successful to becoming a master in the sales profession. I made more than five million dollars in commissions over three years and invested the money well. I am now semi-retired and live half the year in Germany and the other half in Australia, which is where I was educated. The sales profession has given me much and I choose to give back by investing in one student each year, pro bono. I do this as my gift back to the profession that transformed my life and to partially fulfill my obligation to make a positive difference in the world.

You may be skeptical but the results speak for themselves. Every one of my students has at least tripled their income the year following their mentorship. One of my students increased his annual earnings fifteen-fold. I receive many applications each year but I accept only one student. To this person I am completely committed for twelve months. I assist them in unlocking the secrets of RSVP just as my mentor did for me.

Although your father built a compelling case on your behalf, I need more information from you directly before I can make my decision. Federal Express will provide me with the date this package was delivered and you have forty-eight hours only to complete an on-line assessment of your sales abilities. On the back of this letter is a web address and password for you to complete a Sales Aptitude Test for Professional Selling. It should take you approximately forty minutes and please ensure you input both of our e-mail addresses for result notification.

Should you clear this initial hurdle, and if I offer you the mentorship, it will be with strict conditions. I will not enter into any dialogue until you have completed the assessment. I will contact you via e-mail once I have done the necessary analysis of your results. Regardless of the outcome, the compass is yours to keep as a gift.

Yours sincerely,

Damien Drost
Sales Mentor

His immediate instinct was to phone his father to confront him about the uninvited interference. He knew, however, that he needed to calm down first. He would do some research before calling the next day.

Joshua was skilled in tuning search engines and the most obvious place to start was the business social networking sites. It was on one of these in Europe that he eventually found Damien Drost's profile. It was, however, in German but at least he had a picture. He wanted information in English and Damien had been educated in Australia. Universities were goldmines and he spent hours visiting campus and alumni sites but without success. Joshua did other searches and eventually found a site dedicated to the Drost family name, but nothing about Damien. He also searched using RSVP but all he got was a dating site and other irrelevant results. In the end he was left only with the German site and decided he would have to find someone to translate it later.

He wondered where Sylt was located and looked on Google Earth. He also found a link to the history of the island and read with interest about it being connected to the German mainland with a long causeway named after Paul von Hindenburg. During World War II it was a fortress air-base and had been pounded relentlessly by the RAF. Now the island was an exclusive German beach resort for the rich and famous located near Hamburg. Joshua decided to go to the Strand Hotel website: www.strandhotel-sylt.de. He saw the hotel's phone number and, although he had no intention of actually speaking with Damien Drost, he wanted to confirm this was where he actually lived. He dialed and wondered if calling would prove to be a mistake.

"Hello, do you speak English? Could you please confirm Mr. Drost's apartment is number seven?"

There was a prolonged pause before an officious man with a heavy German accent spoke. "I am sorry sir. The executive apartments are penthouse residences and not part of our hospitality operation."

"I need to mail him a letter. Can you just confirm his apartment number please?"

"Are you listening? They are private residences. I cannot help you."

"I see. Thanks anyway." He replaced the handset in weary resignation.

Damien obviously had money and no need to work in a large city. It was getting late and he was tired, frustrated and needed to sleep. Joshua's curiosity was stronger than the initial feelings of resentment concerning his father's uninvited actions. The on-line test could wait and he would call Mark in the morning. As he powered down his computer he thought about Damien Drost's offer; it seemed very generous but too good to be true.

It was 8.25am when he phoned his father's direct office number. "Hi, it's Joshua."

"Are you okay? Is something wrong?"

"Everything is fine. Who's Damien Drost?"

"He contacted you! Is he offering to take you on?"

"I haven't agreed to anything. Why are you interfering in my life again?" Joshua bit his lip. He realized he had made a wrong move and put his father on the defensive.

"I'm not going to interfere. It's just an introduction."

"But who is he and what did you tell him about me?"

Mark lowered his tone. "I'm sorry but he agreed to consider you on the strict condition that I don't discuss it with you, or with anyone else for that matter. What I can tell you is that you can trust him and he's very well qualified. This is a great opportunity."

Joshua tried another angle and was determined to get an answer. "What's with the cloak and dagger stuff? I've seen his profile on the internet – it's in German but I'm going to get it translated. Surely you can tell me something about him?"

"No. I've signed a confidentiality agreement that specifically states I must not interfere. Surely that's a good thing so far as you're concerned. These are his conditions, not mine."

Joshua couldn't decide whether he was grateful or annoyed. "I know I should thank you for trying to help but I didn't ask you to do this."

"It's between you and Mr. Drost now. He's the best in the business but it's up to you."

"What if I don't like him?"

"It's not about having a mentor you like. It's about working with someone who can make a difference. Just be honest with him and see what happens."

"Are you implying I'm not normally honest?"

"Not at all. I'm late for a meeting but we can talk later if you want to. I have to go." Mark terminated the call.

Joshua sat brooding over the fact that he had allowed the same old negative buttons to be pushed during the conversation. As he calmed down, however, he formed the view that Mark really had sought to help rather than interfere. He needed to make a decision and phoned the office to tell them he would be late. Joshua headed for his favorite café.

As he stirred his espresso he reflected on the last twenty-four hours and the huge range of emotions he had experienced. Maybe it was the effect of caffeine on an empty stomach but he felt detached and objective toward his life. He considered why he felt so frustrated and wondered if he was in the wrong profession – selling could certainly be lucrative but was it really what he wanted to do with his life?

Many things happen by accident but lasting success is not one of them. Joshua knew this fact but clichés were easy. Other than an absence of failure, what did he specifically want? He had been wrestling with the question since London and began scribbling random thoughts in an attempt to create clarity. He conceded that his father was right. This *was* an opportunity and it could determine whether professional selling should be his career. He decided to do the test.

Joshua knew from experience that poor test results were often the result of not reading the instructions properly, rather than from not knowing the correct answers. He typed the password and input his and Damien's e-mail addresses. There was no time limit. Forty minutes later he was finished. A message appeared advising that his results would be e-mailed. The test comprised theory and practical multiple choice questions. He had labored over many of them and was anxious to score well; he knew he had only one chance to impress. Joshua regarded himself as highly capable but felt a little uneasy. Many questions clearly had more than one correct answer and he had been torn between responding honestly or with what he perceived would be scored as being correct. He launched his e-mail application and waited.

He had not been this apprehensive since waiting for his university entrance scores. His final year at school had been lived on a knife edge. His teachers agreed that he was a bright student with outstanding potential but hampered by distracted inconsistency. When focused, there was no stopping him but he was easily diverted; especially by the students from the neighboring girl's school. Joshua did just enough to get by and it frustrated all those who saw his real potential. Despite his nonchalant demeanor with others concerning school and university, Joshua knew the world measured everyone according to scores, qualifications, titles and income levels. In the last six weeks of school he developed manic tunnel vision and lived on a cocktail of caffeine energy drinks. It worked; he finished in the top ten percent of the state. But now Damien Drost was assessing him and there had been no way of ensuring he knew the right answers.

The computer signaled there was a new e-mail in the in-box. His stomach churned as he read the results. The overall score was disappointing but Joshua was dismayed with the individual results for closing and objection handling. These were meant to be his strengths but he had bombed badly. *Surely there's a mistake?* But there was no starting over and Damien Drost would be looking at the same results.

He went to the office where his worry over the test scores was overshadowed by concerns with his boss's reaction to the disappointing meeting the previous day. Michael Blunt was a demanding manager, with high standards, and he had made no attempt to hide his annoyance with Joshua's handling of the failed sales process. The animosity was mutual. Joshua had a problem working for someone who did not respect and support him. The day dragged by as Joshua avoided contact with Michael.

After work, Joshua went to the driving range to escape his thoughts. Each strike was intended to release frustration, yet he was still churning and balls sprayed erratically, mocking his determination. He stopped and reflected, breathing deliberately, choosing to become lost in the purity of golf. All other thoughts faded as he became consumed by his quest to swing perfectly through the ball. It worked. By the time he shouldered his golf bag, his mind was clear.

He stopped for take-out on the way home and ate it from the plastic containers while standing at the kitchen bench. When he eventually logged on to his e-mail, it was late in the evening but the middle of the day in Europe and there was nothing from Damien. Joshua gave up waiting and went to bed, resigned to the inevitable. He wasn't angry or frustrated anymore. Instead, he felt sure of only one thing as he pulled up the covers – the selling profession was not for him.

Joshua woke with the test results on his mind. If there was an e-mail, he would face the bad news after a shower and with a clear head. The water seemed to cleanse his thoughts. The decision to quit the selling profession felt right, and he rationalized that the test was merely an academic exercise. *So what if I didn't do well? I know how to deliver in the real world.* Years of selling had conditioned him for rejection and he regarded it as a necessary part of his career, but this would be one of the last rejections he would have to endure. He felt that Damien Drost's intervention would be the catalyst for his change of career. He made a cup of tea and settled in front of the screen. The inevitable e-mail had indeed arrived. What he read took him completely by surprise.

Hello Joshua,

By now it is your morning and you probably had an uneasy sleep – unless you had given up after seeing your scores. The results alone do not enable me to make my decision. I therefore need you to complete one final task and you have twenty-four hours to respond. Complete the following sentence. 'To change my life, I need ...'

As previously, there will be no additional dialogue at this time. Just answer the question truthfully. Search within. I look forward to your reply.

Damien Drost
Sales Mentor

Joshua was amazed. He was still in the running despite his poor test results. But the question was perplexing. He considered the possibilities all day but was unsure of the best response. That evening he sat in front of his laptop staring at what he was about to send. Beside him were hand-written notes for potential options: the right opportunity, the right support, the secrets of success, money, my own business. What he now saw on the screen was his own revelation and the truth he had come to accept in the last twenty minutes. He hoped it was the right answer for Damien. He whispered it. "To change my life, I need to first change myself." He hit the send button.

He watched television while regularly checking for a reply. At 10:45pm he received it.

Hello Joshua,

The results of the on-line test were only ever going to reveal areas needing attention but your completion of the sentence told me whether or not I should invest my time in you. Your answer indicates that you accept the need for personal change and believe that success comes from within rather than external factors. I trust you were sincere in your response as this is wisdom beyond your years. I am pleased to offer you a twelve month mentorship but there are strict conditions.

I value my privacy and do not seek any form of promotion, publicity or unsolicited contact outside my network. You must therefore agree not to divulge to anyone that I am your mentor.

You will not ignore any question I pose, nor will you engage in any form of posturing. You will resist the temptation to tell me what you think I want to hear but instead be completely honest. You will be committed to learning through change and to making our relationship work. You will complete every task to which you commit. Clarity is essential in your learning and will be facilitated exclusively through e-mail correspondence. There will be no phone calls, no blogs, no instant messaging. The benefits of getting your thoughts in writing will become self-evident. E-mail is an efficient means of exchanging the correspondence between us regardless of geographic location. We will meet face-to-face twelve months from now but not before.

I trust you accept your father's judgment that I am equipped to help you and we will therefore not waste valuable time in establishing my credentials. Your reply to this e-mail should begin by acknowledging your agreement with the terms of our engagement above. If you break our contract, I will not hesitate in terminating our arrangement. I will invest substantial time, effort and money in the coming twelve months but I will not require any form of monetary payment from you. Time is precious and this is why the conditions of your mentorship are essential.

You stated correctly. "To change my life, I need to first change myself." Nothing can change for the better until we do. But how deeply do you believe this? Acknowledging reality is the first step in transforming any situation but what do you think of this next statement? You, Joshua, are living exactly the life you desire, and right now you have everything you want.

I know you have many questions. Feel free to ask anything you wish but in accordance with the conditions of our agreement documented in this e-mail. You have a unique opportunity and I am fully committed to your success. I look forward to getting to know you, Joshua Peters, and to ultimately meeting you face-to-face and celebrating your transformation. The twelve month clock is now ticking.

Damien Drost
Sales Mentor

The correspondence-based relationship had begun. Joshua went to bed feeling surprisingly optimistic; a feeling that had been absent for some time. He slept blissfully unaware of the huge challenge that lay ahead.

Chapter Three: Dialogue of Secrets

It had been two days since Joshua sent his e-mail and he was anxious for a response. He had confirmed agreement with Damien's terms but was flummoxed by the bizarre proposition. He was unhappy at work and definitely did not have what he wanted in his personal or professional life. What he had was not what he wanted at all, nor what he felt he deserved. Yet he agreed that he must change in order for his life to be positively different. His e-mail had echoed the conundrum. He confirmed that he needed to change, but that he disagreed with the assertion that he actually had what he wanted in his life. He sought further clarification and also asked about the difference between coaching and mentoring. It was evening when he arrived home and saw the reply.

Joshua,

Thankyou for confirming our contract. We have begun well and I commend your honesty. This e-mail has been sent to you from the club lounge at Changi Airport in Singapore while on my way to Australia. I am planning to live on the east coast during the southern hemisphere summer but e-mail will remain our exclusive means of communication. I trust your deliberations over my last question highlight the value of putting your thoughts in writing.

Some would argue that the difference between coaching and mentoring is merely semantics, but there can be fundamental differences. Both are outcome focused but a coach is often a skills practitioner. In essence, coaches show you what to do and how to do it, and they focus on improvement of attitude and skills with emphasis on process execution. A coach is concerned with the mechanics of a profession and with the effective application of the necessary skills, but their approach to motivation can sometimes be perceived as external in nature.

Mentoring goes far deeper and, although capable of covering the same areas as a coach (and some coaches can also be mentors), they go beyond practitioner to the far more important matters of why, when and with whom you should engage. A mentor gets you working internally and is a sounding-board. Mentors often spend far more time asking questions than providing instruction and direction. A mentor brings experience, understanding and sound judgment because they've already successfully done what the protégé, or student, is seeking to achieve. In many ways I have already walked your path, Joshua, and my role is to equip and challenge you, at every level, to make you accountable for being the best person you are capable of becoming, professionally and personally.

The origins of the word mentor come from Greek mythology. Homer's Odyssey tells the story of Mentor who was a trusted servant of the mortal hero, Ulysses, who had a son named Telemachus. Ulysses charged Mentor with the personal development of his beloved son, and with specific focus on the areas of courage, character and attitude. Mentor functioned as a non-judgmental conscience – a mirror and an unrelenting point of accountability for Telemachus. Mentor did this by asking Telemachus fearless and profound questions. You, Joshua, are my Telemachus but I am no demigod.

The Oxford Dictionary simply defines mentor as an experienced and trusted advisor. A coach may bark instructions but my goal is to assist you in facilitating your own learning, where you truly embrace new ideas because they are yours. You can only really commit to change if you sincerely want it in your life. Sustained learning only occurs when you internalize and seek to change yourself as a result of committing to your own education and betterment. I am working with you, not just because I think you can become great, but because you already have greatness within you. In the same way that Mentor was accountable to Ulysses, I will be called to account concerning my investment in you. Be assured that I am focused on achieving the best possible outcomes in you from our time together. Most importantly, just as with Mentor and Telemachus, our relationship must be based upon trust, honesty and profoundly confronting questions. Please do not tell me you agree if in fact you do not. If two people agree all the time, then one of them is redundant!

You asked if there is a dichotomy in having exactly what you want, yet also knowing that you need to change. Your e-mail clearly indicates that you are not happy with your life and you are therefore wondering how you could possibly have exactly what you want. Paradox is not contradiction. Let me ask you another question. If you really are unhappy and genuinely want to change, what would you need to believe for the statement to be true? (I am living exactly the life I desire and, right now, I have everything I want). Think about the law of reciprocity and let me know what you conclude.

Joshua, although I would like to focus on sales mastery as soon as possible, the results of your on-line test revealed some serious deficiencies in your base-level understanding of professional selling. We must ensure your sales fundamentals are solid because they are the foundation on which we will build. Review the Value Quadrant for Professional Sales Agents below. In which sector do you mainly operate? Answer based upon how you behave rather than what you think is theoretically the case.

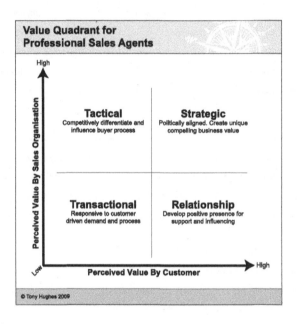

In the interests of time, I will cover these principles of professional selling and I want you to comment on all aspects in your next e-mail and let me know to what extent you agree or disagree. Before I get to the principles, allow me to summarize the recent history and evolution of professional selling. I do this because I fear you are stuck in the past. You need to evolve from 'push selling' to 'attraction selling'.

Professional selling has existed for thousands of years and can simply be described as commercial influence. Modern corporate selling began to take shape following World War II and in the 1950s there were two forces that combined to forever change the sales industry. One was psychology and the other was process methodology. These disciplines conjoined to manifest in a five step method attributed to Dale Carnegie.

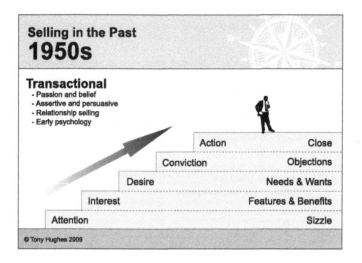

The process was described in the acronym AIDCA. In the above illustration the seller works up through the five steps to secure a buying commitment. This methodology works best in commodity, retail and direct consumer selling but fails to address complexity and strategy. Amazingly, there are still sales people today that practice this style of selling in complex corporate sales environments and they transparently adhere to the AIDCA five steps:

· Attention: through 'sizzle'
· Interest: aroused through features and benefits
· Desire: by linking the above to buyer needs and wants
· Conviction: from the seller in overcoming objections
· Action: by actively and assertively closing for commitment

The acronym was later abbreviated to AIDC, with the C standing for Close. In the 1960s and 1970s psychological techniques became more sophisticated but the approach was still one of manipulating the sale and persuading the prospect. There was much emphasis on personality and charisma and the only substantive new element to be added to sales practice back then was greater analysis of the statistical aspects of success. Problems persisted in large complex selling and in the 1970s, AIDCA was usurped with a focus on Features (and Functions), Advantages and Benefits – FAB. But this new FAB emphasis meant that sales people often became trapped below the level of real power, due to the bottom-up approach. In this era, David Sandler led in developing sales methodologies. Discipline in sales process inputs became the hallmark of effective sales management; while sales people focused on conveying the message of features as benefits. Vendor 'benefits', however, do not always translate to tangible business value, and the sales person's audience often consisted of recommenders and influencers within corporations rather than real decision makers.

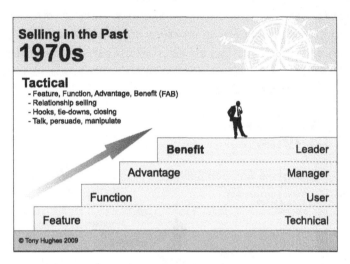

During the 1970s and 1980s, large corporations made considerable advances in how they managed the procurement process. They devised buying techniques designed to foster supplier competition, thwarting clever and charismatic sales people. Sales techniques that worked in the past increasingly became barriers to success, especially in more complex environments. Professional buyers became better educated and more sophisticated and did not respond favorably to clumsy or manipulative selling behaviors. Consider how prospective clients today view outdated sales practices from last century:

- Assertive or persuasive: perceived as aggressive or pushy
- Persistent: perceived as annoying and not listening
- 'Positive questions': perceived as rhetorical and manipulative
- Premature 'features and benefits': perceived as having no understanding or too expensive

Throughout the 1980s, there was greater awareness of the fact that aggression from the sales person created defensiveness with the customer, but that trust and understanding created cooperation. It was in this context that the psychological practice of Neuro-Linguistic Programming (NLP) came to the forefront of the sales training industry. Although not invented by Anthony Robbins, he popularized NLP and applied the principles to the sales profession. This new trend matured in the 1990s and focused on building trust subconsciously to create influence.

During this period, however, there was serious research being done concerning successful sales be-haviors measured from the perspective of professional buyers. This research was led by Neil Rack-ham from Huthwaite who developed SPIN Selling ©, the forerunner of today's value-based approach to professional sales. Huthwaite documented a methodology that revolutionised professional selling by focusing on problems, the implications, and the specific business benefits of resolving them by implementing solutions. Neil Rackham's influence and contribution to professional selling is second to none. Sadly, even with his revolutionary approach, many sales people continued to operate below the level of real power. The vast majority persisted with their feature, function, advantage, benefit mantras. Old habits really do die hard, but things were changing.

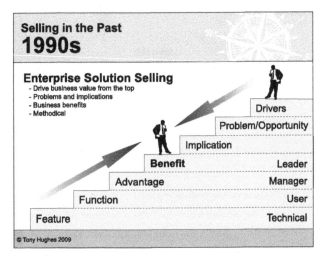

A number of sales process methodologies emerged in the late 1980s and 1990s as best practice for qualifying, managing and strategizing complex sales opportunities. They remain highly relevant today and promote a top-down approach aligned to the political and economic power in a buying organization.

The most successful sales professionals see themselves as problem solvers with specific domain expertise. They value their time and the time of others. They don't waste valuable resources or emo-tional energy trying to convince people to buy something not genuinely needed. This is because to do so, they would violate their personal values and professional integrity. High achievers carefully invest their time with the right people and ask the right questions. Consider the following summary of today's values-based approach which is predicated on trust, understanding and integrity:

· Genuine interest in the customer
· Thorough enquiry concerning their problems and opportunities
· Full understanding of the business needs

- Identifying specific benefits and priorities
- Negotiating how to proceed and implement

Values-based selling is in stark contrast to the AIDC and FAB methods from last century. Instead, this modern and ethical approach is fully aligned with the customer. The best professional buyers define their relationship with sales people as the process of reaching progressive agreement concerning the purchase of something they need and can afford. In this customer-centric model, the sales person's role is to fully understand the customer's requirements and conditions for complete satisfaction. They then validate the suitability of what can be supplied to exactly meet the customer's needs.

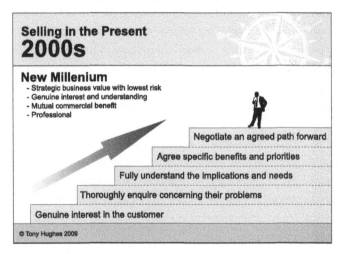

The role of a sales professional is changing. In the past, it was the marketing department that 'created' value, with sales people having the role of communicating it. Yet the term, value, is usually a euphemism for generic solutions to specific markets or vertical industry segments. Anything generic can easily become commoditized, vulnerable to margin erosion and competitive pressures. Even the biggest vendors need to also be niche specialists. Today, both sales and marketing people need to create and communicate value, but this can only be achieved with customer intimacy.

Enough history, there are timeless principles I now wish to cover. These are not fads, and there is no new truth – just contemporary application of proven laws for success. Suffice to say that clumsy, outdated or manipulative sales techniques should have no place in your life. Values-based selling means that you adopt a customer-centric approach, focused on creating real value through genuine understanding, solving problems and helping people make mutually beneficial buying decisions.

The selling profession demands genuine belief in yourself, your employer and your product (service, software or hardware). This is important because, at the most basic level, selling is the transference of belief. People buy emotionally and then use factual information to support or justify their decision. To put it another way, people make buying decisions with their emotions and rationalize with intellect. In every sales encounter, someone buys. Maybe not the product or service but certainly an attitude or belief, which is a precursor to any commercial transaction. The issue is who has the stronger belief – the sales person or the prospective customer? Words can never substitute for emotional sincerity. The buyer must know that the sales person's belief or conviction is genuine before a level of trust can be established.

In addition to belief, having a positive attitude is also essential. This is far more than enthusiasm and should not be perceived as arrogance in any form. A positive attitude is one of optimistic purpose that attracts opportunities and resources. A positive attitude embraces a genuine desire to seek the best outcomes for others. Having purpose, means you will always have a reason for being with someone and a desire not to waste time – yours or theirs. Genuine empathy and understanding through listening must create and maintain balance in the positive attitude equation.

Beyond belief and attitude, competence in dealing with people is the next essential ingredient. I define 'people skills' as 'tactical sales skills' and these include, at the most basic level, having a great smile and a warm, friendly and confident handshake. Beyond the way you make a positive first impression, your competence must then manifest itself in being fully engaged and completely interested in the other person. This should be evidenced by maintaining positive eye contact, actively listening and asking insightful open questions.

The final foundational element is discipline, which is the habitual practice of doing the right things, the right way, at the right time. Beyond work ethic, these are the inputs that create, qualify, develop, close and leverage opportunities in a sales funnel. Do not confuse activity with effectiveness. The world is full of busy fools. Look at your business card; what title is printed under your name? I am sure the words: Professional Visitor do not appear. You are employed to sell and every meeting must result in a sale or the progression of a profitable sales process.

So, Joshua, do you have compelling belief in yourself, your corporation, and what you offer your customers? Do you really have a great attitude and project yourself as confident and knowledgeable without appearing arrogant? Are you a person of sincere intent? Do you have purpose in the way you invest your time and interact with others? Are you fully engaged every time you meet someone? Do you plan to ask great questions? Are you habitually disciplined in your approach to the sales process and do you have a solid work ethic in doing the right things at the right time? Are you tactically capable in execution?

Some experts boil all these fundamentals down to just two words: skill and attitude. Is one more important than the other? To answer this, imagine you are a sales director seeking to hire a new sales executive. What are the attributes of the ideal candidate? Write them all down – there should be dozens. Once you have completed the list, use two different colored highlighters to categorize each attribute as either attitude or skill. Some will be both, so count them twice. What are the scores for each category?

Is attitude the same as motivation? If you take someone who is naïve and inept but you then successfully motivate him or her, what sort of person do you now have? Finally, Joshua, define what professional selling means for you. These questions may cause you to doubt yourself in the sales profession. Allow me, therefore, to give you some reasons to persist.

Professional selling can pay comparably with the legal, accounting or medical professions. Unlike these vocations, however, you do not have to sacrifice years of your time and substantial sums of money in obtaining the necessary qualifications to practice. In addition to financial rewards, the sales profession provides unrivalled freedom and flexibility for those who are truly successful.

Although professional selling provides the allure of financial reward and a flexible work environment, it attracts many who are ill-equipped. A significant number burn up and vanish early in their careers, attracted to selling like moths to a flame. These misplaced individuals are often insecure and lazy yet pursue a profession that demands hard work and the ability to deal with constant rejection and disappointment. You, Joshua Peters, can align to worthwhile values but success also demands emotional toughness and a disciplined work ethic.

Professional selling is about helping people buy something that solves their specific problems. The very best sales people create value in doing this masterfully for their customers. There are very few sales people who really understand this. Many of your competitors are unenlightened operatives, predominantly relying on relationship-based selling principles and the often false assumption that they have a market-leading solution or superior value that gives them some kind of edge.

Outstanding results come from thinking and acting differently. It is to your advantage that very few people are willing to do what it takes, but rather hold onto limiting views that they are doing their best or doing what has worked previously. Most people rely on the law of averages to achieve mediocrity and they hope for good fortune to over-achieve. The reality for the vast majority is that their best efforts need to be much better.

You, however, can become one of the few. It will require positive belief and attitude combined with excellence in execution through skill and discipline. On this foundation, we can build strategy which, combined with masterful execution, creates spectacular success. But I am getting ahead of myself. We must first ensure that the basics are right and then we will move on to the RSVP principles. I look forward to your reply.

Damien Drost
Sales Mentor

Joshua felt intimidated by what he had just read and was amazed Damien was coming to Australia. His stomach began to churn as he contemplated the implied expectations. As he read the e-mail again, he wrote each of Damien's questions on the top of separate sheets of paper. The questions raised by Damien were anything but straight forward and he was still preoccupied with the proposition that he had exactly what he wanted in his life, including the things he did not want! He read Damien's words again out loud. "Think about the law of reciprocity." He sat brooding before it hit him. "We attract what we radiate!" It now made sense. He started writing furiously to get all his thoughts on paper.

Joshua sent his e-mail two days later. He had labored over many issues before settling on the words Damien would read. The most difficult was his definition of selling and he had been honest in his response. Joshua created a correspondence folder and dragged the sent e-mail into it. He wanted a chronological record of their dialogue. *Maybe this will make a great book one day*, he thought.

Hello Damien,

I will do what it takes to succeed under your guidance. I am sincerely committed to making the best of our year together even though it is confined to the medium of e-mail. I appreciate your patience as I adjust to your mentoring program and although I would very much like to speak with you, I am beginning to see the value in writing everything down for self-reflection.

Let me begin by addressing the most difficult issue I have wrestled with since our dialogue began. You assert that the undesired aspects of my life are exactly what I want. Please don't take offence but, in the spirit of honesty as requested, I must say that I have a bias against new-age, self-help psycho-babble or propositions that business success hinges on some Judeo-Christian version of karma. I have nonetheless come to agree that we all attract what we radiate; the law of reciprocity as you pointed out. I would, however, like to change the word 'desire' to the word 'deserve' so that the statement reads: I am living exactly the life I deserve today. I do accept responsibility for my situation and I have never embraced being a victim. I have what I deserve at present and I need to change and become a person capable of getting or attracting what I really want.

You asked me to define selling and this proved to be quite challenging. I looked up the word selling in several dictionaries and this was alarming. Definitions include: swindle, trickery, corrupt bargaining, betray for money, cheat, hoax, deceive, and disappoint. In Roget's Thesaurus, other terms are used including: hawk, peddle, falseness, fraud, sham, sleight of hand, hocus-pocus, chicanery, hypocrisy, delusion, snare, trap and ambush! You were right, all this self-examination has caused me to doubt the selling profession and I guess there is no shortage of negative examples out there.

On a positive note, the dictionary also describes selling as: inspiring with desire to possess something, giving information concerning value, being enthusiastic about, finding purchasers, winning acceptance, approval or adoption, and being commercially successful.

But how do I personally define selling? I agree with you, Damien, that it is the transference of belief supported by logical and factual information, and I once heard Anthony Robbins describe selling as, "changing someone's emotional state." Although I agree, I am against any form of manipulation, especially if it contravenes someone's best interests by selling them something they don't really need or cannot afford. I enjoyed reading your summary of the history of selling and I agree with your views concerning how it should be today. One course I attended taught me to think of selling as the process of helping someone make a positive decision that is in their best interests (provides genuine value) and is profitable for the seller. In simple terms, selling for me is: influencing someone to make a positive buying decision.

My frustration with selling, however, is that potential buyers have no problem with wasting my time and do not always tell the truth. This is the very trait that sales people are stereo-typically labeled with! To avoid having my time wasted, I ask strong qualification questions and ask for the order early. I have found, however, that closing quickly does not always work when selling in larger corporate environments. But surely successful sales principles are universal? My first sales manager taught me that the ABC of selling was: Always Be Closing.

I thought your summary of the foundational principles of sales success was interesting. I agree that belief, attitude, skill and discipline are essential prerequisites. I already knew this but I guess the issue is to what degree I actually embody the principles. I must admit that the belief factor in my current job is not where it needs to be. My belief in myself, however, is strong and I think this compensates for some of the shortcomings with the product and corporation. I am sure you will want to explore this more and I do not mean to gloss over the importance of what you said with the four elements of success, it's just that I really do already agree.

I liked the distillation of the principles down to skill and attitude but the concept of belief is a little abstract. You asked me whether skill or attitude is more important. I did the list as requested. Here are the attributes I came up with for the dream employee:

Persistent	Honest	Confident	Fun	Teachable
Work ethic	Passionate	Team player	Accountable	Friendly
Disciplined	Optimistic	Empathy	Competitive	Stable
Energetic	Visionary	Leader	Mature	Sincere
Thorough	Consistent	Listener	Competent	Thoughtful
Experienced	Integrity	Committed	Enthusiastic	Engaged

I was amazed when I started categorizing them as more than 90% were attitude! Before doing this exercise I would have said that both were equally important.

I considered your question about taking someone who is inept and motivating them. I think the result would be to have a motivated idiot. In my opinion, motivation is no substitute for competence, and competence equates to skill. Attitude and skill are both essential but if you have the right skills then it must be attitude that differentiates.

You also asked whether attitude is the same as motivation. Not in my opinion, because it is possible to have a person with a great attitude but no real ambition. Having a great attitude does not necessarily mean you are motivated but I think having ambition with goals creates motivation.

I studied the Value Quadrant and I'm unsure about the use of the various terms. I would like to believe that I fit somewhere in the top half between tactical and strategic but I think the term, strategic, is cliché and over-used in selling. I am looking forward to you explaining the differences.

I want to learn and I want to succeed. Feel free to be brutal in your next e-mail. I am sure there are some things you wish to challenge and explore.

Your student,
Joshua Peters

P.S. Thanks for the compass. May I ask its significance? Could you also please provide an English translation of the inscription? On a lighter note, I always thought that Telemachus was the god of working from home over the internet using a Mac computer – only kidding! Thanks for explaining mentoring.

    The next few days went quickly for Joshua. The self-examination was a welcome distraction from his difficult work environment. His boss, Michael, had formed the view that the crucial deal had not slipped into the next quarter but rather had slipped into the clutches of a competitor. Joshua and Michael were at odds concerning whether they should try to salvage the situation or just wait, hoping the competitor would stumble. Michael detested inaction and did not suffer fools, or incompetence, gladly. He progressively adopted a hostile attitude toward Joshua.

    Joshua constantly checked his e-mail. He was keen to discuss his work situation and the deal he was certain had been lost. He wondered what he should have done differently and if anything could be salvaged. He especially wanted to move on from esoteric theory and what he regarded as self-help gobbledygook.

    Late in the day, Joshua received the inevitable letter via e-mail confirming that the deal was lost. He phoned to request a debrief but they were reluctant. He pressed further and obtained a token commitment that they would organize a meeting once they had finalized a contract with the other party. After forwarding the e-mail to his boss, he headed home early. Joshua knew that the next day would be unpleasant; Michael Blunt would be most displeased. "The joy of selling", he said to himself sarcastically. *It really is a bipolar career.*

    Joshua had learned long ago, however, that the sooner he put a loss behind him, the sooner he could get on with winning other business. Once home, he flicked the light switch, put his keys in the usual spot and checked his e-mail. Damien had replied.

Hello Joshua,

It is good for me to be in warm and sunny Australia. What a wonderful contrast with winter in Germany! Sorry for the delay in my reply but I have been getting organized so we can focus together. We are making good progress and soon we will be able to move on to the principles of RSVP.

I am glad you see the value in writing things down and crystallizing your thoughts. Your definition of selling is excellent and you clearly have sincere motives. It is good that you detest manipulation but belief in what you offer is far more important than you think; we will explore this later.

Although selling can be negative (manipulative or with unbalanced value for the parties), it can also be of great benefit to buyers and the process can be conducted ethically, for mutual benefit. At one level, selling is simply a form of communication. Everyone sells; some just do it for a living. When a parent asks their child to pack toys away, when a man asks a woman on a date, when a person is in a job interview – these are all selling situations. The tragedy with the sales profession is that it is full of amateurs and, in truth, is not a profession at all. There are no formally recognized qualifications or degrees, no peer standards body, and no consequences for malpractice. Yet selling can be approached professionally. We will get back to selling, and your two major weaknesses, but let us first finish our dialogue concerning foundational principles.

I was not offended in any way by your statements concerning new-age psycho-babble but there are universal truths that have stood the test of time. The law of reciprocity is one of them. It is good that we agree on this truth. Your sincerity in applying proven ethical values will be the cornerstone of your success in professional sales. Integrity should pervade everything we do and is essential for anyone seeking lasting and meaningful success, or aspiring to personal or professional leadership.

I am also happy that you resolved the tension you perceived in the two statements concerning change and having what you want or deserve right now. You understand that to change your world you must first change yourself. Who you are, is the force behind what you do and in turn what you attract into your life. Let me take this one step further; who you are, springs from your beliefs, values and attitudes. Think about what defines you as a person. How do you want to be thought of? Our beliefs, values and attitudes are often formed unconsciously and that is why it is so important for you to choose your employer, personal environment and the people in your social life very carefully.

Do you really know what you believe and do you truly understand your values? Are they genuinely yours and do you emotionally and intellectually own them? Knowledge and knowing are two completely different things. You need to move from mere intellectual values to virtues, which are internalized. Never underestimate the power of your beliefs, values and attitudes as they will either sabotage or underpin your success. Your most valuable lessons will come from real world application of what you believe. Let us now discuss some important points in your last e-mail. I will then introduce you to the first RSVP principle.

Your comments concerning attitude and skill were right on the mark. You are correct in stating that both are essential and that skill (competence) alone is not enough. It is attitude that differentiates high performers and leaders. Your comment about the 'motivated idiot' was also insightful. There are, however, very few of these people in professional selling because they are usually screened-out when someone has to fund a substantial salary for them. Employers always have a range of candidates that appear to be equally competent but skills alone are not what make a sales employee successful. Skill is a prerequisite, not a differentiator. Employers care about a person's ability to positively influence and deliver results, while also being a good cultural fit. Many qualified and knowledgeable people miss out on jobs or promotions due to poor attitudes. No-one really cares about what you know or your qualifications. They, instead, care primarily about themselves and what you can do for them. This is the universal law of self-interest, and it is dangerous and naïve to violate it.

You also answered correctly concerning the fact that having a great attitude does not necessarily equate with being highly motivated. You are right in saying that goal driven ambition is what creates motivation. We will discuss your goals at a later time.

Enough praise. Let us now turn to what needs to change. You identified your weaknesses but I am not sure that you fully understand the gravity of your problems. Symptoms are not necessarily causes.

Your first two problems are that you open sales calls poorly and you attempt to close prematurely. This was evident in your test results and confirmed in your last e-mail. The techniques that work in small and simple sales do not work in large or complex selling situations. The ABC of selling, as you put it, only works when selling low price and low value commoditized products or services. Closing prematurely in a corporate sale will only damage your credibility and alienate the buyer. Any attempt to close should occur only after the seller has a complete understanding and the buyer's agreement to move forward. Closing can be defined as obtaining progressive agreement to move forward and this is an excellent approach but closing for the sale as a way to test the buyer only creates undesired objections and mistrust.

Your old sales manager probably also told you that objections are opportunities to close but in professional enterprise selling that statement is wrong. Objections occur when a sales person tries to move forward without fully understanding the situation or before the buyer is ready. Aggressive qualifying and premature closing will absolutely damage your chances of success in large or complex sales environments. Objections are for amateurs and simply prove that the sales person has made a mistake. Instead of qualifying hard and closing early, what should you be doing?

The next problem is your belief, or put more accurately, your lack of belief. You do not truly believe in your corporation, product and service. This must surely create frustration for you but what is the real cause of your lack of faith? Make no mistake, Joshua, lack of emotional attachment to what you sell is a serious problem. Be completely honest in your response.

You asked about the significance of the compass and although we will discuss its purpose more fully toward the end of your mentorship, consider the fact that moral values hold us together, individually and corporately. It is essential to anchor yourself to values that can hold you in good stead in both prosperous and challenging times. Many a rising star has come crashing down due to avarice. Trust and integrity are prerequisite in all interactions and small moral defects easily magnify into cata-strophic errors of judgment or trust-destroying behaviors as the stakes increase. Unethical values cannot be successfully masked and eventually pervade every area of life. You can segment your time and activities but not your values and behaviors – you bring all of yourself to everything you do.

You requested that I translate the inscription: TRUE NORTH – OD DAS VEILS but there is no need as it is mainly in English. Das, is the only German word in the inscription and translates to: that is. The word Od is English and can mean: a hypothetical force pervading all of nature. It's a handy word to know when playing Scrabble.

Let us discuss your position on the Value Quadrant (now with archetype roles assigned) and what the four categories mean. Individual value in the workplace is not determined by knowledge but rather by a person's ability to positively influence and deliver results. All sales people move between the quadrants based upon their value proposition and customer needs.

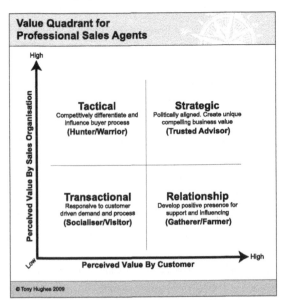

The bottom left quadrant, Transactional, represents the lowest value for all concerned. A transactional sales person can be likened to a 'professional visitor' offering only marginal value due to their inability to differentiate or exert influence. The Transactional quadrant is the realm of commodity products or services where sales success is usually dependent on representing a strong brand. Transactional selling is most subject to price sensitivity as customers seek to drive down price for what they perceive as commodity products and services. Buyers want responsiveness to their procurement process and expect sales people to assist them in transacting with best commercial value. In the Transactional quadrant, the seller is responding to client demand and participating in the buyer's disempowering (for the seller) process of reducing price. The sales person's role represents limited value and pays accordingly.

As a sales person progresses in their career, they tend to move out of the bottom left quadrant to become either an account manager focused on incremental business through maintaining and developing customer relationships or they become a business development manager, seeking to generate new business in more competitive environments. But transactional sales people usually struggle to evolve and attempts by them to position 'solutions' are often perceived merely as the bundling of products and services. More worrying, is that there is often a lack of understanding from both buyer and seller concerning genuine value in the delivery of outcomes and management of associated risks. Instead, there is myopic focus on features, functions and price. Although the transactional sales person may seek to use tactics and relationships to position their value or outmaneuver the competition, their limiting characteristic is dependence on recommendations from technical and middle management people. They operate well below those who set the agenda or hold real economic power.

Relationship selling (the bottom right quadrant) is important because people buy from those they like and trust. Positive relationships are therefore prerequisite for success at any level. Relationships must, however, be built with the right people in the buying organization and, as already stated, transactional/relationship sales people are usually limited by having relationships with lower level and mid-tier operatives. All sales people leverage relationship skills in the role of account manager (bottom right quadrant) or business development manager (top left quadrant), but the level of genuine influence is what actually defines the value of a relationship for the seller. On the other hand, lower level buyers define relationship value by the perceived level of responsiveness and trustworthiness of the sales person.

The top left Tactical quadrant is populated by sales executives or business development managers seeking to influence the buyer's process and requirements. Here, the sales person employs tactics to differentiate and overcome the buyer's efforts to drive down price through commoditization and competition. Sales people operating in this quadrant are usually assertive and competitive, positioning unique solutions and helping purchasers identify differentiating value. Tactical sales people tend to also suffer from being stuck with mid-tier relationships, and they easily focus wrongly on features and functions. The terms, 'hunter' and 'farmer' were coined by the insurance industry in the late 1800s and refer to producers (those who signed new customers) and collectors (those who collected the premiums). Contrary to the stereotypes, the best farmers are actually hunters within existing accounts, and relationship competence is essential to all selling.

A sales person makes a significant jump in the value they offer an employer when they move from responding to transactional demand (bottom left), to influencing the buyer (bottom right), or tactically competing (top left). The giant leap, however, in value for both employer and customer is achieved when the sales person operates in the top right quadrant, strategically creating value for all parties. This quadrant is where buyer and seller value is balanced and where the return on investment is high for both parties. Value is maximized and price becomes less important as the focus moves to managing risks in realizing the business benefits of delivering high value outcomes.

Moving away from transactional selling into any other quadrant is often labeled 'solution selling'. Beware of this cliché term, however, as 'solution selling' can manifest as the sales person acting like the cure looking for a disease. When you're a hammer, everything looks like a nail. The concept of solution selling is valid but only if it is preceded by a consultative approach to understanding the actual problem that needs to be solved. Solutions are an integral part of strategic selling but no strategy can be effective without trust, value and excellence in execution.

The top right quadrant is, therefore, populated by the very few who operate strategically with excellence in the execution of tactics and management of senior relationships. The very best sales executives masterfully engineer business value through alignment to the seat of genuine political and commercial power within the customer organization. They recognize that demand creation is achieved through early engagement and by understanding and aligning with serious problems or opportunities. They also know that differentiation is achieved through becoming a trusted advisor, with an intimate understanding of the customer's operational constraints and potential risks, internal and external, in the delivery of business value.

Being strategic is, therefore, evidenced by proactive demand generation with effective strategy to defeat the competition while building compelling business value. You, Joshua, do not sit in the top right quadrant. You drift between being a relationship and tactical operative, dependent on mid-level relationships for recommendations rather than decisions. Although this assessment may seem harsh, I think you know, deep down, that this is the case. If not, let me ask another question to highlight the issue. Do you get price objections at some point in every sale? I don't mean the type that occurs during negotiations, but rather, early in the sales cycle. I know you will answer, 'yes'. The reason for this is that you think that features are benefits, another issue revealed in your test results.

Product or service features are not necessarily benefits. A benefit is only so if it solves a specific acknowledged problem for the client. Touting numerous features early in the sales-cycle, hoping they will be perceived as benefits, can actually create price concerns in the mind of the buyer. Price is only relevant if they want what you are selling, and cost must never outweigh the benefits of purchasing. This is often expressed in terms of the cost/benefit equation.

When was the last time you had a one-on-one meeting with the ultimate decision maker in an organization? I do not mean that they attended a group presentation but, that at your request, they met with you exclusively. The real measure of a Sales Master is their ability to have meetings with senior executives, focused on creating business value. This is in stark contrast to lower level meetings focused on competitively responding to technical and functional requirements. Review your calendar of appointments over the last three months. It will not lie.

In summary, it is essential for you to consider the following truths and decide what changes you need to make in the way that you operate:
- Features are not necessarily benefits
- Closing prematurely damages the sales process
- Objections are for amateurs and evidence of mistakes
- Price is only relevant if they want what you are selling
- Problem solving is far more important than solution selling
- No solution should be proposed without understanding the problem
- The size of the sale directly relates to the size of the problem or opportunity

I promised that we would cover the first of the RSVP principles in this communication. Here it is.

Be fully there. Pay attention and execute with excellence.

When you RSVP to an invitation, you commit to being there. Selling is no different. Successful execution of any strategy or tactic demands you pay attention and be fully engaged. When you are with someone, business or social, be fully there! This may seem absurdly obvious but it is vitally important. Sadly, very few people do it well. The key point, is that you are never distracted and are fully focused on the other party. You seek to understand before being understood. They, not you, are the most important person at the meeting and you are committed to understanding their needs and agendas. What do they want and, more specifically, what do they want and need from you? What operational, environmental and financial constraints are they working within? What is their personal agenda and motivation? What are the politics within the organization and how will their selection and decision processes work? What are their real problems and the tangible benefits that can be derived from implementing solutions successfully? These are just a few of the questions.

Being fully there, means you turn your phone off and eliminate distractions. It also means you fully prepare for the meeting by having an agenda and doing your homework. You listen, really listen, and ask insightful open questions. Not simple situational questions about their corporation's activities, the number of employees, their revenue, and the like. Those types of questions will annoy the other person because you should have done this basic research before meeting with them. Again, learn to ask insightful open questions and then listen like you have never listened before.

In my early days in the software industry, a CEO with whom I had developed good rapport looked at me very seriously.

"Do you know the real difference between a software salesman and the actual software?"

He asked in such a dead-pan manner that I had absolutely no idea how to respond. I sat there open mouthed as he leaned forward and lowered his voice.

"Damien, you only have to punch information into the software once."

We both laughed but I got the message.

I will finish this e-mail with something very important. Your test results revealed that you lead into a sale by positioning your product or service early and forcefully. This means that you suffer from PPS – Premature Presentation Syndrome. There is a better way. People do business with those they like and trust, and trust is built on genuine understanding and shared values. Listening is the key to influence and questions are the key to genuine understanding.

Joshua, please consider the following as a potential career-changing revelation. Problems must come before solutions. Your product is not the product – you are the product! Consider all of the above and tell me what you think. But more importantly, tell me what you will do differently.

Damien Drost
Sales Mentor

Joshua did not agree with everything he had read and he felt uneasy with how Damien had nailed the issue of incongruent beliefs. Deep down, Joshua had always thought that to be successful in selling he had to be casual with the truth. He thought back to some of the guidance that previous managers had given him. 'Don't lie, just don't tell them everything', and 'tell them what they need to hear'. These phrases echoed in his head but none more so than what one of his sales managers had jokingly said. "You've made it in sales when you can fake sincerity." It was said with humor and he had laughed at the time but it never sat well with him.

Joshua snapped out of his mental diatribe with aggravated curiosity. *How did Damien gain so much insight from a test and a few e-mails?* He was convinced that his father had colored Damien's opinion and it irritated him greatly. He was smart enough to know never to send an e-mail in anger. He decided to mull over the content of what he regarded as Damien's pontifications but his initial thoughts were definite. *Surely you have to establish credibility early and take control. You have to tell them about your product or service in a powerful and compelling manner, so that you earn the right to ask questions and qualify them, so that no-one's time is wasted!*

There was much to think about over the next few days and Joshua was convinced Damien was over-emphasizing esoteric concepts. He disliked the Germanic psychoanalysis. *Maybe Damien is related to Freud*, he thought.

In the next few days, Joshua considered Damien's assertions constantly but resisted the urge to call his father to ascertain the degree to which Mark Peters had meddled. He resolved to deal with Damien's perceptions via the power of the pen, or in this case, the keyboard. The e-mail he was about to send was the result of some positive self-realization but also designed to motivate Damien to move on.

Hi Damien,

Your last e-mail took some digesting and some of the points you made were difficult for me to accept. I fear that my father has tainted your view of me but I trust you are dealing with me on my own merits.

Much of what you wrote I already knew but I must admit that I do tend to listen, waiting for an opportunity to speak, rather than listening to truly understand. I guess this is just my desire not to waste time. I do recognize that I need to prepare for meetings with better questions, so thanks for the insights on listening and preparing properly.

You asked me what I should be doing instead of qualifying hard and closing early. I still think it is important to qualify a prospect early so they don't waste my time, but I've linked your question to one of the other points you made: "The product is not the product." I've thought about this a lot over the last few days and I am excited with what I now believe. My product is what the customer may be interested in (my corporation's solution) but I am what they need to buy before we can transact business. I am selling trust and understanding so that we can explore together the potential suitability and value of what my corporation is offering. This is quite a revelation for me and it will take some time and effort to break my habit of leading with product and service features, but I have made a conscious decision to do so from now on. I will make a real effort to understand them and their problems as a pathway to building trust and earning the right to sell my solution.

I disagree with how you rate me in the Value Quadrant. Although I do tend to get price objections regularly, these help me qualify a prospect. I am fairly strategic and I don't agree with your assessment of me being a tactical sales person.

Now to the most difficult part of your e-mail where you raised my 'lack of belief'. It is true that I feel a bit conflicted in the selling profession but why is that such an issue? A plumber does not enjoy unblocking a sewer-pipe but that is how he makes a living. Surely selling is no different? My frustration is not caused by any integrity issue, it's caused by potential buyers who waste my time and tell me lies. I am also frustrated by having a boss that does not fully support me.

I thought about the meaning of the compass and I guess it relates to my direction. My father has always harped on about having a moral compass and I do believe in doing the right thing but I guess we can cover this later. I really would prefer that we discuss some new skills or techniques.

Your student,
Joshua Peters

Every day without a reply from Damien intensified Joshua's misgivings concerning his last e-mail. To make matters worse, he had an ominous telephone conversation with his boss, summoning him to a meeting. Joshua had artfully avoided a face-to-face encounter since sending the e-mail confirming the deal was lost, but Michael remained committed to addressing what he regarded as ineptitude in his employee.

The brief conversation in Michael's office was brutal. He told Joshua that he should start looking for another job if he lost another deal that required executive approval for special discounting. The hostile lecture reminded Joshua of being chided when he was a school boy. He resented being bullied but avoided inflaming the situation. Michael reinforced his threat with what he regarded as a clever piece of pointed humor.

"Success is all about execution – the trick, Joshua, is not to be next."

Joshua apologized through gritted teeth and walked out seething. Once he was clear of Michael's office, he muttered his feelings.

"What a load of crap."

"What did you say?" His boss had followed him to close the door.

Joshua turned around. "I've got to stay on track."

Michael was unconvinced but let it go. "Get on with it then."

It was two more days before Damien's reply appeared and Joshua started reading it at work. He abandoned it in annoyance after the first paragraph and struggled to concentrate for the rest of the day. As he contemplated Damien's negative comments, he felt the world was against him. That evening, he read the e-mail in its entirety.

Hello Joshua,

I am compelled to challenge your last e-mail. Please stop evaluating yourself based on what you think. Instead, assess yourself based on what you do. Intellectual ascent to the theories of selling is of no value unless it impacts how you behave. I am sorry to inform you that the philosophies and beliefs you espouse do not match your actions. You really need to be honest with yourself. Do you want to feel right or do you want to be successful?

Logic and facts are used for rationalization, merely supporting beliefs, rather than creating them. Belief is a matter of the heart and, therefore, most effective when accompanied by positive emotion. Joshua, do you 'have the faith'? Do you carry deep conviction concerning the value you offer and the integrity with which you operate? Do you believe in your corporation, the people you work with and the value of your product or service?

There is enormous freedom in facing and accepting the awful truth about something. Look in the mirror honestly, Joshua. Do you over-rate yourself? Are you living in denial about what is holding you back? To gain something you must first make room for it. The best way to improve most things is to reduce – cut away – rather than add. The baggage of our past is not what holds us back – we hold on to it. Joshua, what baggage do you need to let go of?

Your profession rewards proportionally to the challenges being overcome. You must become the person worthy of the success you seek but your biggest hurdle is your lack of belief. Recognize that you are the problem, yet also the answer and the opportunity. Success is determined more by your ability to unlearn wrong or limiting beliefs than by absorbing new information or charging forward with bravado. You asked me for new skills or techniques but success is achieved through attraction, not by pushing and not by any form of manipulation. I will not promote sales gimmicks or trickery.

Telling people things does not equate to effective communication but when you genuinely listen and ask thoughtful clarifying questions, the other person becomes receptive. Empathy and rapport occurs automatically when there is genuine interest, understanding and goodwill. Be quick to listen and slow to talk. Forget about being interesting. Instead, be interested. The reason for their question is far more important than your answer.

Consider this statement: Joshua Peters is the product, and the product is 'problem resolution'. You are committed to a process that has integrity; you find people with serious problems and help those who have the money and motivation to do business with you. You are completely committed to the process, not the financial outcome. Can you make these last few sentences your affirmation? If so, you will remove all negative pressure while you are selling.

I have one last thought for you. If you choose to fire your boss and change employers, never forget this inescapable truth – no matter where you go, you are always there. If you are the problem, then changing jobs will solve nothing. Even if your boss is difficult, I am sure there are things he can still teach you. The very best sales people succeed despite their boss, not because of them.

Dare to embrace the awful truth.

Damien Drost
Sales Mentor

"Arrogant self-righteous sauerkraut!" Joshua stormed around the kitchen until his emotions were eventually in check. He then reluctantly concluded that Damien's e-mail had merit and returned to the computer.

The glow of the screen illuminated one side of his face as he gazed into the dimly lit corner of the room. He reflected on the fact that, years earlier, he had drifted away from his family's values as he sought to establish his place among his peers and express himself independently. The turbulence of adolescence had fuelled conflict with his father and he could now see that his moral compass had been misdirected by ego and testosterone. Disengagement seemed to pervade his life and he was haunted with various regrets. *The legacy of religion*, he thought. Sitting alone in the darkness, he wasn't sure what he really believed in or stood for.

He had thrown it all away but was conscious now that he'd failed to replace it with anything of significance. His lust, greed and impatience were poorly balanced by feelings of guilt, fear and frustration. Behind the façade of confidence was a boy yet to truly become his own man. The truth was, despite his persona, he doubted his own capabilities. He inevitably concluded that Damien was right – he had to align his head with his heart, intellect with emotions, and beliefs with actions. If only he could reconcile and harness every aspect of his being. Then he could be a force to be reckoned with.

Damien's provocation had worked. Joshua turned to the screen and began to write as never before. He poured out his heart on the keyboard and hoped that mentor also meant confidant but he didn't really care what Damien thought of his ramblings. The point, for Joshua, was that he was being real, dealing with the truth of his own state. He was finally addressing the issues that had prevented him from giving himself fully to what he pursued. Regardless of where his career went, he wanted a definition for success that he could believe in at every level.

Hello Damien,

Thank you for confronting me. My last e-mail was quite rude and I apologize. You are right – I have been my own worst enemy in my career and I accept that I need to be a person worthy of the success I seek. I am now beginning to accept that my thinking is what determines my success and that I have a number of limiting beliefs and attitudes. I hope you're neither an atheist nor the Grand Master of a bizarre success cult but please allow me to ramble a little to explain the baggage that has been weighing me down and why I am ready, I hope, to now let go ...

Joshua's e-mail went into painful detail concerning his rejection of his parent's values and his turbulent relationship with his father. He also explored his true thoughts and fears concerning success. The honesty was raw and touched on the factors that limited his world-view and his ability to progress. His e-mail continued.

... I therefore choose to let go of my baggage and live truly and passionately. I want to forgive and be free – free of regret and free of the opinions of others. It will take time but I am committed to achieving this in my life. I now understand that selling can be fully aligned with my beliefs and values. From this point forward I resolve to live congruently and committed to the right sales process. I have chosen to own the affirmation you provided for me. "I, Joshua Peters, am the product. I find and solve serious problems for those who have the motivation and resources necessary to do business with me. I am fully there for people when I am with them. I build trust and understanding by listening actively and asking insightful questions."

Incredibly, I have this strange sense of not caring what happens now. If I do the right things with sincerity and competence, the rest should take care of itself. I look forward to what you have in store for me next.

Your student,
Joshua Peters

Joshua went to bed in the early hours of the morning and slept incredibly well. At 8:15 he woke to the ring of his mobile phone. As he rubbed his eyes and looked at the clock, it suddenly occurred to him that the sales meeting started in forty-five minutes and he had a minimum thirty minute drive. The last thing he needed to do was antagonize Michael Blunt any further. He scrambled into the shower. Minutes later, he roared down the road to do battle with peak-hour traffic.

The sales meeting was uneventful. Later that day, Joshua accessed his private web-mail and saw Damien's prompt response. It pleased him greatly to know that he and Damien had finally, truly connected. The posturing, stilted honesty and impatience had been replaced with genuine dialogue between someone eager to learn and someone wise, rich in experience and generous of spirit. Joshua smiled as he read the opening words of Damien's communication. This was the first sign of genuine warmth he had detected from his Germanic mentor.

Mein wunderbarste Joshua,

You bared your soul in that e-mail and made a monumental step in changing your world. I feel now that I am beginning to truly know you. Please forgive my harshness in previous communications but a jolt is sometimes necessary to create awareness.

I am pleased you understand that true freedom comes from within and I commend your courage in facing the reality of your internal challenges. In answer to your question, I am neither an atheist nor part of a success cult. I do, however, believe that our internal battles are more difficult than anything the business world can present. Meaning and purpose are essential ingredients for success. Your values are therefore an asset rather than any form of liability.

We can now move on to more concrete matters, so let us discuss the tangible aspects of success in selling. We will get to the RSVP principles soon. For now, I would like you to consider the seven sins of selling. We have touched on some of these already, so please review our e-mail dialogue to date. Tell me which ones have been revealed and what others you think comprise the seven sins?

Damien Drost
Sales Mentor

Chapter Four: Myths and the Seven Sins

Joshua had sent his e-mail to Damien concerning the seven sins before leaving for work. He had nominated: lack of belief, thinking features are benefits, and closing prematurely. Beyond these three, Joshua thought he would be guessing and therefore did not nominate others. He hoped Damien would respond quickly. He was keen to learn about the key pitfalls of selling and then move onto the substance of RSVP.

Although Joshua was feeling better about himself, things were not going well at work. Michael had insisted on attending the loss review with the ill-fated deal and Joshua feared it would reignite negative dialogue. The debrief they received however was surprisingly candid and he attributed this to the disarming introduction to the meeting by Michael.

"We really appreciate you making time to meet with us and please be assured that we respect your decision and process. Our goal today is simply to understand and learn from not being selected. Anything you can share with us is appreciated."

Joshua also asserted himself early in the meeting with well prepared questions and surprised even himself with how they uncovered the real cause of losing the business.

Driving back to the office, the pair reflected on the fact that they had been the lowest price and had a technical solution that was acknowledged to meet the requirements. Although not said directly, they lost because they did not have the necessary relationships with the right people. Joshua had been outsold, plain and simple. The competition had a strong relationship with the CFO and the external consultant who influenced their key technology decisions. The customer had selected the opposition for 'strategic reasons'.

Joshua had always had an awareness that he was stuck at the wrong level but had not wanted to offend his contacts and supporters by going above them. He believed it was essential to honor their process and he seemed to have built a strong relationship with the project manager. Yet every time he asked for meetings with more senior people he was told it could only happen once they were ready to negotiate. Joshua had wrongly thought that the comment was a buying signal. He had failed in the fundamental skill of bypassing the gatekeeper who sought to prevent access to people with real power.

During the loss review the CFO and project manager had been kind enough to say that Joshua had done a good job in representing the corporation and that it was a very difficult decision. This was, however, cold comfort. Coming second was the most expensive way to lose because they kept investing heavily right up until the bitter end.

Back at Michael's office, Joshua was asked a very direct question. "Why did we lose the deal?"

"It's my fault. I should have had direct relationships with the actual people making the decisions."

Michael was expecting him to attribute blame elsewhere and had mentally prepared a brutal progression of questions but he now seemed unsure of what to say next.

Joshua broke the awkward silence. "They agreed that our solution would do the job and they highlighted that price was not a determining factor. I've learned from this – next time I'll make sure we have the right relationships."

"Okay, let's not lose another opportunity like this again. I meant what I said previously – you cannot afford to lose another deal this way if you want a career here. I expect a formal loss review, fill in the paperwork and schedule the meeting with me for next week."

Joshua stared his boss directly in the eye. "I'll do the paperwork but why do we need to meet again on this? We know why we lost."

"Because I said so – just do it."

Joshua intensified his gaze. "I respond better to positive motivation."

"And I respond better to competence."

Joshua's heart was pounding as he left. Despite Michael's bravado and continued threats, he had largely disarmed his boss by simply accepting responsibility for failure and demonstrating that he had learned. He was keen to share the experience with Damien.

That night, when Joshua arrived home, he went straight to his computer where Damien's next e-mail was waiting for him.

Hello Joshua,

The three sins you nominated were correct but there were more within our correspondence. Not to worry, here are the seven sins of selling for professional sales. Every initial statement is untrue.

Sin number 1: Selling is the transference of information. No! Selling is actually building trust and transferring belief. Information can easily be sourced by customers without the assistance of a sales person. What value is the sales person if they do not distil all the relevant information down to what actually matters to the client? Remember, people do business with those they like and trust. Information and facts serve to support an emotional decision to buy.

Sin number 2: Talking is the best way to influence. Only if your goal is to bore people into submission or negatively push them to your competitor. Words account for only 7% of received communication. People think at 500 words per minute and you can only talk effectively at 125 per minute, so unless you match the words with intonation, and engage the other person visually with congruent body language, they will tune out. Effective communication is actually about asking great questions and actively listening by clarifying your understanding.

Sin number 3: Features are benefits. Not necessarily. Benefits must specifically solve acknowledged problems relating ultimately to time, money, comfort or risk. Prattling on about spurious features early in the sales process creates distracting noise and potential price concerns, preventing the buyer from focusing on the real value you offer in meeting their business needs.

Sin number 4: Objections are opportunities. Not so. Objections actually indicate that the sales person has sought to close prematurely or that they do not fully understand the needs of the buyer. Objections are not buying signals, nor are they opportunities to close. Objections do need to be overcome but they are usually generated by amateur sales people. It is always better to avoid objections by first having them expressed by the client as problems. Only seek commitment once full understanding and buyer readiness has been confirmed.

Sin number 5: The product is the product. Not really. Selling the product, service or solution is the third and final sale in any engagement. The prospective client first needs to be sold on your worthiness (credibility) for investing their time and effort. The next thing they need to be sold on is trust. Can they actually trust you with the information you are requesting and can they trust you to competently and ethically make recommendations in their best interests? If these first two sales are made, then selling the solution becomes very achievable, once you have aligned with their buying criteria and process. The product is problem resolution, through the sales person, and the buyer will engage effectively once corporate credibility and personal trust has been established.

Sin number 6: Skill and knowledge determines value and success. Although these are important prerequisites, the real differentiator in the market is positive attitude and ability to influence. People don't care about what you know. They instead care about what you can do for them. This is why having a positive attitude and proven ability to deliver is vital. Beyond qualifications, this is what employers really look for in prospective employees.

Sin number 7: Success is just a numbers game. Avoid the busy fool syndrome. Work ethic is important and understanding the required activity levels for building and maintaining a sales funnel is essential. However, moving from selling simple commodity products to complex high-end solutions, means success is more about effectiveness than mere activity. This means doing the right things, with the right people, at the right time. Understand and honor the required activity levels for a healthy pipeline but recognize that to progress a prospect to becoming a customer, it is not about numbers – it's all about people, process and strategy.

There are many myths in business. You need to give further thought to these seven sins. Tell me which of these need your repentance. Carefully consider the reality of how you actually engage in the real world. I look forward to your response.

Damien Drost
Sales Mentor

Joshua carefully reviewed the list of selling indiscretions and felt reasonably attuned with most of the information. There were a few things, however, that leapt out at him for self-reflection and he considered his deficiencies. He went to bed musing on how his attitude toward Damien had changed, and he drifted off to sleep feeling a certain kinship with his mentor.

It was 7:00am and Joshua sat drinking his second espresso. He had been typing vigorously for almost an hour, recounting the post mortem with the lost customer and the subsequent meeting with Michael. He then moved on to some valuable lessons he had learned.

... and the special price I tried to use to close the deal made absolutely no difference but did create a problem for my boss by triggering visibility with those above him when he sought approval. They told us that price was not a factor and I could hardly believe it. The second main thing we learnt was the importance of having influential relationships with senior people.

Losing this deal has taught me some valuable lessons and reinforced the key points you've been teaching me. But the most amazing thing was how my boss just backed-off when I accepted responsibility for losing the deal, explaining to him what I had learnt.

I have thought long and hard about the seven sins of selling and, although I am by no means perfect, I genuinely believe I am embracing the beliefs, habits and actions necessary for avoiding these traps. I am firmly focused on delivering real value to my customers by sincerely focusing on how I can help them through understanding their problems and requirements. I will seek to work with them on the basis of establishing trust, credibility and understanding. I am beginning to really understand who I need to be and how I must operate, in order to be successful.

Your student,
Joshua Peters

Strangely, it was five days before Joshua received a reply. He wondered if Damien was sick or maybe travelling. As he read Damien's words in the long awaited communication he understood why there had been a delay.

Hello Joshua,

You may have been wondering why this reply has taken so long. I have been carefully considering what we should cover next, or more importantly, whether we need to revisit lessons to date. We will keep moving forward but be cautious with your confidence – it can be the feeling you have just before you understand the situation. Confidence can also manifest as a lack of preparation or arrogance.

Success can teach little but instead may reinforce weakness or malpractice. Failure, on the other hand, causes self examination for those with the right attitude as they learn from their mistakes. Winning may be good for the spirit but losing can be educational and motivating if embraced in the right way. Congratulations on the few things you picked up from losing the deal. Strive also to learn from the experiences of others.

I was delighted to read of your excitement in seeing the power of accepting responsibility with your boss. You are beginning to use well considered questions in meetings. I am also happy that you understand the importance of having relationships of trust with the right people. This is the perfect time to reveal more of RSVP.

The R stands for Relationships, and most sales people wrongly believe this to be their strength. This is because many sales people have a disempowering view of the role that relationships play in strategic selling. They invest time and emotional energy with the wrong people, the ones they are comfortable dealing with. The relationships that make a difference are with the people that are initially resistant to meeting with you. Sales relationships need to provide far more than support; they need to provide powerful influence and accurate information.

Every buyer seeks Return On Investment (ROI) from a purchasing decision, but the seller also makes an investment in the sales process. In complex solution selling, the costs are substantial. The sales organization, therefore, needs their ROI but to obtain their return on the selling investment, they must first have Relationships Of Intelligence, Integrity and Influence within the buying entity – this is The New ROI ©. A Sales Master understands that ROI needs to be reciprocated with powerful relationships providing accurate, insightful, differentiating information.

The S of RSVP stands for Strategy. Relationships alone are not enough if you wish to be a Sales Master. I must say, Joshua, I am concerned that you did not identify the lack of strategy as a cause for losing that important piece of business. Most risk in business comes from not knowing what it is that you don't know. The process of formulating strategy largely addresses this risk because you are forced to test assumptions and gather all the necessary information before making decisions and executing.

What do you think the V and P stand for in RSVP? Please also let me know your thoughts concerning the specific deficiencies in strategy that contributed to losing the opportunity.

Damien Drost
Sales Mentor

Joshua was a little miffed after digesting the e-mail. Damien had offered both praise and a cautionary reprimand. *Thank goodness he didn't regress into the self-help stuff*, Joshua mused. *Finally I have half the RSVP riddle. Surely the P stands for Price.* He believed he had three quarters of the equation but struggled with the V.

He could not escape the constant distraction of wondering what had caused Damien to hesitate in moving forward. Damien may have decided to move on but Joshua needed to resolve the issue for his own peace of mind. He re-read his previous e-mail to Damien through fresh eyes and could see the problem – he had come across as if he had 'arrived' by paying only scant attention to the seven sins.

He had to uncover what the V stood for and restore Damien's confidence in him. Joshua pondered the RSVP acronym endlessly over the next few days and it came to him while driving home.

Hi Damien,

I re-read what I wrote to you and I apologize for being glib in my response to your question about the seven sins of selling. I guess I was focused on sharing the loss review and subsequent conversation with my boss. I revisited the seven pitfalls and wrote an affirmation that I will read every morning over breakfast so that I remain diligent in seeking to avoid the traps.

Here it is: 'I have a great attitude and genuinely care about my customers and their outcomes. I believe in the value I offer. I am a subject matter expert and problem solver. I sell trust by being a great listener and by asking insightful questions so that I fully understand my customer and their problems before exploring potential solutions. I distil information in order to focus only on the things that actually benefit the client by solving their specific problems. I confirm the client's satisfaction throughout the sales process and only seek to close when I am certain we have agreement.'

You are right to raise your concerns with my over-confidence. I have never heard that definition: The feeling you have before you understand the situation! From now on, whenever I feel confident, I will pause and reflect on this definition.

I know you will be horrified at the following admission but I am committed to being honest. I have been thinking about strategy as it relates to the lost deal and I guess the problem was that I have regarded a relationship strategy as my only strategy. I must also admit that my relationships lacked senior influence and failed to provide accurate competitor information. I love the concept of ROI and I will change my thinking and approach, so that I can influence senior people and get better coaching from supporters of our solution within the customer's project team.

But surely product marketing and management are responsible for determining product strategy and formulating the value proposition that we in sales take to our target markets? The sales training I've had focuses on being able to pitch on the basis of features and benefits with specific expertise in target industries. Strategy is my biggest weakness and I am looking forward to learning as much as possible from you in this area.

Thank you for revealing the first half of RSVP! I think the V is for Value and the P is for Price. Am I correct? Actually, having just re-read this, is V for Value proposition?

Your student,
Joshua Peters

Joshua sent the e-mail feeling optimistic that Damien would be impressed with the content. He had apologized and acknowledged his weaknesses with regard to strategy. He felt sure that he had solved the RSVP riddle.

That night, Joshua watched television in blissful distraction. Work was becoming less important than his mentorship and he felt he had little to learn from Michael Blunt. He had not told Damien but he was committed to a change of employer, sooner rather than later. Joshua had formed the view that sales people were 'hired guns' and wondered whether Damien would agree but decided to leave the question for another time. The next morning he checked his e-mail with little expectation that Damien would reply so soon.

Hello Joshua,

A quicker response compared with my last e-mail but your correspondence was worthy of prompt attention. You correctly identified the reason for my reticence in my last communication. I commend your positive affirmation for countering the seven sins of selling. Think of it as your statement of the seven virtues! If you can live your affirmation intuitively, you will have begun your journey toward sales mastery which is unconscious competence (being instinctively capable) in doing the right things, the right way, and at the right time.

I am sorry to say that you have not fully grasped the ROI concept. Please give it more thought. Positive relationships are essential in all selling environments yet most sales professionals develop relationships with the wrong people. Think about the deal you lost. Your weakness was not your ability to build positive rapport, but with whom you invested your time and emotional energy.

Remember the Value Quadrant? It illustrates the difference between low value transactional selling (professional visitor) and being strategic in creating genuine value. Transactional/relationship selling is often price sensitive and the predominant value of the sales person is defined by the relationships they build with their customers. Although solution sales people need to be excellent with relation-ships, they must also develop and execute tactics within a well conceived strategy while also man-aging complexity. A relationship strategy is important but 'relationship selling' is not an acceptable strategy on its own. Do you understand what I am saying here? Relationships are valuable because they enable you to gather information, understanding and support.

Relationships with the wrong people, on the other hand, can inhibit success because they provide misinformation, trap you at the wrong level, or align you with losing political or commercial agendas. It is very rare for someone to do this to you intentionally but many people within organizations are sim-ply outside the genuine sphere of influence. It is essential to be politically and commercially aligned with the power-base within an organization if you are to succeed. The more dependent a sales person is on relationship selling, the more they belong in the world of selling low value commodity products, or transactional selling.

High value solution selling, however, demands that you understand the customer's problems and align with political and commercial drivers – measures and outcomes. Positive relationships are good but should be with the right people and desired by them because of the perceived value you offer. No-one likes being sold to but everyone wants people around them that can help in achieving their desired outcomes or objectives. You need to help and ask, rather than tell and sell.

You must also distinguish between relationship selling and a relationship strategy. The problem with relationship selling is that it is the default operational mode of most sales people and the only kind of strategy they know. I have every confidence that strategy will become your strength and we will deal with this in detail soon enough. For now, I want you to let me know what the most important thing is in developing effective strategy. Please think carefully before you respond.

Joshua, RSVP is not as obvious as you may think. You got the V almost right and the P completely wrong. V is Value creation and value proposition but the P does not stand for Price. Although price can exclude you, it only matters if the customer wants what you are selling. Think further and consider why sales people so often get their forecasting wrong. You are doing well and I look forward to your reply.

Damien Drost
Sales Mentor

Joshua was surprised that he had been wrong concerning the meaning of P. He rinsed his cup and headed for the bathroom. For some reason, Joshua did his best thinking under a hot shower. The misty steam engulfed him as he focused on the strategy question posed by Damien, but he could not escape his fixation on the P. As he dried his hair he concluded that it must stand for either Position, Performance or Process, but which one? He continued to mull it over as he drove to work.

He descended the office car-park and felt mildly alarmed upon realizing he couldn't remember the journey in. *It is amazing how the brain takes care of repetitious activity*, he thought. Maybe one day soon he would instinctively execute sales process just as Damien alluded. He turned off the ignition and, sitting in near-darkness, reflected on the concept of strategy. He thought about military history which was his favorite subject at school. It occurred to him as a revelation – *strategy depends upon accurate intelligence*. The answer to Damien's question concerning strategy was having all of the necessary accurate information.

As he headed for the elevator, he refocused on the P and was determined to get it right – no more guessing. He pressed the elevator call button as Damien's advice echoed in his head: *Focus on the reason sales people get forecasting wrong.*

He had arrived in the office just in time for the regular sales meeting. The quarter was drawing to a close and the blow-torch was being applied to Andrew, one of the low performers. Everyone felt a little uncomfortable and Joshua was thankful that he was having a solid quarter. At the end of the meeting, Michael emphasized the need to deliver results and then asked the team if they had anything they wanted to discuss. Without thought, Joshua jumped in.

"Why do you think we struggle to forecast accurately?"

Michael was a little bemused. "There are two main reasons: Not enough coverage in the pipeline, and not truly understanding the customer's buying process."

Joshua looked like he wanted to ask another question but Michael had no intention of indulging him.

"The meeting is over but stay focused on closing business. There are only thirteen selling days left in the quarter."

Joshua decided he did have something to learn from Michael Blunt after all and asked him if he had time for a coffee. They met twenty minutes later in a quiet corner of the café downstairs, and Joshua began to quiz his boss.

"Why did you say we miss our forecast because we don't understand the customer's process? Surely closing business is all about us driving the sale?"

For Joshua, it was like watching a locked car door close just as the realization hit that the keys were still in the ignition. He immediately followed-up before his boss could speak.

"I'm sorry, Mike, that really wasn't what I meant. I know business closes based on the customer's readiness, not external pressure. It's just that I'm working with a new sales methodology. Have you heard of RSVP?"

"No, but forget about fads, you can't get away from the basics."

Joshua nodded. "I agree but I've been trying to figure out what the P stands for and you've helped me come to the conclusion that it's definitely Process – the customer's process."

Michael appeared cautiously interested. "What do the other letters stand for?"

Joshua was keen to see what his boss thought but felt uneasy talking about a subject he barely understood. "Well, the R is for Relationships. The S is for Strategy and the V is for Value proposition."

"Hmm – if you have those areas covered in a deal and you truly understand their buying process, it would be hard to lose."

Michael then reached into his coat pocket and magically produced a piece of paper – it was the forecast.

"Let's use this RSVP thing to talk through a key deal you still need to close this quarter."

For the next thirty minutes, basic RSVP questions revealed the vulnerabilities and additional information he needed. After the meeting, Joshua went upstairs to access his web mail.

Hi Damien,

The P is for Process – the customer's process. Have a great day. I will send you an e-mail tonight. Thanks again for everything!

Your student,
Joshua Peters

Chapter Five: The Choice

Joshua closed the quarter strongly and people around him were beginning to notice a change, not just in results but in him as a person. He had developed a self-deprecating sense of humor at work. The most liberating aspect of Joshua's new life, however, was that he freely admitted mistakes and said he was sorry. He had embraced these new values in professional life and was experiencing the benefits but deep down, he knew he needed to expand the ethos into his personal life. He had already lost Mandy but felt there was plenty of time to salvage the relationship with his father.

In his career, the mentorship was going well and he could see the value of Damien's approach in allowing lessons to unfold within the context of real life experience. It was for this reason that he recognized the indecent haste with which he was pushing for RSVP revelations. It was time to pull back and defer to Damien's experience in the pace and delivery of new information. The e-mail he was about to send reflected his desire to ensure that he really had taken hold of the new ideas in his life.

Hello Damien,

It felt good to finish the quarter ahead of quota and my relationship with Michael, my boss, has improved over the last few weeks. I've been re-reading our correspondence and I noticed that I've been rather impatient for new information. I will instead focus on applying what I've learnt.

In line with this, I've been thinking more about the first RSVP principle: being fully there. In my personal life, I think this is why my girlfriend left me. She always seemed to want to talk while I was busy (often watching television) but, in truth, I wasn't there for her. I think I've often been distracted instead of being focused, but I've been making a conscious effort lately to live this principle at work. I've been attending meetings without my laptop, and leaving my phone in my pocket on silent. I'm amazed by how many people sit in meetings working on their laptops, doing e-mail or taking calls when their phone rings! The scary thing is that I was one of those people. I've come to see that these distractions substantially damage the effectiveness of any meeting but people just seem to accept this behavior as normal.

I've decided that any meeting I run will have an agenda and printed on the top will be a statement about being fully there. I am going to do everything possible to ensure people are on time and that there are no distractions. I've also noticed how much more effective I am with customers now that I seek to become absorbed by their needs rather than my own. I am now getting so much more information and people seem really willing to open up. I've also found that people are beginning to ask me what I think, whereas I used to be the first to jump in with an opinion. Thank you for this change in me.

I am a big step above where I was previously and I still don't understand RSVP beyond the headings, and that's okay. I know you will reveal these things at the appropriate time. I should let you know that I am going to do a bid review at work later this week and although we will use the corporation's standard account planning documents, I will lead with the RSVP concepts to help decide if we should invest in the opportunity. My boss sees the benefit of applying clarity of thought to our account plans where there is just too much detail.

I have been paying special attention to the ROI concept (Relationship of Intelligence/Integrity/Influence) and can see that I really did not understand what you had originally told me. It is not about me influencing them; it's about developing senior positive relationships with the people who influence the decision, and who provide accurate information to assist in our strategy. Relationships within the customer's organization need to go beyond being supportive, they must help engineer the deal. Am I on the right track here?

What should I be doing to reinforce the information you've already given me? I will keep working on 'being fully there'. I'm already noticing that it is becoming easier – not that I am masterful, but I am beginning to become instinctively capable. I've really worked on meeting people well, by having a firm, warm and friendly handshake, matched with smiling eyes and having a genuine interest in them. Anyway, I just wanted to say that I will keep working on being fully there but what else should I focus on in order to go from knowledge to knowing?

Your student,
Joshua Peters

Later that day, Joshua sent out the meeting invitation for the session that would decide whether they would bid for a potential new customer, Zenyth Corporation. The calendar invitation included an agenda and on the top there were instructions for the attendees.

Opportunity Review: Zenyth Corporation
Please be on time and 'fully there'.
No e-mail or messaging, no working on your laptop and no phone calls.
We will start punctually and finish ahead of schedule if possible.

Joshua was waiting for additional information which he expected to have prior to the meeting. This would be his first attempt at using the RSVP process in a group and he was looking forward to it. That night he made dinner and ate as usual in front of the television. Although he only intended to watch the news, it was several hours before the intermittent rolling of the screen created enough irritation to prompt him to turn it off and check his e-mail. It annoyed him that he had wasted most of the evening but he felt better when he saw that Damien had replied.

Hello Joshua,

You are making outstanding progress! Congratulations on a great quarter but more importantly, congratulations on the change within you that is being noticed by others. You deserve the positive results and recognition.

You asked me what you should do to move from knowledge to knowing. We learn best through experience and we become masterful at something through repetitious practice of the right things. The answer, therefore, is to learn through doing until it becomes instinctive.

I am very happy that you are seeking to become masterful at being fully there, especially when first meeting someone. You also made a very astute observation concerning meetings and how people attend but rarely engage 100% with their mind and emotions. It is both ill-mannered and unproductive to be distracted by electronic gadgets, especially e-mail and messaging. You are right to encourage people to be fully there when you lead a meeting. It will be interesting to see how others respond to you in this regard.

At the risk of heaping too much praise, you also did well to recognize that the more we know, the greater awareness we have of just how much we do not know. A little knowledge can bring arrogance, but knowing brings wisdom. Ignorance produces prejudice and, in business, it results in bad decisions. My advice is to be tolerant and to learn how to gently influence those around you who are relatively unaware.

It is good that you are beginning to work with RSVP and that you have the support of your boss. Now is the right time to introduce you to the RSVPselling.com website where there is an Opportunity Qualification Tool which will assist in your meeting later in the week. This approach need not replace the strategic selling methodologies and tools a business already uses. RSVP is a process but also a way of thinking strategically for covering the essentials without the necessity for complex documentation. It is a way of easily focusing on the important elements in winning business and running an effective campaign.

I was sorry to hear about your girlfriend leaving you but am glad you see the benefits in addressing non-business issues in your life. Everything is interconnected. I have something else important for us to discuss. I want you to finish this sentence: 'To do something great with my life, I must first ...' The answer is not 'change', as we have already dealt with that issue. It is good that you accept the reality that you must be the change you want to see in your world and you are making excellent progress in this regard. Here is a clue: Examine the contents of your home. Success is a process, not an event. Both success and failure are the result of thousands of tiny cumulative decisions that form habits.

Good luck for your meeting and make sure you employ strategy in addressing relationships and competitor positioning. Remember that the power of RSVP is in its simple clarity, not complexity. Explore the website as it will reveal much.

Damien Drost
RSVPselling™ Sales Master

Joshua noticed the change in Damien's e-mail signature title and was annoyed that he had not discovered for himself that there was a website for the RSVP concept. He focused, however, on something else in the e-mail. He was glad Damien had advised him to consider strategy for relationships, and the competition, but wondered why price was not included. He opened the agenda document and eventually decided to delete all references to price. He wanted to replace it with the topic of competitors but was unsure who the real threat was or how they would position. There was clearly more work to do before the meeting on Friday but at least now he knew what he didn't know – or so he thought.

Damien's latest question was intriguing. "To do something great with my life, I must first …" He started a list of possible endings: be great, be ready, be a leader. The list went on but nothing felt right and he re-read Damien's e-mail, focusing on the clues provided. "Success and failure are processes determined by habits. Examine the contents of your home." He repeated it softly but nothing he had written down related to the contents of his home. It was late and he was tired. He hoped the answer would come to him in the morning.

The new dawn brought no revelations concerning Damien's latest riddle. He decided to focus on the Zenyth deal and the task of gathering more information, especially about the competition. At work, he began exploring the RSVPselling.com website and completed the Opportunity Qualification Tool. The results painted a rather bleak picture concerning whether they should marshal their valuable resources in pursuing the potential revenue at Zenyth.

At the end of the work day, he planned to examine everything in his home, item by item, until he had the answer to Damien's latest task. He put a pot of water on the stove and the gas burner whooshed to life. As it steadily came to the boil he fired up his laptop and sent a quick e-mail.

Hi Damien,

The website is fantastic but the Qualification Tool gave a negative score and highlighted a number of areas we need to address. Thanks for the tip on strategy; I have been gathering additional information all day to prepare for Friday's bid review.

I will send a more detailed e-mail once I feel I can answer your latest riddle. I am really stuck; any chance of another clue?

The water was boiling and Joshua dropped a generous handful of spaghetti into the pot before placing the bolognaise sauce into the microwave. "Thank God for mothers", he whispered. Clare Peters was of Italian heritage and made fantastic lasagna and bolognaise that seemed to taste better the longer it was left in the fridge. He had just grated fresh parmesan cheese over his steaming meal when he heard his laptop. He grabbed his glass of red wine and went to take a look. It was from Damien. *That was fast*, Joshua thought. He hit print and took the single page to his kitchen table so that he could read and eat at the same time.

Hello Joshua,

Here is your clue: Time is precious.

I will be surprised if you go to bed tonight without having the answer.

Damien Drost
RSVPselling™ Sales Master

He still felt in the dark and circled a few of the possibilities that had potential linkage with objects in his home. "To do something great with my life, I must first – read." He had the beginnings of a reasonable library of business books. *Surely this is it*, he thought, *reading changes people because they hear their own voice and engage their imagination – or maybe not*. Joshua focused again on the three clues: Something inside his home, habits create success, time is precious. He started talking to himself again. "To do something great with my life, I must first – get organized." His home was rather messy and he knew that clutter created distraction. Damien certainly seemed obsessed with Germanic efficiency. Joshua knew he wasted time looking for things as a result of being a bit disorganized but wondered if the answer could be that simple.

Neither of these options seemed compelling. He wondered if it was about getting rid of something, or maybe introducing something new. Spending lots of time reading did not seem to fit the third clue. Maybe the answer really was to eliminate clutter and get organized. As Joshua slid his dinner plate over to make room for writing more on his sheet of paper, the remote crashed to the floor. He bent down to pick it up – *the television remote!* "To do something great with my life, I must first turn off the TV!" It was a perfect match for the three clues. The television consumed several hours of his time every day and watching it formed an insidious time wasting habit. To Joshua, it seemed basic rather than profound, but there was no doubt in his mind.

Hi Damien,

Thanks for the extra clue. To do something great with my life I must first turn off the television! I am sure that, as a result, I will have time to be better organized and to develop the positive habit of reading. Am I right?

I feel prepared to lead the bid review and will focus on the overall strategy while working through RSVP with the Qualification Tool. Thanks again for your input and advice. I will let you know how it goes.

Your student,
Joshua Peters

Joshua went to bed comfortable with the concept of watching less television and reading more. He drifted off to sleep feeling the next day would be good.

It was 6:30 Friday morning and Joshua sat reading Damien's latest e-mail. Communication between them had been frequent in the last few days. The bid review meeting for the Zenyth account was in a few hours.

Hello Joshua,

Good luck with your bid review today. I know you will do a capable job and I look forward to hearing how it goes.

Yes, television was what I was looking for. It may not strike you as profound but you must make room for the change you seek – you need space for thinking. TV is the biggest time waster in most people's lives and computerized entertainment can fit the same category. Worse than merely wasting time, television also propagates fear and prejudice, and seduces viewers into feeling that happiness comes from being entertained. The goal of life is not entertainment or self-absorbed escapism. Happiness should be the by-product of finding purpose and meaning in being part of something truly worthwhile.

You cannot make a difference while being addicted to television or computer games. To do something great you must, therefore, eliminate mind-numbing television. The brain waves of people watching it border on hypnosis. Some television is worthwhile but not much. It is a time thief and should have little place in the life of someone committed to changing their world.

Maybe you intellectually recognize television viewing as an unproductive and negative habit but just to affirm this view and give it emotion, consider how much sitting in front of television really costs you. Divide your annual income by the number of hours you work per year. Now, how many hours per week do you spend watching television? Multiply the hours by fifty-two. Now do the math; multiply your television hours in a year by your hourly income. This is one measure of the potential cost, but don't worry, it's only money – or is it? What will you do about it?

Lasting success is the result of our positive choices and habits. Success is rarely an event; it's a process. The key to living a successful life is to develop the right habits and make the right choices. We must thoughtfully choose our environment and beliefs as they create outcomes within us. Finally, Joshua, if your success gets ahead of your capability – or worthiness – it will be temporary. I sincerely believe your success will be fully sustainable when our time together is through. There is much food for thought here and I look forward to your reply.

Damien Drost
RSVPselling™ Sales Master

He wants me to commit to the cult. In Joshua's mind, Damien had taken self-help psychobabble to a new level and he didn't like it. Now it was clear that Damien wanted him to go all the way, but Joshua loved television and was saving to buy the very latest wide screen technology ready for the next football season.

As he headed out the door, he patted his father's old television and smiled. "I won't let him take you away."

It was a beautiful day and he lowered the roof as he eased out of the garage. He enjoyed the trip to the office and focused on the meeting he would be running. Damien's disturbing e-mail could wait until evening. At work, he completed the RSVP Opportunity Qualification Tool again but with more optimistic responses – the results were still less than satisfactory.

It was 10:00, and everyone was in the boardroom except Phil, one of the two pre-sales engineers. Joshua started without him.

"Thanks for being here on time and may I ask you to put your phones on silent. The purpose of this meeting is to decide whether or not we bid for the Zenyth account. I've already circulated drafts of the account plan and there are some details missing, but I think we have enough information to make a decision. Rather than get into a lot of detail with the account plan, I would like – "

"Hi everyone, sorry I'm late." Phil had arrived.

"Hi Phil. Anyway, rather than work though the account plan, I would like to address four key criteria for determining if we should bid. They are: relationships, strategy, our value proposition, and what we know about their buying process. If all four of these don't line up, then I think we should withdraw."

Joshua projected the RSVP Opportunity Qualification Tool for Zenyth on the screen. Michael leaned forward and started taking notes. He was only partially listening as Joshua continued.

"Let's begin with relationships. Go to page seven of the account plan where I've listed all the key people involved in the decision process and project but I can't seem to identify an executive sponsor. This is important because we don't yet understand their business case and what's really driving the project."

Joshua stepped through the relationship questions on the screen and then flipped the white-board, revealing an organizational chart of sorts, highlighting who he thought were the key people. He had referenced them in the account plan document but he summarized what he knew about each person, including their bias and drivers. The group asked some good questions and Michael seemed impressed, busily noting additional information that was needed. It was obvious that their coach within Zenyth was only mid-level in the organization and that a number of key senior relationships were not covered.

Phil was renowned for having his laptop as an appendage and he had powered it up while Joshua was drawing on the whiteboard.

"Phil, what's the laptop for?"

"I have to check something before my next meeting."

"If you need to be somewhere else, that's okay. But if you're in the room, we really need you to be here."

Phil was taken aback but feigned a smile. He closed the lid on his laptop. "Sorry, I'll get focused but I will need to leave early to prepare for my next meeting."

"We will probably finish ahead of time anyway."

Joshua continued. "If we bid for this, we will need a strategy for covering all the key people and crafting a unique value proposition. But I'm not completely sure about who our biggest threats are or how they'll engage. I know Zenyth will have the usual suspects on the short-list but there might also be a few niche players in the picture. The danger is that we are neither a best-of-breed player, nor the bidder with the strongest brand or technology. That's why we need to approach the deal a little differently."

Joshua went on to highlight the very serious problem of not fully understanding the customer's business case and prerequisite project outcomes. The Opportunity Qualification Tool served as a constant reference for the group as they stepped logically through the issues and their weaknesses.

"We need to identify the unique aspects of what we offer, technically and commercially, that matter to them."

Joshua stopped talking and smiled at Phil who looked up with a sheepish grin and stopped composing his text.

"Ah – sorry." Phil's mobile device disappeared into his coat pocket for the remainder of the meeting.

Joshua moved on to how they could align their technology and service offering to the biggest business problems and drivers within Zenyth. It was clear, however, that this was difficult without having all the necessary information. They needed a meeting with a key Zenyth executive to discuss the business case and the driving factors behind the project. Once they identified the executive sponsor for the project, Joshua would need a way of establishing credibility to position himself as someone worthy of their trust. He knew that executives resented priming sales people with basic information. The team explored all this for about fifteen minutes before Joshua stood and moved to the big screen.

"The Opportunity Qualification Tool shows what needs to change if we are to bid but there is something we need from Zenyth." He moved to the whiteboard and wrote ROI in big letters. "The main reason we need to identify the executive sponsor for the project is so that we can get our ROI – Relationship Of Influence."

Michael smirked but Joshua continued unperturbed.

"We need to truly understand their drivers, selection criteria and procurement process. We also need to know whether this deal is, for them, more about risk or reward."

Phil was unimpressed. "You know we are a good technical fit – surely we will bid? We can beat the tier-one competitors on price."

Joshua glanced over at Michael while Richard from marketing added his weight to Phil's rhetorical question. "We certainly need clients in this industry segment. Presence in this vertical is a key part of the marketing plan – I think we should go for it."

Michael looked like he wanted to speak but Joshua jumped in first. "Unless we have a unique and compelling value proposition, and have access to the executive sponsor, I think we would just be making up the numbers and wasting our time. The Opportunity Qualification Tool doesn't lie."

Michael leaned forward and nodded. "Yes, I'm with Joshua on this, we always talk about qualifying out before we qualify in. Joshua is right on both counts." Michael paused briefly and glanced at Joshua. "Let's reconvene when we have more information and a better idea of how we can win. All four scores in this qualification tool need to lift dramatically if we are to bid. This was a good meeting Joshua, can you stay for a few minutes?"

They had finished twenty minutes early. Joshua closed the door and wondered what his boss wanted to say.

"Josh, grab a seat. I've been harsh with you in the past but I just wanted to say how well you ran that meeting. That qualification tool is good and I like the way you're thinking. I'm sick and tired of us bidding for business where we are destined to come second."

The RSVP process had highlighted substantial gaps and Michael was supportive as they reviewed the list of questions and actions together. Joshua knew what information was needed before they could meet again to discuss whether they would bid, and if so, what their strategy would need to look like.

After the meeting, Joshua left a message on Phil's voicemail. "Hi Phil. Sorry if I was hard on you in the meeting today but I'll buy you lunch and explain. I've learned that there's magic in being fully there. It will make sense when we get together, let me know what day suits you."

At the end of the day, Joshua headed for the pub to meet his friends and watch Friday night football on the big screen. His team lost but was still in the race for the finals. He was tired when he arrived home but watched the late night sport anyway.

Joshua woke feeling refreshed and cooked eggs and bacon, which was a Saturday morning tradition. He mopped-up the last of his runny yoke and munched on the toast. He considered Damien's exhortation concerning television but eliminating it completely from his life was a radical concept. *Everything in moderation – maybe I'll just watch sport and news.*

He hovered over the keyboard reviewing his attempts to justify television where he had argued that everything in moderation was alright. He made a link with eggs and bacon – too much was unhealthy but a few times a week was okay. The comparison was lame and he decided to close the incomplete e-mail, saving it into his drafts folder. He would head for the café and read the Saturday paper. He hit send. "No!" He hastily sent a follow-up to Damien.

Hi Damien,

Please disregard the previous e-mail. It was only a draft and sent by mistake. The comment about moderation was something my father used to say to me. I'm struggling with your television challenge but will write to you before the day is over. The meeting went well yesterday!

Joshua

Reading the Saturday paper at his local café was also a ritual he thoroughly enjoyed. Nearby, couples laughed and talked together and it reminded him of his past life with Mandy. He knew he wasn't yet comfortable with being alone. Ninety minutes later, he was back home getting ready for golf and was surprised to see that Damien had replied.

Hello Joshua,

Sorry but I did not see your follow-up e-mail until it was too late. Here is another eggs and bacon analogy: The chicken was involved but the pig was committed. The issue is not one of moderation.

You are your father's son but it is time to cast your own shadow.

Damien Drost
RSVPselling™ Sales Master

Joshua drove to golf thinking about the habits in his life. He had not been playing well for months and although he knew what was wrong with his swing he couldn't seem to fix it. He had reinforced bad habits for so long that any necessary corrections felt impossibly unnatural. Joshua had a hitting mat and net in his garage and had spent the last few weeks practicing drills to shorten his back-swing and stop collapsing his left arm at the top. He felt he was making good progress, until he stood over a ball during a round to make a full-blooded swing. He was determined that this round would be different.

The game had gone well and Joshua stood on the fifteenth tee, two shots under his fourteen handicap, with four holes to go. He had played smart and stayed out of trouble by swinging within himself. He had employed good course management and avoided his trademark 'death or glory' shots. His short game was solid and, by minimizing the number of errant shots off the tee, he had avoided trouble and frustration.

The fifteenth tee was elevated, presenting a beautiful vista of the tantalizing dog-leg par five. It enticed the player to hit over the water with a driver to shorten the hole and played like a long par four if this brave shot was executed well. Just last month, Joshua had crushed a drive on this hole and had marveled at the purity of the shot as it climbed over the water with a slight draw and then bumped along the fairway in perfect position. On that day, he reached the green with his fairway wood and two-putted for a tap-in birdie. All subsequent visits to the fifteenth, however, had yielded very different results. All involved water and bad language.

His regular playing partner, Anthony, had a club handicap of nine and had safely hit his drive sweetly across the lake. He turned to Joshua and engaged in predictable mind games.

"Don't think about the water."

"All I can see is the fairway."

The head of Joshua's driver hovered as he looked up to again visualize the planned flight of the ball. He momentarily practiced the take-away, flexed his knees and started the back-swing – he abruptly broke away and laughed.

"This is so stupid."

He headed for his bag, put the driver away and returned with his three wood. Anthony mocked with unrestrained laughter.

"I'm being smart for a change. Three wood, five wood, then eight iron."

That was exactly how he played the hole. He reached the green in regulation and two-putted for par. Not long after, the pair shook hands on the eighteenth green. It had been a long while since Joshua had beaten Anthony.

"Well played Josh. Here's your twenty bucks. You only have to beat me for the next ten weeks in a row to break even. You still haven't broken those bad habits your dad taught you when you were a kid. He has the swing of a one-hinged rusty gate."

One of Joshua's positive memories was playing golf with his father but that was a long time ago. After a couple of beers, Joshua headed home to confront the television issue. He ordered pizza, opened a bottle of wine and started writing to Damien, recounting the bid review meeting. Before long, a knock at the door signaled that dinner had arrived.

The delivery man headed down the path, and Joshua went to eat in front of the television. He felt a twinge of guilt as the box came to life. He eagerly stuffed pizza into his mouth as he watched the news, sport and weather. He realized he was being drawn into the next program and abruptly hit the power button. It faded to black. The laptop screen projected an eerie light within the room. "Habits." He continued to mumble the word as he went through to the garage to think and hit balls. He was determined to replace his old bad swing habits with new correct ones. He focused on having a square take-away and high hands at the top of his backswing.

After a few dozen ball-strikes, his mind focused less on golf technique and more on the television problem. TV addiction had been a major source of conflict when he lived with Mandy. Within a few minutes he was decided – the television would go. He rested his seven iron against the wall and strode inside. His phone rang but Joshua ignored it. He typed his e-mail to Damien with conviction and felt empowered by his affirmative action. He wanted to make a statement concerning his commitment and he approached the task with single-minded dedication.

Joshua struggled to carry the television into the garage. He moved the car outside, closed the garage door, ran a power cord and connected the portable antenna. He pointed the remote and pressed the button – the demon came to life. After rummaging in the workbench drawer he found his safety goggles.

Saturday night offered trite, meaningless programming. Joshua channel-surfed until he found the perfect context for termination: World's Dumbest Criminals Caught on Camera. Joshua slowly pulled his driver from the bag and then found a new ball which he placed on the rubber tee. He parted the Velcro of his glove, the ominous ripping sound seemed appropriate. Joshua flexed his fingers and made a fist to ensure the fit was snug. He stretched the elastic strap over his head to position his goggles. He was ready.

An advertisement bleated and it helped him to harness the negative emotions he felt toward the time waster. His thoughts turned to his shot. *Loose hands, smooth swing*. He practiced the take-away and then paused, closing his eyes. This was a life-changing statement and he wanted to soak up the significance of what he was about to do.

Joshua worried whether the ball would penetrate the screen or ricochet back. *No holding back.*

"Fore!"

He executed the perfect drive. The ball pierced the techno-color screen like a missile, the spectacular fireworks lasting only an instant. Acrid smoke drifted from the dark hole at the centre of the shattered façade. Joshua unplugged the unit and leaned forward, inspecting the broken glass, poking with his club head to create a bigger hole. He was straining to see the ball among the imploded and charred remains.

"What are you doing – are you crazy?" Mandy stood in the doorway, aghast.

Joshua turned around, shocked to see her. "It's a new interactive golf game." He chuckled as he said it.

"You're drunk – nothing changes."

Joshua stretched the rubber strap and repositioned the goofy lenses above his forehead.

"No, I'm not. This TV was stuffed and fixing it would have cost more than it was worth."

"I hope you haven't lost your mind as a result of me leaving you?"

There was an awkward silence. "You do still drive me crazy."

Mandy looked away and Joshua changed the topic. "Why didn't you knock? I could have been entertaining someone."

Mandy smiled mockingly. "I don't think so."

"Well, you still should have knocked, or called."

"I did both but you obviously couldn't hear anything else over the blaring TV. The door was unlocked anyway and I heard you yell, and then the explosion."

"Mandy, there's a good reason for all of this."

She didn't want to know. "I'm just here for the TV remote."

"I assumed you'd bought another one?"

"I did but it broke earlier this week and they're expensive."

Joshua paused as he removed the goggles and golf glove. "Come inside and talk."

"No. I'm meeting friends for dinner and I need to get going."

Joshua couldn't avoid showing his disappointment as they went inside and searched for the remote control unit. He noticed her looking judgmentally at the open bottle of wine. A few minutes later they were standing at the front door. He didn't want her to go but Mandy held out her hand.

"I'm just happy you didn't get to keep our television or the cost of inventing your new interactive golf game would have been much higher."

Joshua forced a smile as he handed over the controller. Their fingers briefly touched.

"I'm sorry about the past but I am changing."

"Well, it doesn't look very promising. I hope you don't go back in there and take to the microwave with your pitching wedge." Mandy's humor had always been dry but now it was tinged with bitterness.

"I did what you always wanted me to do when we were together. I've eliminated television as a distraction. Mandy, so much is different – can we talk sometime?"

"I don't think so – I'm late." She turned and headed down the path. Joshua was oblivious to her emotions as she walked away.

"Promise me you won't tell anyone about the TV?"

She waved her hand in the air as she disappeared into the darkness.

Joshua sighed and headed for the shower. A few minutes later he emerged from the bedroom with wet hair and dressed in shorts and a t-shirt. He threw the pizza box in the rubbish and wiped the table clean. As he lifted the wine bottle he realized it was almost empty. *Another habit I need to change.*

It was 11:30pm when he hit the send button. Joshua went to bed feeling strangely liberated, but longing for Mandy.

Hi Damien,

The bid review went really well and the RSVP methodology is amazingly powerful. Even though I barely understand the basics, I was still able to lead the meeting using the Opportunity Qualification Tool to focus the conversation. I am very much looking forward to truly understanding RSVP beyond the headline concepts and what's on the website. I totally trust that you will reveal things when I am ready.

My boss spoke with me after the bid review and said he is keen to do whatever he can on this deal. He is clearly impressed with my attitude and new-found ability to work a deal in the right way. It seems that I am starting to get the support I need to be successful and I am sure it is because of your influence. I am changing and people are noticing. I can really see the law of attraction in action now. My boss wants to invest in me now and it must be because I am competent, to a degree. Thank you for your patience, I can now see how the self-development side of things really works.

I want to tell you how golf went today. I decided to play with the right attitude and, by that I mean, I played within my ability and managed the course and my emotions well. I shot a score two shots better than my handicap. I now understand that my lack of 'unconscious competence', when taking a full swing, has been my biggest handicap. I compensated by playing to my strengths rather than my weaknesses. I will work on drills with the practice net in my garage for as long it takes to develop the right swing habits. I will invest a few evenings each week working on this now that I have the available time – I have literally killed the television.

Success is a decision – well, many decisions I guess. I made a statement by smashing it with a golf ball. I hit the perfect drive straight through the screen! It was old and the tube needed replacing anyway. I agree that television is a time thief and I can reintroduce myself to TV at some stage in the future when my mentorship is through. I must say that this was radical for me and a big sacrifice, but one I made willingly. My father once told me that the two biggest things that change your life are the people you meet and the books you read. I guess I will now have time to read more books! Do you have any recommended reading for me?

Thanks Damien, looking forward to your reply.

Your student,
Joshua Peters

When Joshua surfaced on Sunday morning there was an e-mail waiting for him. He read it eagerly over breakfast.

Hello Joshua,

Well done with the television! Sometimes in life, it is good to burn your bridges. I know the decision was not easy. Congratulations on removing any possibility of merely plugging it back in during a moment of weakness or boredom. I am pleased that you are keen to develop the beneficial habit of reading. There is an excellent list of recommended books on the RSVPselling.com website. The first book you should read is *SPIN Selling©* by Neil Rackham, as it reinforces the basics of professional sales and perfectly complements the RSVP concepts. The second book is *Good to Great* by Jim Collins. It covers the essentials of business leadership, so let me know your thoughts after you've read it. The *Sales Tips* section of the website also provides an overview of the ten laws of relationship selling and the ten laws of strategic selling. We will progressively explore some of these laws during our time together but, rather than me put them in an e-mail, go to the website and study both the lists directly.

It sounds like you did well in using the Opportunity Qualification Tool to focus the meeting. Your knowledge of the RSVP concepts is better than you imagine and your patience in waiting for the details will be rewarded.

I don't play golf but I believe that it's incredibly difficult, and that it reveals one's character. You seem to already understand this but here is something you may have not considered. Strategy and execution are equally important, and interdependent. You can stand on the tee of an intimidating hole, having the best strategy in the world, but if you cannot execute the shot, your strategy is of no value. I am sure you will find other practical insights within the game.

Damien Drost
RSVPselling™ Sales Master

Annie was about to move interstate to start her career with an elite law firm, and Clare had organized a family lunch to congratulate and farewell her. Joshua arrived, determined to ensure the interaction with his father would be positive. Mark had also made a conscious decision to avoid anything that could ignite smoldering emotions. They all focused on Annie's cadetship and potential career. After they'd helped clear away, Mark invited Joshua to play chess on the veranda. He hesitated before responding.

"Okay, just one game and then I'll have to go."

Clare arrived with coffee. "It's good to see you both doing something together again."

Joshua looked up and smiled just as the phone rang inside. Clare headed for the kitchen to answer it.

The next few moves made it clear to Mark that he was destined to lose unless Joshua made a mistake. He did not. Mark was check-mated after being forced into exchanging his rook.

"Well played Josh. I'll make sure I'm more focused next time."

There was a long pause. Mark waited for eye contact with his son.

"Josh, a group of guys I know are going to walk the Kokoda Track in New Guinea. It's a grueling ten days but if I paid for you, would you consider coming?"

"You mean hiking over the mountains in Papua New Guinea?"

"Yes, like they did in the Second World War to stop the Japanese being in a position to invade Australia. It's physically and emotionally tough, but you're fit enough. Everyone who does it says that it is life changing. You gain a small insight into the price that was paid for our freedom."

Joshua wasn't ready for that level of interaction with his father. He appeared to be mulling it over but was actually searching for a plausible and inoffensive excuse. Mark, on the other hand, knew that his son was fascinated by military history and decided that a brief history lesson might arouse the necessary interest. Perhaps the conversation could establish safe common ground and a chance to reconnect.

"Most people don't know it but the Americans also crossed the Owen Stanley Range fifty kilometers south-east of the Kokoda Track. The Australians had by far the toughest job because they had to fight the Japs all the way, but the Yanks had more difficult terrain to negotiate with their unprepared battalion of a thousand men. The Americans had to drag themselves over Ghost Mountain which was three kilometers above sea level, a thousand meters higher than the Australians encountered on Kokoda. They struggled along the narrow and slippery Kapa Kapa Track in constant cloud. When they stopped moving they froze and when they trudged along they were drenched in perspiration. Some fell to their deaths off sheer cliffs in near zero visibility, but it was malaria and other diseases that debilitated seventy percent of the force even before a shot was fired. Fifty kilometers to the north, the Australians were engaged in muddy, brutal and bloody close combat."

Joshua seemed only notionally interested but Mark continued unperturbed. "The Americans and Australians were both spent forces when they emerged on the other side of New Guinea. They combined for an allied assault on the Japanese port strongholds of Buna and Gona. They'd taken almost two months to struggle hundreds of kilometers, and both forces had been devastated for different reasons. They were ordered to take the Japanese strongholds at any cost. By the time the ports were taken, the Americans had lost almost ninety percent of their troops."

"I thought the New Guinea campaign was exclusively Australian?"

Mark became more animated. "Don't get me wrong, the Australians paid a terrible price on the Kokoda Track, and it got worse on the coast, but the Americans suffered and fought side by side with our Diggers. This trip is extra special because we will link with six Americans. Four of them had relatives who lost their lives there in the war. They'll do the Kapa Kapa Track over Ghost Mountain, and we'll do Kokoda."

Joshua shook his head. "You need some training on how to sell a holiday."

"We'll struggle along different paths but we'll come together on the other side."

Mark paused, struck by the unintended gravity of his words. Joshua fidgeted uncomfortably in his seat before his father eventually continued.

"The two groups will rendezvous at the same place that the allied forces did more than sixty-five years ago. You'll have six months to prepare. Will you consider doing it with me?"

"Sorry. It just isn't a good time for me with the mentorship, and with my job. I need to knuckle-down and work hard. Thanks for the offer but I can't."

Mark did his best to conceal his disappointment. He knew not to push. "I understand. It was a long shot but I thought I would ask."

Annie was going to another farewell event being held by her university friends. She came to say goodbye and caught the end of the conversation.

"I keep telling him that Kokoda is a bad idea. There was another fatal plane crash last month. If you don't get killed flying in, then you could die from a heart attack or some exotic tropical disease."

Mark reassured his daughter. "It's not as dangerous as the press would have you believe. I'm going for a thorough medical before the trip. Statistically, they're not due for another plane crash for eighteen months, so I should be okay."

Annie shook her head. "What is it with you men? If it's not dangerous, it's not fun. You torture yourselves and think it's a great experience!"

Joshua smiled. "Anyone who pours hot wax on themselves and rips their hair out by the roots can't talk."

As Annie left, Joshua marveled at how much his little sister had grown into a confident young woman.

Mark changed the subject. "Thanks for being here. I can't remember the last time we played chess. How's work going?"

Joshua sat back and paused before responding. "Actually, it's going really well. The mentorship is making a real difference. I don't think I ever thanked you for organizing the introduction?"

"Don't mention it – where do you think it will take you?"

"Selling is okay but it can be very frustrating. People really waste your time and buyers aren't always honest."

"They would think that's the pot calling the kettle black but I know what you mean. Most people think success is about being clever but I've discovered that success has far more to do with your capacity for being screwed around. Selling has never been easy but it's rewarding."

Joshua shrugged. "That may be so but I'm hoping it can lead to something better."

"Regardless of what you end up doing in your career, selling is a fundamental business and leadership skill. But if you move out of sales, you'd probably need to finish your degree."

Mark could see that he had crossed the line.

"I thought we'd agreed you wouldn't lecture me anymore?"

"You're right. Let's talk about something else. How about another game?"

"No. I really do need to go."

Just then, Clare appeared on the veranda. There was something wrong. She looked sternly at her son.

"That was Mandy on the phone." Joshua braced himself. "She called because she is worried about you. She said you smashed the TV with a golf club – is that true?"

Joshua looked down and exhaled. "Yes, but the tube was shot anyway and..."

Clare interjected. "We raised you better than to destroy things. Did this Damien character put you up to it?"

"No. I wanted to make a statement that TV is a waste of time."

Clare continued. "Extremism is the cause of most of the world's problems. I don't like this mentor arrangement even if you did recommend him Mark."

Mark spoke calmly. "There is no way that Damien Drost would have told him to smash my television."

"I'm not a kid anymore. I don't have to stand here being interrogated. I'm off, thanks for lunch."

Joshua turned and marched out, pausing only to retrieve his keys and wallet from the sideboard. He fought the urge to slam the door as he left.

Mark and Clare stood on the veranda watching as Joshua's car roared down the street. She turned to her husband and sighed. "Don't tell me that we're back to the bad old days again."

Mark was staring blankly down the street and spoke in a thoughtfully detached manner. "Conflict can serve a purpose."

Clare erupted. "No! Conflict has nearly destroyed this family and I'm worried about this Damien character. He seems to be a dangerous influence." Mark was about to respond but Clare wasn't finished. "Joshua keeps this relationship shrouded in secrecy. How do you really know he's not some con-man with an agenda?"

Clare was verging on tears and Mark couldn't bear to see her distress. "It's okay – he's not."

Joshua was speeding toward home and dialed Mandy but it went to voicemail. "Thanks for not saying anything!" Joshua brooded for the remainder of the day and struggled to get his mind off the argument with his parents. He became gainfully distracted by washing his car. He then swept the garage and cleaned up the mess from the television episode the night before. After pouring the bits of glass into the shattered cavity, he pushed the defunct picture box into the corner and covered it with an old sheet. *Broken and hidden away.*

He organized his home office and books but was still haunted by how upset his mother had become. He rang his parents and got their answering machine. He didn't leave a message. It was Sunday night and he missed watching the usual programs. He went to bed early, having second thoughts about his decision to live without television. *How do I make things right with my family?*

The following morning he was at the regular weekly sales meeting, feeling tired. He was uncomfortable with Michael highlighting Zenyth as an example of how to effectively work an opportunity. The deal was far from being in good shape and he didn't like the implied pressure. When the meeting was over he headed for the elevator but was intercepted by Tania, one of the established sales people and a consistent performer.

"Hi Josh, can I buy you a coffee? I would like to ask you something."

"In about an hour if that's okay? I have something I need to do now."

Joshua went and organized flowers to be sent to Mandy with an apology card. He wrote inside, saying sorry for the outburst on her voicemail. He also asked if he could see her to explain everything.

Back at his office foyer, he met with Tania in the café. She was keen to understand why Michael's opinion of him had been so positively transformed. "He is clearly impressed. What are you doing differently?"

"I'm just trying to work a little more strategically. I'm using a simple process to try and ensure I have everything covered but I'm sure he will start picking on me again when I screw up."

"I know you don't have much time now, Josh, but could we get together later to talk about my Pharmtech deal?"

Joshua could not resist, and figured teaching something was the best way to learn. "Sure, how about breakfast tomorrow?"

After his meeting with Tania the following morning, Joshua sent a text message to Mandy asking if they could meet. Days later, there was still no response and Joshua decided it was best not to pursue or pressure her.

Clare, on the other hand, had called to say that she and Mark were happy to put the television incident behind them, and that they trusted Joshua's judgment concerning Damien Drost. There would be no more interrogations.

Several weeks had passed and work had never been better. Joshua enjoyed helping Tania and was meeting with her regularly. He was amazed with the power of simply asking RSVP questions to expose weaknesses in a deal. *If only the RSVP principles could solve the problems in my personal life*, he thought after one of his meetings.

Joshua's own Zenyth opportunity was progressing well. He had exchanged various e-mails with Damien that were helpful in maintaining his focus on obtaining all the information he needed to formulate the right strategy. Through Damien's guidance, Joshua was becoming increasingly aware that the key to strategy was having the right information and that the purpose of relationships was not just for support but also for gathering accurate intelligence. The RSVP process had resulted in them moving to a position of cautious optimism concerning their ability to win. They were now firmly 'qualified in' and investing in a strategy to change the rules on the competition with a unique value proposition that was aligned to the customer's business problem and budget. They had identified an executive sponsor, Bill Trench, and Michael would work that relationship while Joshua engaged with the project manager and his team. They had worked hard to gain insight into what the competition was doing and to understand the Zenyth decision drivers and buying process.

Michael was acting as a resource for Joshua and the change in their professional relationship was nothing short of amazing. Joshua concluded that Michael did not 'have it in for him' after all. He was just a harsh task-master and people needed to earn his respect. Joshua was responding to various work e-mails when Michael came by to invite him downstairs. They sat in the café and discussed Zenyth before Michael changed the subject.

"Joshua, Tania told me yesterday that you've been helping her on the Pharmtech opportunity. I was grilling her this morning and she started covering the RSVP concepts just like you. It was good stuff. She's never been particularly strategic, more of a relationship seller, but Tania is changing. This RSVP thing seems to work but I am yet to be convinced that it doesn't conflict with our existing sales tools."

Joshua nodded cautiously. "The qualification tool is better than anything else we've used."

"Yes, but it's not a process, where are the other tools and documentation?"

"I don't see any clash, we can keep using our same tools. RSVP is all about thinking the right way in using any methodology."

Michael nodded and took a more positive tone. "I liked the fact that I didn't need to drag out any documents to ensure she was covering all the bases. It was just a focused conversation leading to specific actions for strengthening our position."

"Then there's no problem. Was that the only reason you wanted to talk with me?"

Michael's body language became quite formal. "Joshua, I don't make this offer lightly and it depends on you winning Zenyth. There's going to be an opening for a team leader role in another part of the business, reporting to me. It's an entry level sales management position. You demonstrated the ability to help Tania and you've come a long way since I had to beat you up over losing that deal. You would be running a small team – what do you think?"

Joshua was speechless. It wasn't that long ago that Michael threatened him with the sack if he lost another important deal. Their relationship had changed but he did not like Michael's egocentric style or bullying manner. Emotionally, Joshua was still committed to winning Zenyth and then resigning.

"Mike, I don't know what to say. This is a huge decision and I need to think about it. Are you really sure about this? I'm a bit young to be managing a team, even a small one."

"I've given this a lot of thought. Everyone in your new team will be younger than you and selling more commoditized products and services. It will enable you to establish yourself as a manager without any baggage around existing peer relationships. Just consider the offer, and take as much time as you need."

Joshua felt distracted for the remainder of the day. He was currently selling solutions based on bundled products and services to large organizations. The promotion would mean moving back down to commodity products being sold to smaller customers. He was in awe, however, with the positive outlook in his career. That night, Joshua sent an excited e-mail to Damien, ignoring the fact that the offer of promotion was conditional upon winning Zenyth.

Hi Damien,

I had the most amazing conversation with my boss today. He offered me a sales management position running a small team! I must say that, although this is flattering, I think it would be a mistake. Even though I've begun to understand the basics of how to use the RSVP concepts, I am yet to deliver a serious deal using it and I lack any experience as a manager. I still have much to learn and am looking forward to understanding the detail within the RSVP concept.

My boss found out that I've been helping Tania with her Pharmtech deal because he noticed she was talking RSVP every time he asked if she had the deal covered. Michael seems to like the fact that RSVP works without the need for complex account plans. He thinks that capturing progressive snapshots of the Opportunity Qualification Tool throughout the life of a deal is the best way to drive a sale. What do you think?

It feels daunting to be seen as a potential leader when I still have so much to learn. I've been told that most sales people make poor sales managers. Do you agree? Anyway, I think I should decline the promotion and focus on winning Zenyth. I know you want me to come to my own conclusions but I really value your advice. What do you think I should do?

Thanks again for suggesting books for me to read, it felt like I devoured them. Attached is a Word document summarizing my thoughts on the key principles of leadership.

I look forward to your reply.

Your student
Joshua

Joshua wanted to share his success with his parents but felt, despite his mother's assurances, that the television incident was unresolved. Maybe it was a sense of guilt, maybe it was really about the brokenness of everything else with his family. It had been weeks since the argument but he knew that the passage of time didn't automatically fix things. Time had not resolved the issues with his father during his years in the UK. He wanted to do something tangible and bought a modest flat screen television he thought would fit in Mark's study. He organized for it to be delivered to his parent's house with a hand written note.

His mother called late the following day to say they appreciated the gesture of the new TV but that they really did not need another one. She insisted that he should take it once he was ready to have a television back in his life. She also said how much Mark had enjoyed playing chess and encouraged him to visit again for a family meal. Joshua arrived home to find Damien's latest e-mail.

Hello Joshua,

Congratulations on being offered the promotion! Your boss correctly identified the key benefits of RSVP. In essence, it is strategy as a way of thinking, with or without complex account plans, enabling sales people to move naturally from relationship selling to strategic selling. This is what he has seen transpire in you and Tania. The RSVP way of thinking enables someone to effectively evaluate, strategize and manage a sales opportunity in a boardroom with an account plan or even in a café, on the back of a napkin.

Joshua, I would have preferred that you sought my counsel before 'mentoring' someone but I am not going to tell you to stop. In some ways, it is good that you are passing on the knowledge that you have gained and begun to help someone else. Be cautious, however, as mentoring requires experience and commitment and you are not yet fully equipped. Now that you are working with Tania, the important thing is that you are transferring what you know to be true, rather than conveying theory. You can assist best by helping her focus on what is actually important. Resist the urge to tell her what to do but instead focus on asking her the right questions. The RSVP Opportunity Qualification Tool is ideal for facilitating this process and I am sure you have already sent her to the website. Your boss is right in wanting to capture regular qualification tool snapshots of an opportunity as it progresses, and you should do this with Tania.

You said that very few sales people successfully make the transition to sales management. Although there are exceptions, you are correct. The reason for this is that most high performers are successful because they are competitively egocentric. Good sales managers are different in that they are driven by the success of others and put the needs of their team before their own. The skill of managing requires high EQ (Emotional Quotient) combined with experience and maturity. Great sales managers embody all of this and are also genuine leaders. The sad reality, however, is that most sales managers get trapped in bureaucracy and spreadsheets, reports and administrative processes. Sales leaders, on the other hand, are rare. My advice to you is to aspire to sales leadership rather than sales management.

I therefore think your instincts in this matter are correct. It is too soon to make the move to management. Your summary of the principles of leadership were insightful but let me ask you this question: What is the difference between a leader and a manager? As part of your continuing progression as a leader among your peers, please also consider how you can apply this advice from Eleanor Roosevelt: "Great minds discuss ideas. Average minds discuss events. Small minds discuss people." I look forward to your reply concerning these questions.

After you finalize your decision concerning the promotion, we will explore the detail and nuances within the RSVP equation. To help you make this important decision, Joshua, think about who you want to be, what you want to do, and what you want to have in your life – this is the essence of defining your goals.

Damien Drost
RSVPselling™ Sales Master

Finally, Joshua would receive the details behind the acronym – but only after he resolved his career choice. His youthful ambition was pulling him in the opposite direction of his logical rationalizations. In truth, Joshua overrated himself and the opportunity to leap into management was dangerously enticing. His head and heart said 'no' to the promotion but his ego said 'yes'. He lay in bed, torn between the two options, struggling to surrender to sleep.

Chapter Six: The Goal

Joshua continued to be tempted by the lure of promotion. Logic and emotion were tugging in opposite directions. He pushed that issue into the background as he worked on his response to Damien's questions. The first topic to address was goals and he knew he lacked purpose in the activities that filled his life. He had attended a number of seminars where goals made it onto the agenda. One cited the alleged old example of a university study where only 3% of students had specific written goals when graduating and when surveyed twenty years later, this minority made more money than the other 97% combined. Despite this, he had always struggled to have his own goals written down in detail with dates for achievement. There had been one exception, and it was the sports car he aspired to own. Pictures had wallpapered his fridge for nine months before he had purchased it.

Damien's questions echoed in his head. What did Joshua want to do? Who did he want to be? What did he want to have in his life? He now had a framework for defining his goals, beyond material trinkets, and the more he thought about the answers, the more he became aware that possessions and trophies figured little in any meaningful definition of success.

Reading *Good to Great* by Jim Collins had introduced some revolutionary thinking for Joshua concerning leadership, and he had already provided Damien with his feedback. The book articulated a character-based leadership model focused on service to others. Joshua had long thought that leadership was all about persuasion through individual vision and charisma, but not anymore. Beyond the lessons in the book, he sensed that the difference between a leader and manager was somehow linked to his yet-to-be articulated goals.

It was 11:30pm and Joshua lay in bed staring up at an inverted abyss as his thoughts meandered, contemplating the questions posed by Damien: his goals, his career choices, the differences between being a leader and a manager, and the meaning of Eleanor Roosevelt's quote. It all slowly came together. Joshua had an epiphany and leapt out of bed muttering his thoughts as he powered up his laptop. It was the early hours of the morning when he sent his e-mail.

Hi Damien,

I have labored over your questions and made a decision concerning the promotion. I said that I was not ready to step into this role but the truth is that I've been really tempted by the offer. But I cannot justify taking a management role when I am so young and do not understand the detail behind the RSVP concepts. I know that I am not ready and I will tell my boss that the answer is 'no'.

I have thought about your question concerning the difference between a leader and a manager. I know that the best leaders are very determined and serve their cause and their people, rather than beat their chests and tell others what to do. Managers drive work and monitor process. Leaders inspire, set the agenda, and define the culture. I think the most important difference, however, is that a leader does what it takes to succeed, regardless of the obstacles.

More important than all of this, I've had a revelation that brings together all the questions posed in your e-mail! Leadership and my goals are linked. I want to be a person of influence and make a difference. This is my mission, and my career goals and life choices will flow from these things. My goals will be defined by these values and I believe success will follow. Eleanor Roosevelt's quote will be something to which I aspire in my work and personal life: I, Joshua Peters, will focus on great ideas, not events or people. Gossip will have no place in my life. I will be a leader by serving and committing to those I carefully choose.

In line with all this, I've made the decision to resign after I secure Zenyth and receive my commission. My boss is prone to arrogance and bullying, and I want to move from tactical selling to higher value and more complex enterprise sales. I really want to focus on creating and delivering value. I am keen to find an environment in which I can seriously apply the RSVP concepts, selling real solutions that address substantial problems for big organizations. I would like to move into the software industry but I really value your input and guidance. What do you think?

I will write down my specific goals but do you have any suggestions concerning the format and best way to approach this?

Your student
Joshua

It was early the following morning when Damien Drost's in-box was opened. As he read, he was deeply touched by the profound change in his student. He now knew the investment in Joshua was worth all the time and effort.

Joshua was running late and skipped breakfast. The day was filled with meetings and he was busy learning more about Zenyth in an attempt to bridge the gaps in their knowledge. Michael had begun a positive relationship with the project's executive sponsor, Bill Trench, and was also seeking information and support. They had no idea of the budget or business case, and were still guessing about the competition. Joshua was focused on obtaining all this intelligence and today was when he hoped to find one of the missing pieces of the puzzle.

Relatively junior people often have knowledge of budgets and competitors that they easily or inadvertently divulge. At 3:00pm Joshua was having coffee with Paul Brown. It seemed like a casual and innocuous get-together. Paul was keen to meet because he saw Joshua as a source of information and potential assistance for his own purposes. He was an IT systems administrator at Zenyth and, after six years of loyal service, he had been passed over for promotion twice. He was now looking to move to a vendor or service provider and Joshua's corporation seemed an attractive career option. They discussed Paul's aspirations and background, and Joshua promised to e-mail him with the contact details of two senior managers with open positions. The two men stood and shook hands.

"Thanks for your help Josh, I really appreciate it."

Joshua smiled warmly. "It's the least I can do. Send me your CV and I'll get it in front of the right people. No promises but I think we could benefit from having some-one with your skills and background."

He had no problem committing to this because he knew Paul was a capable individual. As they stood to shake hands, Joshua asked the question.

"Paul, I don't want to put you in an awkward position but do you know who the other companies are that have been short-listed by Zenyth for the project?"

Paul smiled and nodded knowingly. Seconds later, Joshua had his information.

Back at the office, Joshua researched the two competitors and their offerings. The next internal planning meeting would be definitive and he was keen to share the new information with Michael. He called him from the car and felt particularly posi-tive by the time he arrived home. He hoped that Damien had replied, and he was not disappointed.

Hello Joshua,

You are rapidly maturing in your approach to business. I am pleased that you have decided to reject the offer of promotion. Selling provides freedom and a wonderfully challenging learning environ-ment.

I agree with your comments concerning leadership but here is the definition I was looking for. The dif-ference between a leader and a manager is profoundly simple: A leader owns outcomes, a manager owns process. Managers do their best but leaders refuse to be victims, they do what it takes. The very best leaders in sales and business are engineers of strategy, not warriors of persuasion.

You have done well in first focusing on your mission: to be a person of influence and make a differ-ence. I have reviewed your three affirmations, contained within past e-mails, and have taken the liberty of creating a subset that could be combined with your mission to become something you truly own and strive to live.

Here it is: I am a person of positive influence and I deliver results. I am fully there for people when I am with them. I choose carefully those to whom I commit. I make a difference by focusing on great ideas, and gossip has no place in my life. I have a positive attitude and lead by serving. I build trust by listening actively and asking insightful questions. I ensure full understanding before exploring potential solutions. I believe in the value I offer and am a subject matter expert and problem solver. I care about people and outcomes. I make a difference with the things that matter.

Believe it or not, the above are *your* words, Joshua. Success is all about being the person worthy of it and you have chosen this path. If you live what you have articulated, then your success will be significant and prosperity will follow. This is because real leaders attract success and the loyalty of those aligned to their cause. The leader ultimately defines the culture of any enterprise.

I would like you to read your mission statement again and develop a list of goals as they relate to eight areas in life. Ask yourself, who you want to be, what you want to do, and what you want to have in your life, concerning:

· Physical health
· Recreation
· Family relationships
· Social friendships
· Career or business
· Finances
· Spiritual or charity
· Education or personal development

Once you have done this for all eight areas, ask yourself three more questions for every goal: why, when, and how? The least important of all these questions is, 'how?' The lower a person's station in life, the more they tend to focus on how to do things. The more successful the person, the more they focus on the 'why' and 'when'. Yet, beyond all this, there is an important truth concerning the value of your goals but we will discuss this toward the very end of our time together.

Balance in life is essential. Imagine your life as a wagon wheel with eight spokes radiating from the centre. Draw it on a sheet of paper and label the spokes in accordance with the eight areas of life. Place a 1-10 scale on each spoke from the centre, radiating out. Now rate how you are addressing each area by placing a dot along each spoke. A score of 10 means that you're completely focused on this area and it receives much of your time and energy. A score of 1 means that you don't regard this area as important or you do not spend time or energy on it. Now re-draw the circumference of your wagon wheel by connecting each of your dots. How round is your wheel of life? The more out of balance the wheel, the rougher the ride tends to be.

There is a substantial amount of work in thinking and documenting all of this. Do not rush the process and test the values behind your desires by constantly asking yourself why you want something. I encourage you to take your time and write it all down in a journal. Remember that no matter what your criteria, the passage of time is essential for providing perspective in measuring ultimate success and value.

Some time ago you asked me about the compass and we discussed its relevance concerning stable values to anchor you through the storms of life. There is however another important analogy here. Right now, Joshua, close your eyes and point north. Open your eyes and identify an object along the line you were pointing and then go and get the compass.

Establish true north. By how many degrees were you out? If you are not travelling far, then being out by a few degrees has little impact, but if you are going a long way, an error of just a few degrees makes an enormous difference to your ultimate destination. This is why a compass must be referenced constantly throughout a journey and the user must understand the variation between magnetic north and true north, while also ensuring nothing interferes with its accuracy.

There is something else you need to know about the compass – it has the answer to a question that has been nagging at you since the beginning of your mentorship. We will deal with the ultimate meaning at the end of our engagement. For now, let me say that you have done well in defining your mission and keeping 'true north' in mind as you establish your goals.

Earlier in our correspondence you compared the selling profession with that of a plumber. I resisted responding with the comment back then but you must avoid merely, *going through the motions*, especially with setting your goals and determining what drives you. The value of any process is determined by the commitment of the participant. My next e-mail will reveal the detail within RSVP.

Damien Drost
RSVPselling™ Sales Master

His thoughts turned to the compass and he was intrigued by the claim that it held the answer to a question that had been nagging at him. He thought the meaning of the inscription was resolved but studied the compass once more. He again opened the hinged cover revealing the engraved inscription. TRUE NORTH – OD DAS VEILS. *True north – a force that is hidden.*

"What is it that's hidden?" He said it slowly as he articulated his thoughts.

Decoding the obscure message could wait. For now, he would focus on his goals, just as Damien had requested. As he began to close the lid he noticed a tiny notch directly above the hinge. He hurried to the garage and returned with a set of miniature screw drivers. He placed his smallest blade inside the slot and levered it. To his amazement, the engraved plate popped out and tinkled onto the table; then a tissue-thin piece of folded paper wafted down beside it. He sat there open-mouthed as the secret compartment revealed another engraving inside the lid: MARK TRUE NORTH. Joshua had two engraved texts. He now carefully unfolded the delicate sheet, seeing that it revealed an incomplete statement: The Joshua Principle: ...

"Mark true north – the Joshua principle."

He said it repeatedly as he looked again at the original engraving on the false plate lying separately beside the compass: TRUE NORTH – OD DAS VEILS. He sat perplexed, mumbling combinations of words. Finally, he had it!

"Mark my true north by writing down my defining principle."

The concept of The Joshua Principle is what was hidden inside the compass. But the more he thought, the more uncertain he became. He had no idea what the principle could be. He was sure, however, that the inscriptions within the compass meant that this principle would be the marker – his true north – for directing his career and life.

Joshua felt certain that defining his goals and choosing the balance and focus in his life, across all eight areas, would be instrumental in defining The Joshua Principle. He smiled as he thought about something his father had said to him before he had headed to the U.K. *Your idea of being balanced is to have a chip on both shoulders.* His thoughts were racing, and he decided to take a drive to find a store that sold quality journals.

Over the next few days, Joshua was frantically busy. By day, he was focused on preparation for his final internal strategy session to ensure they won the Zenyth account. By night, he worked on documenting his goals and priorities in his journal. He also focused on answering the why, when and how questions posed by Damien. Frustratingly though, The Joshua Principle had not emerged as being self-evident.

On Friday morning he ran the strategy session for the Zenyth opportunity. The previous day, Michael had taken Bill Trench to lunch, Zenyth's executive sponsor for the project. Bill was General Manager, Customer Support and the person most impacted by current problems. Bill stood to benefit most from their potential investment and he had given Michael valuable coaching at lunch.

"You certainly have a great solution for us but you're beyond our budget. Don't leave yourselves priced out when we ask for a best and final offer."

A presentation to Zenyth was scheduled for the following week and Joshua's team felt confident that they now understood the competition. There were two other inferior vendors competing for the business. These two companies were not industry leaders and were renowned for discounting. Joshua and his team knew they had superior quality and a unique value proposition, but would certainly be more expensive. Michael and Joshua had read recent internal loss reports for both companies and they interviewed their own sales people involved in the defeats. Armed with the competitive intelligence and the comments from Bill concerning budget constraints, they had obtained approval to bundle additional service levels at no extra charge and discount an additional 5% if Zenyth would commit to an initial twenty-four month contract term.

Joshua was aware that management approval of special discounting required Michael to attach his own credibility to the opportunity. The deal had a high profile internally, and losing would potentially cause Michael to invoke the threat made months earlier. At the very least, he would withdraw the offer of promotion. They were, however, both confident that Bill wanted to buy from them and that he was just posturing for a better price. Joshua felt prepared for the presentation the following week and left work on Friday afternoon confident that the opportunity would close.

Once the deal was won, Joshua would be able to resign as planned. Michael would be disappointed in losing his highest achiever, but maybe learn that his management style needed some adjustment. Although Joshua had come a long way since the mentorship had begun, he was about to learn a powerful lesson – something his manager would also share. Joshua had been wise to involve his boss in the Zenyth deal and although Michael Blunt was an experienced sales manager, he had failed to ask Joshua or Bill Trench the right questions. For now, they were both blissfully unaware of the realities at Zenyth. They lived in ignorant hope.

That weekend, Joshua sent another e-mail. He had been considering the enigma of the compass for days and now he was ready to articulate his thoughts.

Hello Damien,

I am very impressed with your commitment to my training and the time and effort you are investing in truly educating me. I discovered the secret compartment with the additional inscription and piece of paper. Although I am yet to define The Joshua Principle, I think I have unlocked the riddle of the inscriptions.

I believe that The Joshua Principle is what's hidden (veiled) in the compass, and I need to define it as the primary value by which I will live my life. It will be my 'true north', guiding me in making decisions, and it will mark me in the eyes of others as it influences the way I live. Re-reading this now I feel like I am writing just like you Damien! This is all very well but the problem for me is that I have no idea what this defining principle is. I bought a journal and am making good progress in documenting my values and goals as they relate to all eight areas of life. I will keep working on The Joshua Principle but I really would appreciate any input you can provide. Surely there are many principles that serve as guidance in a person's life?

As requested, I have further considered the difference between a leader and a manager. I agree completely that leaders own outcomes and refuse to be victims. I especially liked the comparison and analogy of an engineer versus a warrior. I think that too many sales people and managers are driven by ego. I will seek to adopt a leadership model based upon service and determination.

The Zenyth deal is going extremely well and we have achieved unofficial status of preferred vendor. I managed to have a casual meeting with someone on their project team who is leaving soon and I found out who our two competitors are. I know we are better positioned than the competition and neither of them is a major player. We have a stronger solution and better service levels but are priced above their current budget. We have our final presentation next week and I will let you know how it goes. My boss, Michael, is cautiously optimistic. He had lunch with their executive sponsor, and received positive feedback and some good coaching concerning our price. I think they can obtain more funding but we will offer additional value and a discount to close the deal.

I will resign once I receive my commission for Zenyth. Michael does not bring the best out in me. He will be disappointed but I know I'm doing the right thing for my development and career. Do you have any advice about how I should approach the task of finding the right new job? Thanks again for the compass, it will be an heirloom. I will keep working through my goals and values, and hopefully The Joshua Principle will become self-evident. Can it be a collection of principles?

Your student,
Joshua

Joshua did not look at his e-mail or work on his goals all weekend. Instead, he went cycling on Saturday morning before playing golf. That night, he went to a party he hoped Mandy would attend. She never showed, but the old friends he saw were a painful reminder of when they had been a couple.

On Sunday, he arrived home at dusk after watching the football. He glanced at the empty space that the television had once dominated. He was glad it no longer counted in his personal life but he momentarily wished he had it to distract him from his loneliness. His life was becoming more balanced, yet in the area of personal relationships, he remained unfulfilled.

He turned his attention to the laptop. The eerie glow of the computer screen gave the room a mystical ambience. He had his reply and read with anticipation, wondering if he had guessed correctly concerning the meaning of the compass inscriptions. It quickly became evident that this e-mail contained the detail Joshua had sought for months.

Chapter Seven: RSVP Uncovered

Hello Joshua,

Keep working diligently on your journal and ensure there is emotion in your goals. Include pictures of the things you want, and images of the feelings and experiences you wish to create. Relentlessly ask 'why' and 'when' questions with everything you seek. The 'how' will materialize if your goals are time-bound and driven by emotion.

Congratulations on finding the secret compartment. You obviously gave the inscriptions much thought and I am happy enough with your conclusions. You are right to focus on your goals and values as part of the process for defining The Joshua Principle. Here is a question that may help in your quest: If the goal of life is to find purpose and make a difference, what determines the real value of any activity or pursuit?

In my last correspondence, I promised to reveal the secrets of RSVP. We shall do this now, in the context of the Zenyth opportunity, and you will not like what you are about to read – I think the deal is at risk. Early in our dialogue, I wrote to you stating that confidence can be the feeling you have, just before you understand the situation. Indeed, Joshua, confidence can be the paradise of fools.

Although you did well in discovering the two other short-listed competitors, I was very concerned to hear that they are both commodity discounters, neither of them being a quality solution provider. If it is true that your proposal is outside Zenyth's budget, then there are many things that can go wrong, despite being advised that you are 'preferred'. One of the laws of selling is that a sale is only a sale once you have the customer's money in your bank account. Do not let confidence lull you into a false sense of security.

Has the project sponsor (the senior executive who owns the business outcome) announced you publicly as preferred vendor? Internally is okay but it must be to a broad audience so that any reversal of the decision will have the consequence of damaging their personal credibility. Their willingness, or not, to make this announcement will uncover whether you have really defeated the competition – external vendors or internal options. A positive announcement will stymie attempts by anyone to kill or delay the project. I will come back to this when we cover the S within RSVP.

There is a foundational business principle which triggered the concept of RSVPselling™– it is the law of risk. Risk mainly comes from not knowing what you don't know. Someone or something can always be working against you and it is, therefore, wise to be alert and in a state of healthy paranoia. RSVPselling™ is designed to overcome risk in the selling process but needs to be underpinned by the relentless pursuit of relevant information. Accurate intelligence is essential in formulating and executing winning strategies. I fear, Joshua, that you do not have all the necessary information concerning Zenyth. Revisit your corporation's strategic selling tools and consider the concept of 'red flags' for identifying these risks and creating place-holders for the information that needs to be obtained.

RSVPselling™ is not intended to replace existing selling methodologies an organization uses but sales people are busier than ever. Following process, without understanding, is no substitute for thinking and executing strategically. Disciplined planning and thorough documentation is important but success is ultimately determined by the way a sales person thinks and operates. You must, therefore, know more than how to do something, you must also know why you are doing it, because this gives you the ability to be flexible and adapt as a situation evolves. Responding effectively is far better than reacting hopefully. All too often, account plans, opportunity assessments, bid reviews and other documents are completed as a result of sales management coercion but not embraced as a living part of the sales process. Don't just go through the motions. Instead, use your tools to make a difference.

If, however, an organization does not already have sales process tools, then RSVP can be a simple and effective methodology on its own. You already understand the first principle of RSVPselling™ which is: being fully there with excellence in execution. The balance of the RSVP concept simply

requires that four main questions be continually asked:
- Do you have the right **Relationships**?
- Do you have the right **Strategy**?
- Do you have a unique and compelling **Value** proposition?
- Do you truly understand the customer's buying **Process**?

Relationships: The first law of selling is that people buy from those they like and trust. Strong relationships with the right people can compensate for many short-comings, and an internal coach (or ally) may provide essential support and feed-back concerning how you need to position your product, service or solution. Be very careful, however, not to rely on mid-level operatives. The people most willing to meet with you are usually those who seek to trap you at the wrong level of influence. You will come to know this type of person as, 'Seymour'. He or she is described this way because they are locked in an endless need to 'see-more' before they feel equipped to make recommendations to the actual decision makers.

Your goal is to create business value, not respond to market demand as a commodity provider. This means aligning to business problems or opportunities and starting at the top of an organization. The reason you are not yet a strategic sales person is that you spend all your time with Seymour. Consider these four types of people in a customer organization and honestly evaluate with whom you invest most of your time.

Technical or project people: They discuss and investigate features and functions. They benefit from the free education that sales people provide and they easily lock you into a seemingly endless cycle of information requests. These people love comparative analysis. They often say that they are in control and that they make decisions, which is rarely the case. The truth is that they only take recommendations up the line and often get told 'no' by people of real power. Think of Seymour (see-more) people as necessary but do not naively hope for differentiating influence or decisions. Respect them because they can say 'no' but recognize the fact that almost never can they say 'yes'. It is with these people that you waste most of your time.

Users or consumers: These people care most about functionality and can be an excellent source of information about what is going on in the organization. Their support is essential but they almost never drive a decision.

Managers and supervisors: They focus on product functions, advantages and perceived value, even if the 'value' is not aligned to business drivers (problem resolution or opportunity realization). Managers can often have hidden agendas and be emotionally tied to incumbent suppliers. Their support is also needed but don't get stuck at this level either. Managers often have no real authority when it comes to new initiatives or investment decisions. Is your 'executive sponsor' at Zenyth merely a recommender? Does he have real power?

<u>Business owners or top stakeholders:</u> These people are the hardest to secure meetings with but they either pull the strings or have the power of veto in any decision-making process. They care about managing risk, achieving outcomes and realizing business benefits. They care little about features, functions or advantages. They instead focus on achieving best value in delivering tangible results as rapidly as possible. They need proof, not promises. I do not believe you spend any one-on-one time with these executives but you instead depend on your boss to do this work. If you are to evolve, you must personally develop these relationships of power.

You may have noticed the progression in areas of interest with these four groups of people: feature, function, advantage and benefit. Say this out loud: feature – function – advantage – benefit. It rolls off the tongue, doesn't it? But it is a hollow cliché! Here is another law of selling. Features are not always benefits. Benefits must solve specific acknowledged business problems.

Most sales people mistakenly talk and act as if all features and functions of their product, service or 'solution' are benefits. Worse than this, the people most willing to engage with you on the customer side usually lack insight and focus concerning the real business issues. They talk in terms of symptoms, rather than causes, and rarely understand the real business benefits or the specific outcomes that must be delivered with finite resources.

What a recipe for wasted time! A sales person mistakenly positioning features as benefits and a customer naively thinking symptoms are problems. Again, think about your 'executive sponsor' at Zenyth – is he really that?

Here is the important issue. You need to build relationships of real influence with the people who own the problem and have genuine power. You need to gain the support of, but not get trapped with, the influencers. The awful truth is that you currently depend exclusively on Seymour types to win business. In large and complex sales environments, relationships need to provide accurate, differentiating intelligence and genuine influence. This, again, is the concept of The New ROI © – Relationships Of Intelligence, Relationships Of Integrity, and Relationships Of Influence. The RSVPselling.com website has a checklist of questions concerning relationships and I encourage you to go and review it.

The most important thing to do in strategically considering relationships is to visually map all of the players within the customer organization. Always ensure you draw an organization chart and then overlay the power-base (real decision makers aligned with economic power) and buying centre (people involved in the evaluation, recommendation and procurement process). It is essential to determine areas of relationship strength and weakness. For every person on the chart, identify their buyer type and consider the checklist questions on the website. Ensure you map your team to their organization and then draw the external relationships that can influence the outcome. This includes consultants, analysts, industry leaders, your reference customers, and your competitor's references.

Only when you have all the information, will you be equipped to formulate a relationships strategy. The strategy will be designed to influence the customer toward your strengths and away from your weaknesses. It will also be designed to deliver the necessary accurate intelligence and understanding concerning their business drivers, business case, funding, buying process, selection criteria, competitor positioning and more.

All of this information will enable you to address the critical issue of strategy, beyond mere relationship selling. Strategic information is obtained through people but ensure information is triangulated by validating the accuracy with multiple sources before finalizing your plans. This means three different people at different levels but be careful not to 'lead the witness' by inadvertently encouraging people to tell you what you want to hear. The more senior the person the more likely their information is accurate. The more junior the person, the more easily they divulge information but the higher likelihood of inaccuracy.

Make every step a positive move and think carefully before acting: Don't be afraid to do nothing while you obtain further information and validate intelligence. Patience and diligence are both important in ensuring that your strategies are based upon accurate information and that they will be supported by the key people of power within the organization. Now to the S of RSVP which is Strategy.

Strategy: Powerful relationships, combined with the right strategy, will nearly always win business. I think you can see that relationships provide intelligence and support. Also, understand that the people of power within an organization often have a preferred outcome already in mind when they embark on a formal process of evaluation and selection. Effective influence is, therefore, best exercised with the customer before their visible or formal process begins. This is essential when selling to government. Once a government entity has formalized their project, they are constrained by strict probity rules that will stymie any attempt to influence or operate outside their defined process. This is not to say that you cannot win if you are not there first but the later you participate in a customer's business case and subsequent buying process, the lower the probability of success. Strategy can be defined as engineering an outcome. The best way to be strategic is to get there first and set the agenda by influencing the requirements and process. The second best way to be strategic is to change the rules to create an unfair advantage. All this should be in the best interests of both you and the customer.

If you cannot get there first, then be cunning. Sun Tzu, the famous Chinese general from ancient times wrote: *All men can see the tactics whereby I conquer but what no-one can see is the strategy out of which victory is evolved.* Effective strategy is completely dependent on accurate intelligence (information). Any plan or campaign should result from fully evaluating your strengths and weaknesses, understanding your competition (including the customer's internal options), and understanding the business drivers and invisible political structure within an organization. Strategy should be designed to ensure that a positive outcome is achieved for you and your customer and in the most efficient manner possible.

Strategy is essential when the buying or selling organization has multiple options, including the possibility of doing nothing. Strategy is important, not just when there are external competitors seeking to out-position you, but also when there are other projects competing for funding or when they have in-house options. Strategy is especially needed when there are multiple levels of responsibility and points of potential veto. Strategy is needed when the decision-making process is complex and not self-evident to an outsider, and when the buyer's selection criterion is multi-faceted or weighted.

Strategy is especially important when considering how you manage the highest areas of risk in a sale. In the software industry, for example, the majority of risk is with demonstrations, reference sites, and competitors. Almost everything else in the sales process can be reasonably controlled. Strategy is the key differentiator when the seller does not have significant brand or solution superiority. Finally, thinking through your strategy is vital when you have a choice of sales engagement options. I think you can see that strategy is essential but must be based upon accurate intelligence because a tactical plan is only as good as the intelligence and strategy that leads to it.

Whatever got your organization to where it is today is no longer sufficient to keep it there, and this also applies to you personally. Your competitors learn every time you beat them and they eventually formulate and execute strategies intended to defeat you. Strategy is also important because product features never win a deal but, instead, can eliminate you, often without you knowing. Benefits need to be positioned strategically, matched against the customer's business needs. With the right strategy, traps can also be set for the competition when they position their own features thoughtlessly. Even in a relationship-driven opportunity, political effectiveness demands strategy because relationships with the wrong people can waste time and inhibit success.

Again, strategy is most important in the context of defeating the competition in whatever form it takes.

That is, traditional rivals, new technologies, the customer's internal resources and other projects vying for funding. There is also a checklist of Strategy questions on the RSVPselling.com website. The list highlights a risk that I suspect you have not considered with Zenyth – sometimes the customer is also a competitor, especially when they go to market without enough funding for a proper solution. What happens if Zenyth does nothing? Are there other priorities or projects competing for funding that could cause this? Do they have internal options for solving the problem, rather than needing to go to external providers?

You cannot develop strategy in a vacuum. What is really going on at Zenyth, Joshua? Just because someone goes to market for a solution, it does not necessarily mean they are committed to purchase. Sometimes they are seeking education or simply do not understand what is required. How will you deal with these questions and issues?

Let us now turn our thoughts to strategy as it relates, specifically, to competitors. Strategic selling should not equate with 'negative selling'. You must never speak of your competition in a derogatory manner externally. Ideally, never mention them at all. However, the competition must be considered because a client buys based upon their interpretation of quality, value and risk; not on reality and facts but based upon their perceptions. Just as you do, your competitors seek to focus the prospective customer on the unique strengths of their product, solution or market position; while possibly highlighting the weaknesses of those they perceive as a threat. Engaging in any opportunity, based upon the rules of a competitor, is guaranteed to waste your own precious time and resources. This highlights, again, why it is so important to be there first, positively setting your own unique agenda.

Once a client has absolutely decided to invest their money in a solution to a problem, you win business by defeating the competition – it's that simple. The customer selects one vendor or option, over another, for a combination of these factors:
- The best brand or reputation for successful delivery
- The best product, service or solution for their requirements
- The best price or value within their budget
- The lowest risk, technically and commercially
- The best or fastest return on investment
- The best understanding of their organization and requirements
- The best relationships, and highest levels of trust
- The best warranty, support and service
- The best contractual terms and conditions

All of the above will be the client's comparative perceptions and result in them forming a view concerning best value for money. The challenge, in a sales campaign, is to set the agenda (for example; the weighted selection criteria and mandatory requirements) around your own unique strengths and value (compelling features that are aligned to delivery of specific business benefits).

Back to dealing with the competition which is, arguably, the most important aspect of strategic selling. Military history reveals four distinct strategies that can be successfully applied to business when engaging against a competitor. Keith Eades, Jim Holden and other business authors have linked these concepts to selling previously. The four well documented strategies for competitive engagement are:

- Head-to-head. When you have product strength or market dominance
- Change the rules. When you need to alter the agenda or criteria
- Incremental. To focus on a small piece of business or coexist
- Containment. To engineer a non-decision so you can re-engage later

Here is a summary of these four strategies. It is important that you become completely familiar with these concepts and that you understand how to effectively apply them in any sales situation. All of this must become part of your own instinctive, yet disciplined, sales process.

Competitive Strategy: Head to head (AKA: Direct or Frontal). This direct strategy works if you have unequivocal brand strength or market dominance. You are not afraid of 'slugging it out' against the competition because you have the best brand, superior product offering and strongest market presence. Most sales people adopt this mode of engagement and the competition's price is often their main point of concern. This strategy is attractive because it is simple, but it's the only kind of sales strategy that most sales people know how to use! The main requirement for the direct strategy is superiority, and your customer base must be well established. To be effective, you must have clear leadership with solution and reputation, and this must be validated from the customer's point of view. Be very careful, however, with smaller customers who often associate product (solution) strength, or market dominance, with unnecessary functionality and excessively high pricing.

Competitive Strategy: Change the rules (AKA: Indirect or Flanking). This strategy is essential when you do not have the leading solution or strongest market position. It is an ideal default position because it necessitates the gathering of information and it forces you to search for unique value that matches the client's specific requirements. This strategy should always be employed when nothing about your solution, corporation or industry presence gives you a compelling edge. It is appropriate when you cannot succeed based on the current engagement rules or selection criteria; typically because you were not there first, exerting influence and shaping the requirements. For this strategy to succeed, you must have strong personal relationships with key members of the buying centre and power-base. Beware of 'fighting the good fight', only to have a mystery senior executive veto the recommendation for your product, service or solution. Seymour types will often falsely give the impression they are buying into your strategy, only to revert back to their original position at the last minute. You must get to the top people of power in the organization if you are to maximize your chances of creating a winning strategy.

Competitive Strategy: Incremental (AKA: Divide and conquer; Divisional, Departmental, Land and expand or Beach-head). This strategy can be a subset of changing the rules in a large opportunity. The goal is to divide and conquer by securing a limited piece of business within a subset or business unit of the enterprise. In military terms, this is your strategy to get 'on the beach' and establish a limited presence, or beach-head, from which you can expand. This 'land and expand' strategy should be employed when you cannot win the whole account (enterprise) but when there is a worthwhile piece of business that will give you an internal reference and influence for larger decisions at a later time. It is also useful when you are not seeking to displace another vendor but rather enhance the customer site (or market) by providing a complementary solution or additional functionality not offered by the competition. This strategy is also appropriate when you decide to coexist with a competitor and temporarily share the account.

Competitive Strategy: Containment (AKA: Non-decision, Delay or Kill the deal). Given the choice between a loss and a deferment (non-decision), there will be times when a containment strategy is the best approach. In simple terms, if you know you cannot win, your goal is to stymie the competition by delaying the client's decision, so you can re-engage under new rules at a later time. This is what your competitor may be doing at Zenyth. But this strategy can be expensive and high risk, and it can potentially cause damage in client relationships. The key point here is that, rather than trying to change the basis for a buying decision, you will work to have the decision itself postponed. But this strategy needs senior relationships and time to execute. It is high risk because it may be seen as negative or working against the client's interests. Any time you consider this strategy, be prepared to invest as it usually demands high cost scoping studies and other resource intensive activities.

In the context of strategy, you should also consider: **Positioning and price.** It is usually best to position your organization and solution as being in, 'The Goldilocks Zone'. Analogous to the fable of *Goldilocks and the Three Bears*, this will mean that you are perceived as not too big, expensive or over-featured; not too small, cheap or inadequate; but just the right size and specifications to meet their needs – current and future. Your organization and offering needs to be perceived as just right, therefore being lowest risk and best value.

It is important, however, to remember that price is only relevant if the buyer actually wants your product, service or solution. A high price, early in the process, may disqualify you before you can sell your value. A low price may create perceptions of inferior quality. Early price positioning should, therefore, be high enough to reinforce your messages of quality and value but not so high that you could be eliminated from the evaluation and buying process on the basis that your product or service is unaffordable. It is equally important to have a strategy for maximizing perceived value, with relevant uniqueness, which makes competing difficult for the opposition.

Lastly, there are critical success factors for strategy. It is essential to have accurate and complete information concerning:
- Business drivers (reduce costs, improve productivity, etc.)
- Buying centre (all the people involved in decision process)
- Power-base (those with political power; identify the puppet master)
- The competition, including internal options and other project funding
- Budget, time-frame, compelling events and non-decision options
- Selection criteria (weighted for functionality, usability, price, risk, etc.)

In relation to the Zenyth opportunity, I suspect that the two identified competitors are not your biggest risk. Although we will cover the P, of RSVP, in my next e-mail, I must alert to the fact that I do not think you truly understand your customer's funding and procurement process. How does Zenyth decide which projects receive money? What is the hurdle rate for project funding? What payback period is expected? What return on investment is required? What is their bias toward in-house solutions or out-sourcing? How do they assess risk and value? What was the basis on which they determined the project's budget before going to market? Can they secure additional funding and, if so, how? Is the current budget truly secured? What is their contractual framework? Are you really preferred vendor or just with your alleged 'executive sponsor'? Is he really just a recommender with a manager's title? Does he control the money?

Right now, you must be feeling rather overwhelmed. Please take your time to fully digest all the information here and on the RSVPselling website. I suggest you push your man inside Zenyth to announce you as the winner within their organization as soon as possible. This will help to uncover the truth of your current position.

I really do not wish to be harsh, Joshua, but I am compelled to convey the truth. You know that strategy is important yet you act without all the necessary information. You also must escape the Seymour Syndrome and begin to build direct relationships with people of real power.

We will cover the last two letters of RSVP in detail once you have had time to digest all this. Most sales people have no problem in grasping the concept of unique value, which is the V, but they fail to transition effectively from features to tangible business benefits. The area most neglected by sales people is the P, which is the customer's Process. Do you really understand the Zenyth process for justifying your selection and commercially committing to your solutions?

Knowing and doing are indeed two different things. You have much to mull over for now. Do not rush your response. Think before acting and involve your boss by strategizing with him.

Damien Drost
RSVPselling™ Sales Master

Joshua felt overwhelmed with the level of detail in what he had read. RSVP had seemed straight forward but now there were many perplexing questions. The biggest realization confronting him was that he spent all of his selling time with Seymours. He was annoyed with himself for selling at the wrong level. On the few occasions, however, when he had gone over the head of his primary contact, it had created serious problems. He was awash with frustration concerning what to do.

Another realization hit him – complex account planning documents really did serve a valuable purpose. He knew that he undervalued their use and his lack of accurate information meant the outputs had often been ineffective. His thoughts returned to what he regarded as Damien's glib instruction to sell higher without any enlightenment concerning how to do so. He manically made notes.

The next day, Joshua sat down with Michael and discussed his newfound concerns with Zenyth but the anxiety was not shared. Michael reluctantly agreed to schedule a meeting with Bill Trench, under the guise of seeking better understanding of their timing, resource requirements and any potential contract issues. The real reason for the meeting would be to persuade him to announce them as preferred vendor, ensuring there could be no reversal or deferment without an unacceptable loss of face for Bill.

Michael gave Joshua an ominous look. "We'll meet with Bill as soon as we can. What's your answer on the promotion?"

"I really do want to discuss it but we need to win Zenyth first. I'm late for my next meeting. Can we talk later?"

It was a rhetorical question and Joshua was walking away before Michael had a chance to protest.

Later that afternoon, Michael phoned to say he had secured the appointment with Bill two days hence. He pushed again for a decision on the promotion and Joshua could delay no longer. He agreed to discuss it the next morning.

That night, Joshua composed an initial reply to Damien and it was midnight before it was sent. Although he wondered what the competition would be trying to do to his Zenyth deal, he felt everything was probably okay. He drifted into a restless sleep, mildly concerned but oblivious to the real problem. He had no idea about the real competition.

Hi Damien,

There was a lot of information that highlighted many things I have never really covered properly in the sales process. I agree with all that you wrote but I am really struggling with the concept of getting directly to the very top person in the buying organization. It's not that I disagree; it's just that I feel ill-equipped to engage in credible dialogue at that level. And more than that, every time I've sought to go over the head of my primary contact, it has always ended badly. Don't senior executives delegate decisions and then, generally, accept the recommendations from their experts if within the budget?

I've rewritten the above in several different ways, and I know you're right, but very senior executives just do not want to meet with sales people. I want to make the transition to selling at the highest level but I feel inadequate in this regard. My main question here is how do I engage with a senior executive who pulls the strings if he has delegated responsibility to others?

Also, I have read, and reread, your insights on the Zenyth situation. I am taking your questions and comments very seriously. We have an appointment with the executive sponsor this week and we will push for him to announce us internally as you have suggested. I am not taking anything for granted but I will be very surprised if either of our competitors have better relationships than us. They will have alienated the key person in the deal if they went over his head. If price is the only concern, then we can use this to get the deal closed.

As suggested, I will give the content of your e-mail much thought. I just wanted to come back to you on the issue of selling to very senior executives, as I do agree that the 'Seymour Syndrome' is a real problem for me.

Your student,
Joshua

Bill Trench was a middle-management veteran at Zenyth, well liked and supported by his team. Bill's ability, however, to get the project across the line was marginal at best. He was a ditherer, and Zenyth's new CEO, David Thomas, had no time for ineffectual plodders. Transformation was needed to fulfill his commitments to the board. Bill was about to be introduced to outsourced self-optimization – retrenchment – and would make way for the CEO's new agent of change, Kirsten Slater. She had been hired six weeks earlier as Manager, Special Projects. Few knew it, but Bill's Customer Service Department was a *very* special project. Kirsten would be calling the shots in just a few short weeks once she was promoted to Director, Customer Service. She made her own decisions and cared little for the status quo. She was being installed to rapidly deliver improved service with reduced costs. Joshua's corporation did not necessarily help with the latter.

Two restless nights in a row meant that Joshua awoke in a zombie-like state. The hot shower had some effect and he mentally rehearsed the difficult conversation he was destined to have with Michael in just a few short hours. He drove to the office in unusually heavy traffic and it drained away the temporary energy surge he had experienced from steam and caffeine. The café downstairs was a familiar environment and Joshua was a well known regular. He was early and nervously sipped on a strong cappuccino to re-energize while waiting for Michael.

"Hi Joshua, where's *my* coffee?"

The two men briefly discussed Zenyth before Michael could wait no longer. "Well, what's your decision?"

Joshua knew exactly what he would say and delivered it with as much conviction as he could muster. "I'm sorry to have taken so long to give you an answer but, even if we win the Zenyth deal, I'm just not ready. I still have things to learn and I need more experience before I make that kind of move. Thanks for offering but the answer is no. Sorry."

Michael gave nothing away with his body language. He just nodded thoughtfully. "I've organized lunch for you and the boss. Just listen to what he has to say. I'll tell him you're undecided, okay?"

"Actually, no, it's not okay. I'm not going to change my mind."

There was a prolonged period of silence, both men knew the next person to talk would not get their way.

Michael finally relented. "I'm disappointed and I think you're making a mistake; but let's get back to the Zenyth meeting. How do you think we should play it?"

Joshua was relieved to have escaped without any more pressure. He resisted the urge to give any additional rationale for his decision as it would simply open the door again. He paused thoughtfully and then raised something at the forefront of his mind.

"Mike, before we cover that, can I ask you for some sales advice? What's the best way for me to get to someone like Bill Trench's boss?"

Michael was bemused. "I admire your desire to sell high but I've always found the best way to get to the key senior people is by mapping executives from our side into their organization. Your job is to manage the sale and work the mid-level relationships. I'll work Bill Trench and decide if we need to go above him."

"Until very recently, I would have agreed but for me to take the next step as a sales person, I need to figure out how to engage with someone like Bill's boss."

Michael grabbed the opportunity. "You know what, Joshua, that's exactly why you should take this promotion. It will give you a genuine management title on your business card. Senior executives are more likely to agree to meet with a manager rather than a salesman. Have lunch with the boss and hear him out."

"No. Let's talk about the meeting with Bill."

Joshua reached into his coat pocket and pulled out a single sheet of paper. He unfolded it and placed it in front of Michael. "This is a list of potential questions I thought could be useful with Bill." They were from one of Damien's e-mails but re-drafted in Joshua's own words. Michael carefully reviewed the list and scribbled notes beside a few of the questions.

"Joshua, these are all good questions but most of them should have been asked a long time ago. You told me that the project is approved and funded."

"Yes. I think it is but I got the information from the project manager. We should confirm it all with Bill directly."

Michael shook his head. "The goal of the meeting is to get him to internally announce us as preferred vendor. These types of questions will probably just annoy him. Let's focus on asking Bill about their timing for implementation and then close based on overcoming any price gaps. If he baulks, we can maybe drill down with some of those questions then; but only then. Okay?"

"Sure, you lead the meeting. I'll ask some of those questions only if appropriate. Let's have me, the salesman, annoy him if necessary, rather than damage your relationship with him."

Michael was now running late for his next meeting and he stood to signal an end to the conversation. Joshua felt relieved that he had dealt with rejecting the promotion. He sat and pondered whether a more prestigious title on his business card could be the key to securing meetings with senior executives. Michael's comments concerning team selling were certainly valid but Damien had been clear that he had to personally interact at the highest levels.

Joshua went to his desk to plan the sequence of questions he would ask Bill if the meeting failed to secure the commitment they needed. He felt sure that Bill would only announce them as the successful bidder if the project was truly locked-in. Later in the day, he sat eating lunch in front of his laptop while checking his personal e-mail. He stopped chewing and focused on the screen.

Hello Joshua,

I was concerned with the lack of scope in your questions but I am pleased that you have focused on the most difficult of all the issues. The problems you face in successfully engaging with the most senior people are indeed challenging. You are right when you state that they do not want to meet with sales people like you. That is why it is so important to be a business person. You need to talk their language and operate as they do. Let me explain how they think and this will help you understand what they need from you.

Commercial enterprises are driven by profit, which is achieved with a combination of margin and volume. Margin is the result of deducting costs from the selling price. Volume is a function of market size and market share. Business prosperity is achieved with focus and specialization. Successful companies therefore have business models focused on either low volume but high margin or high volume but with low margins. Think about Coca Cola compared with Boeing as a simplistic example.

If a business is seeking to improve margins, then this is achieved by increasing their selling price or reducing their costs (COGS: Cost of Goods Sold). If, on the other hand, a business is seeking to increase volume, then this is achieved by gaining more market share or accessing new markets. You must therefore help customers to reduce costs or increase prices through value, or you must help them increase market share or gain access to previously untapped markets. Cost cutting is a tactic, not a strategy, and no organization can cost-cut its way to long term success. A final consideration is the cost of acquiring new customers, and it is far more cost effective to invest in retaining existing clients than replace those lost due to poor service or failure to provide adequate value. When you seek to sell at the very top in a commercial environment, you must align your value with their focus and business drivers.

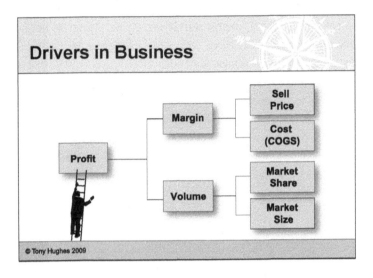

In addition to business drivers, you also need to consider an organization's level of urgency and motivation in solving problems or realizing opportunities. Organizations in either high growth or crisis / survival mode will make decisions quickly but if an organization is in business-as-usual mode, decisions will be slow. Any business in survival mode is desperate to reduce costs and improve cash flow. A business experiencing high growth, on the other hand, will be driven to increase profit and achieve greater efficiencies. The problem with selling to a business that is maintaining the status quo (business-as-usual) is that they can easily do nothing and defer investment decisions. Although they want improved profitability, through greater efficiency and reduced costs, they struggle to commit to investing and can move so slowly that decision momentum is lost completely, through endless analysis. The lesson, in all this, is that you need serious problems in order to create compelling value. Seek organizations that are growing or, depending on what you offer, may be in crisis. Beware of prospective clients that have the option of simply doing nothing.

Government and charitable organizations are not driven by profit. Instead they are focused on achieving outcomes. These 'not-for-profit' organizations either want to improve service value (efficiency and service levels) or they want to increase service volume (the number of people or organizations utilizing their products or services). When you seek to sell at the very top in government or charitable environments, you must also align your value with their drivers and metrics for performance measurement.

You must help them increase efficiency and improve productivity or you must help them to cost-effectively increase the reach (or capability) and utilization of their services. In essence, the drivers are almost always to improve compliance and service levels or to operate more efficiently. Beware of any government employee, however, telling you that their business case is compliance alone. The very top people see compliance as a relatively low level 'tick in the box' issue and will not allocate serious funding in isolation. Compliance may be a driver for some but it is never a business case alone. Compliance outcomes must be the by-product of investing in improved efficiency and service levels.

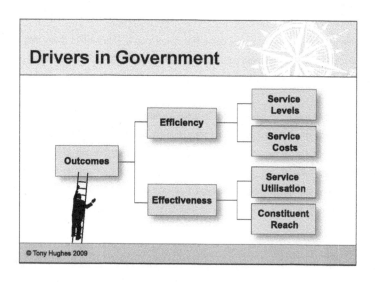

Finally, concerning selling to government, if you are responding to a tender and did not have prior engagement, it is difficult to exert influence with relationships and strategy. If you do decide to bid, and you probably should not, it is vitally important to focus heavily on the V and P of RSVP. Ensure best value and full alignment with their evaluation and buying process.

Now you know what senior executives care about but there are other important considerations in interacting with them. No one likes being sold to and a sure sign of a sales person is when they use manipulative sales techniques and F words! Not bad language but, rather, Features or Functions. Overt or manipulative sales techniques are to be avoided at all costs and this means you must allow the senior executive to be in control. No manipulative questions or closing techniques, just a sincere desire to understand their agenda, drivers, vision, and the constraints within which they need to deliver results.

Senior executives become most annoyed when someone wastes their time, especially by asking for information that could have been sourced elsewhere. Invest in understanding their business and industry, beyond just looking at their website and last annual report. There are many creative things you can do to gain genuine understanding of the problems and opportunities in their industry. Consider becoming a shareholder or take one of their sales representatives to lunch. You could develop a relationship with an independent consultant within their industry and ask where they lag behind the competition or who is threatening their market position. When you meet with the prospective customer's top people you must talk their language, not with clumsy clichés and acronyms but with genuine insight.

Being on time to an appointment means being five minutes early. You wait for them; they should not have to wait for you. Never take more time than has been allocated to you. If the meeting goes well, it is essential to document and commit to follow-up actions and schedule another meeting.

In addition to valuing their time, talking their language, understanding their industry and allowing them to be in control, you must also have proof of your ability to deliver tangible benefits; not evidence of product features. Instead, you must be equipped to discuss case studies and reference sites relevant to them where you have already delivered tangible business value. If you do not have real world examples of where you have already delivered, then it is very difficult to engage powerfully with a CEO. Sales Masters use their customers to do their selling for them but in an intelligently controlled manner.

You need to make the words your own but here is an example of how to set the agenda with a CEO. 'Every organization is unique and I can't promise the same results we delivered at XYZ (your relevant reference customer), that's why we need to invest some time together to ensure that I understand your vision and the outcomes that need to be achieved.' You then need to ensure you have ongoing access and get sponsored down to the appropriate person. 'Our teams are going to be working closely together but I would like to keep you directly informed on how well both sides are staying focused on the business outcomes you need delivered. Project teams can easily become lost in lower level detail and I want to ensure we stay aligned to delivering within your framework. Is that something that's important to you?' Let the CEO be in control. If you have prepared well, and positioned yourself as a business person, the CEO should agree that it is a good idea.

Finally, Joshua, you will need the right relationship established between the prospective customer CEO and your reference customer's executive. This is more important than mapping your own corporation's executives into their organization. Figure out how to get your best customers working for you but in a way that manages the associated risks. They need to tell your prospect about how you are best value and lowest risk, and committed to resolving any issues. Again, every CEO needs proof of performance, not promises, and they will invest time with you only if they believe you can help them achieve their vision and goals.

My next e-mail will have the balance of the RSVP information – unique value proposition and understanding the customer's processes.

Damien Drost
RSVPselling™ Sales Master

Joshua read the e-mail again that night while picking half-heartedly at the cold remnants of his dinner. He pushed the plate away and allowed the information to sink in fully. He made no notes. He was intimidated by the enormity of stepping up. Before long, his tiredness drove him to bed.

The next day, he arrived at the office feeling prepared for the meeting with Bill at Zenyth. He knew Michael did not share his paranoia but Joshua was ready with a series of questions. Later, the three men sat in a café just down the street from Zenyth's headquarters. Michael was leading the conversation while Joshua observed and nodded, appearing to be fully engaged, yet his thoughts gravitated to how he could find an opportunity to ask the questions gnawing at him. Michael was doing a good job in asking about the next steps and probing for meaningful commitment. Bill was candid in his responses but vague on their timing and process for approval to raise a purchase order. He artfully deflected the requests to announce them as the selected vendor and the conversation seemed to go around in circles. Joshua could tolerate it no longer.

"Sorry Bill, I don't mean to interrupt but it's your department, your project, your budget. Surely announcing us will enable you to get the project locked-in?"

There was a long awkward pause. "Joshua, I appreciate your enthusiasm but until the CEO signs off, it would be premature."

Joshua spoke calmly. "I thought the project was already approved?"

"I know how much time and effort you've put in, and I want to go ahead. God knows we need it but the CIO has been in the ear of the CEO claiming the IT department can build a solution for half the price. I keep telling them that it's a pipe dream. The IT people almost never deliver anything on time or within budget, but ..." Bill paused, looking lost for words.

Michael stepped in. "This must be frustrating. We are on the same side, so how can we help get the project over the line?"

He was right; Bill did regard them as allies in his quest to improve service levels. They explored the problems with genuine empathy. Forty minutes later, Bill left on a mission to meet with the CEO, David Thomas, to convince him that the IT department had no chance of delivering what he needed and that the costs put forward by the CIO were vastly under-estimated.

"I so wanted to reach over and choke the life out of you! I thought we agreed that you would let me run the meeting with Bill?" It was a rhetorical question and Michael did not wait for a response. "Anyway, I hate to admit it but you were right – we have a serious problem. This deal is a long way from being ours, Bill is only the recommender. I don't think he would have agreed to sponsor a meeting with me and the CEO, so I didn't ask."

For the next hour, the two men sat strategizing about what they should do concerning their precarious situation. Michael was the senior and more experienced, yet Joshua responded beyond his years.

"Mike, we don't have all the information and we don't have any solid relationships beyond Bill. This is our deal to lose. The biggest risk is that they'll do nothing. If we panic we could actually damage things. Give me a few days to do some homework."

Joshua couldn't bring himself to write to Damien. He was embarrassed by the degree to which his mentor had been right. He wanted to resolve the problem before corresponding and he needed information – intelligence – upon which he could formulate a strategy. He especially needed insight into the CEO and the internal politics. It suddenly occurred to him that one of his friends worked for Zenyth's external audit firm. He would call in a favor, to organize a meeting with someone connected to the Zenyth account. In the meantime, he searched the internet for information on David Thomas, the relatively new CEO.

The next few days were hectic. There had been no word from Bill and, disturbingly, he was not returning Michael's calls. Joshua was, however, meeting with Adrian Chowdrey, Principal Consultant at Zenyth's audit firm. His friend had provided an introduction but was surprised that he had agreed to meet with Joshua. Adrian had demonstrated a reluctance to engage in dialogue with a salesman seeking to hawk to his valuable client. Joshua had used all of his sales skills over the telephone to secure the meeting.

Joshua arrived two minutes early at the city café and spotted Adrian Chowdrey sitting in the corner reading a document. He walked over and introduced himself with a warm smile and firm handshake. His friend had said that Adrian appeared affable but disliked small talk. Joshua, therefore, cut to the chase by explaining his dilemma. He made it clear that they were already preferred vendor and were working with senior management to secure business case approval from the new CEO. Joshua explained that he was seeking insight into how David Thomas operated and the new priorities inside the organization.

Adrian was cautious. "You know I cannot divulge anything confidential concerning my client?"

"Yes. I fully understand and I respect your position, but I believe I'm acting in Zenyth's best interests. This is an important project for them and I'm struggling to help the project sponsor get the business case over the line. I would be grateful for any insights you're able to share."

Adrian paused thoughtfully before he spoke. "What I'm going to tell you is in the public domain, so there's no conflict. I'm still the Principal Consultant for Mawson Industries. I've worked with David for about ten years and he brought us over with him to Zenyth. He focuses on cost control and the bottom line. Let me ask you something. What's the basis of financial justification in their business case?"

"To be honest, I don't know. I think it's based on return on investment, rather than payback period. The productivity improvements don't all drop to the bottom line. It's more about improving service levels."

Adrian looked bemused. "You say you're working closely with senior management but you don't understand the ROI or whether it meets their NPV gate."

Joshua knew not to pretend that he understood. "I'm embarrassed to say that I don't know what NPV means. The executive sponsor for the project has been vague on the approval metrics."

"NPV stands for Net Present Value. Accountants like it but it's not used all that often these days. Zenyth's CFO uses it as his preferred method for assessing any investment."

"What does David Thomas think of NPV?"

"He's not a fan. He prefers payback period and the savings have to be tangible. Everything must be monetized."

"Thanks, I'll raise this with Bill Trench. He's the executive sponsor."

Adrian leaned forward and lowered his voice. "Joshua, listen carefully. Often when a new CEO takes control, he adopts a new broom approach. David has now been in the seat for nearly four months. Do you understand what I'm saying?"

"I think so but Bill seems quite respected within his department and ..."

Adrian shook his head and interrupted. "You should align with the future. Have you met Kirsten Slater?"

Joshua shook his head and did his best to look calm. "Who is she?"

Adrian ignored the question. He didn't want to breach trust. "David achieved big things for Mawson Industries, and they were disappointed to lose him. Do your own homework on the period David was CEO there. Everything you need to know is in the public domain. It will provide insight into what he has planned for Zenyth."

The meeting was brief and Joshua walked out with a sense of foreboding, but worry was soon replaced by purposeful activity. He now had insight, and maybe enough time, to save the deal. He knew they had to engage with David Thomas but first he needed to know more about Kirsten Slater. Back at the office, he rang the Zenyth switch and asked for Kirsten's title and department. The receptionist was helpful and gave him what he needed without fuss.

"She is Manager, Special Projects but I cannot see her department in our system. Oh, here it is. She reports directly to the CEO."

Joshua navigated the Internet and within a few minutes was looking at press archives quoting her as a call centre expert. One article had a photo with a caption: Kirsten Slater – Client Services Director, Mawson Industries. Joshua felt certain this was bad news. David Thomas had brought Kirsten over with him and there was clearly an agenda for doing so.

Bill Trench's buying process had commenced before David Thomas started and Joshua knew he needed to somehow align with what the new regime wanted. He was, however, still working in a relative vacuum and desperate for more information. He downloaded all the available annual reports for Mawson and searched the web for press releases and editorials. He also looked for details on other vendors who had delivered for Mawson. He wondered if Kirsten was working in the background to bring her own supplier relationships over to Zenyth.

His biggest worry was whether he would be stymied, prevented from engaging at the right level to sell the deal all over again. Damien's last e-mail could not have been timelier and it provided insights into what the most senior people in an organization wanted. He knew he needed to have a business conversation with David Thomas, and it needed to result in him being sponsored down to Kirsten. Questions raced through his mind. It was time to write to Damien, but only after he thoroughly researched the suppliers and technical environment of Mawson Industries.

Hello Damien,

You were right about the Zenyth deal and I desperately need some advice. I think our senior contact (Bill) is about to be replaced by someone that the new CEO, David Thomas, has brought over with him from his previous corporation, Mawson Industries. She will have her own agenda and maybe her own supplier relationships. I've done some homework. The good news is that Mawson has a very different technical environment and no common suppliers with Zenyth. From looking at old annual reports for Mawson, David Thomas seems to focus on reducing costs and improving service levels through supply chain innovation, something not directly linked to our project. The driver for our project was improving customer service but I'm now going to see if we can deliver cost savings or other measurable benefits with our solution.

Here is my dilemma: I don't know if Bill Trench is aware of the fact that he is about to be forced out. I discovered this information during a meeting I had with an external consultant who has known David Thomas for many years and is convinced that he will put a broom through the management ranks. Do we abandon Bill or still work with him? Do we tell him what's going on? Should my boss approach the CEO while I work with Bill? Do I go directly to the new person the CEO has brought in? How do we re-engage around Bill without damaging our chances of winning the deal?

My boss has a better relationship with Bill than I do but whoever goes over his head to the CEO is going to cause a problem for Bill. I guess, in hindsight, that I should have developed the relationship with Bill and my boss should have engaged with the CEO. Another issue is that Bill has been very focused on features and price rather than business value. Every time I've attempted to lift the conversation to benefits, Bill simply turns off. I guess he views this as a sales tactic.

I know you want me to sell at the very top so should I personally approach David Thomas? I'm sure my boss will want to do it instead. I think we should let Bill know that we are going above him and ask for his support but not his permission. If Bill tries to stop us, then we will tell him that we're concerned about the project's alignment to the new CEO's agenda, drivers and vision for where he is taking Zenyth. What do you think?

Thank you for the information in your last e-mail. I think I understand and I am committed to behaving as a business person rather than a salesman. I will stay away from features and functions, and focus on business drivers and outcomes. I understand that the effectiveness of a meeting is determined by preparation and the questions I ask. I will focus on their vision and goals and emphasize how committed I am to ensuring that we deliver business benefits by understanding their environment and the sought-after business outcomes.

I forgot to thank you for the tip concerning The Joshua Principle. I am still stuck but will keep reflecting on this and let you know when I have made more progress.

Your anxious student,
Joshua

Joshua wanted to wait for Damien's response before meeting with Michael. He felt sure his boss would seek to take control directly with the CEO and relegate him to dealing with Bill. He wished, more than ever, that he had telephone access to Damien to discuss how to deal with Michael and his bullying management style. He sat in front of his laptop, hoping for a rapid response.

While he waited, he studied the Mawson annual reports again and searched additional press archives. Industry publications had run a number of features that provided invaluable insights into David Thomas, portrayed as a leader who focused strongly on supply-chain efficiency, customer retention and profitability. One editorial show-cased their success and focused on David's view that many companies failed to understand the high cost of customer acquisition compared with the value of investing in customer retention. *'Customer churn is an ugly factor that has to be aggressively addressed by any corporation seeking to improve profitability and market position.'* There were more quotes. *'The management team here at Mawson Industries is committed to more than just customer retention. We are investing to make our customers truly delighted. We are listening to them and earning their support with them becoming our advocates in the market. This doesn't mean we are not focused on new clients, it's just that sustained industry-leading profitability can only be achieved if we have the most loyal customers.'*

The more Joshua read, the more convinced he became that Zenyth's board brought David in to apply the same treatment. It would need to be validated but he nevertheless felt buoyed by the potential to align with addressing their *'leaky bucket syndrome'*, as David Thomas put it. He was publicly critical of companies spending huge sums on expensive sales and marketing programs, only to lose existing customers almost as fast as they acquired new ones.

Bill Trench had simply stated that the project was part of improving customer service but the tender documents had no information concerning the business outcomes they were seeking. The documentation was merely a set of technical requirements and Joshua felt this could be his justification for requesting the meeting with the CEO. They had invested heavily in Zenyth's process and things had stalled. Bill could not articulate the new CEO's vision, to which the project must surely be aligned. He made copious notes with references to source documentation, and methodically linked anything relevant to the public priorities of David Thomas. While he was on a web site, Joshua's in-box registered the anticipated reply.

Hello Joshua,

Every sale must begin and end at the top. Not with functional managers or Seymours. You know this now, so let us do all we can to ensure that Zenyth is not an expensive lesson. The challenges you face are substantial but you are equipped for the job. You must personally engage with the new CEO. The issue is how to best execute while managing the situation with Bill who is on the way out.

Your idea of having a one-on-one meeting with Bill is the right approach but under no circumstances should you tell him that he is about to be replaced. It is highly likely that the CEO has already informed Bill directly and that he is actively looking for another job. If, on the other hand, he is unaware; then it is not your place to deliver the bad news, nor do anything that could result in a negative outcome. Imagine the consequences, if Bill stormed into the CEO's office to confront him, following your potentially shocking revelation. Your actions would have betrayed the trust of your source and created a problem for the CEO.

I am sure Bill is a sincere man and it appears you have built a good relationship with him where there is trust and openness. Bill may be able to provide accurate intelligence concerning what is really going on inside Zenyth but he is now a corporate eunuch, outside the power-base, unable to exert real influence. When meeting with Bill, adopt the position you articulated in your previous e-mail. Do not ask for permission to meet with the CEO. Instead, ask for his support and coaching.

If Bill offers to conclude the transaction before he leaves Zenyth, be politely skeptical and test the likelihood by asking him to explain the business case and how the project aligns with the new CEO's vision and priorities. Also ask Bill to specifically detail the process for gaining approval and issuing you with a purchase order. Remember that you must never lose control by depending on recommenders to do the selling for you. If Bill asks you not to contact the CEO, simply state that your organization has made a substantial investment and that you are under instructions. Set the scene by telling Bill that there is clearly something wrong. Every new CEO seeks to stamp their imprimatur on an organization and you need to gain direct insight into the new vision, agenda and priorities. Don't ask Bill to set the meeting up for you. Instead obtain his commitment that if the CEO asks why you are going direct, he will simply state that he could not provide the answers you were seeking and that you are credible and worth meeting.

You must not abrogate responsibility for getting the account back on track. This is an excellent learning opportunity and you are absolutely capable of salvaging the situation. Although you should manage it directly, do not hide anything from your boss. Michael will want to take over but tell him you are the one who will engage with the CEO. If he tries to bully you, just tell him that you seek his counsel and advice in planning strategy but that you will execute – it's not negotiable.

I agree with your angle on the Zenyth CEO but emphasize that you are concerned about whether the current proposal is aligned with where he is taking the organization. Resist the urge to tell him that you believe there are some adjustments that can be made that potentially deliver better value and a stronger return on investment, as this would be perceived as hollow clichés from a salesman. A final piece of advice for when you first meet with the CEO is to treat it like a job interview. Imagine he is seeking a senior executive to effect change within Zenyth and that you are a proven performer in delivering what he needs.

This point leads me to the balance of the RSVP equation promised to you in my previous e-mail. We've already discussed the fact that relationships with the right people, combined with effective strategy that is based upon accurate information, will take you a long way. You also need a unique and compelling value proposition and complete understanding and alignment with the customer's selection and buying process. Let us now explore the second half of the RSVP equation.

Value: It is essential that you create value for the customer and that the value you offer is embedded within a strong business case. This ensures the necessary funding is secured without risk of competing projects diverting money or resources. But value creation, evidenced by a compelling business case, can only be achieved with intimate understanding of the customer's business through relationships at the right level that create, or uncover, value through solutions to serious problems or the ability to realize potential opportunities.

The goal of a professional sales person is therefore 'value creation' before 'value projection'. Once value is established, you can then focus on your value proposition which must be unique and compelling. In essence, it must provide you with an unfair advantage. Never waste your precious time and resources in bidding for business where the odds are stacked against you. Never gamble by hoping for good luck or competitor ineptitude. Hope is not a strategy. Being dependent on luck is for amateurs. The maxim of, 'selling is a numbers game' can be true but being busy does not necessarily equate with being effective. The 'busy fool syndrome' is more of a problem in the sales industry than laziness. Success depends on doing the right things, the right way, with the right people, at the right time.

Play to your strengths and invest your time and energy where you already have an advantage and offer compelling unique value. Do not be deceived by your own organization's marketing hype. Your unique value proposition must be focused on specific and tangible benefits for the customer, and directly linked to resolution of their specific problems. There is enormous value in being able to deliver solutions within the constraints and political framework of their organization. This can also be part of the unique value equation – your intimate understanding of the risks and how a solution specifically needs to be delivered.

Every organization seeks to balance risk with reward. Always ask your customer what happens if they do nothing, and who is most impacted? Is your solution part of a business case? Is there a compelling event or a very strong driver for buying and implementing the solution? Always ask questions to uncover or clarify these potential deal-killers. Internal competition for funding and resources can often be invisible to outsiders yet stall or undo a purchasing initiative.

Beyond a compelling value proposition, you also need to represent best value for money which is usually assessed in accordance with the following formula. Value For Money = solution being Fit For Purpose plus having the Lowest Risk Profile; divided by the Total Cost of Ownership.

$$VFM = \frac{FFP + LRP}{TCO}$$

It is essential that you meet the exact requirements and be perceived as representing the lowest risk. These two factors are then weighed against the total cost of ownership. All of your assertions concerning value and risk need to be considered from the customer's point of view. Unique value can be derived from a combination of features that translate directly to benefits or from your experience, methodologies and credentials that prove lower risk. You must consistently ask yourself, what do I offer that is uniquely compelling and does the customer see it that way? The most powerful unique value propositions usually include your people, not just your product and service. Remember, one of the laws of selling is that people buy from those they like and trust. The solution is also people and their ability to deliver outcomes. Ensure that you understand exactly how they measure TCO, and over what period. This leads us to the P of RSVP – Process.

Process: This means the customer's selection, negotiation and procurement process, not your sales process. Failure to fully understand and align with the buying organization's processes is a serious weakness for many sales people. Poor process alignment automatically introduces risk and makes it almost impossible to forecast accurately. This is a major cause of frustration and tension with sales management. Unnaturally forcing the pace of business creates tension and resistance. Instead, manage your own organization's expectations and truly understand the customer's timing and process.

It never ceases to amaze me how easily miscommunication and ill-conceived assumptions permeate business dealings and personal relationships. Even when there is a clear understanding at some point, circumstances can easily change and the buyer can somehow overlook advising the seller. You must constantly clarify and confirm your understanding in order to keep an opportunity on track.

Your deadlines are of little concern to the customer. They care about their needs and process. Never forecast revenue based upon your own end of quarter or financial year pressures. The timing for closing a deal must be in accordance with the process and timing of the customer. Never assume that price or other incentives will change the customer's timing. Are you actually aligned to their decision drivers, processes and timing for selection and procurement? The best approach is to understand the date that they need a solution implemented and then validate their commitment to the date by asking what happens if it slips or they do nothing and the status quo prevails. Once you have certainty of their commitment to a date for realizing benefits, identify everything that needs to occur in order to achieve the implementation deadline. Then, working backward from this date with the customer, go through the list and create a time-line, identifying all the milestones. Now you have a realistic time-frame for when a purchase order or contract can be executed.

You should be able to work with your customer to understand and document all the things that need to occur before a purchase order or contract can be signed. Their organization might need to develop a business case and work through a convoluted process for approval and funding. They may need to adhere to an onerous procurement process. There could be critical reviews with steering committees and there may be approvals required from senior management or at board level. There may be inter-dependencies with other projects or initiatives. The good news is that once you understand all this, in partnership with your customer, you are able to work with them to keep everything on track and adjust your strategy and activities accordingly. You are able to execute effectively because you understand everything that should happen as part of their selection and procurement processes.

If you couch your enquiries the right way, you will be surprised by how willing a customer is to share all the information with you. Simply explain that you are committed to working with them cooperatively, and that you are motivated to engage in accordance with their process, requirements and timing. Tell them that you need information on all these things so you can secure the very best resources and support within your own organization. There is an excellent list of Process questions and an Opportunity Close Planner on the RSVPselling.com website, and I encourage you to review those now to develop specific questions you need to ask Zenyth.

Every piece of business has a natural pace at which the selection and purchasing process can be executed. Great sales people ensure that they fully understand the client's requirements, buying process, timing and environment, prior to forecasting when business will close. If all these things are fully understood, then you will not lapse into a situation of creating unnecessary tension with the buyer.

So, Joshua, now you have it. RSVP seems simple enough but I think you already understand that nuance is the essence of mastery. You need to become instinctively capable in all these things. You have a tremendous opportunity with Zenyth to apply everything that you have learned.

Eliminate risk by ensuring there is nothing you don't know. Review the checklists and tools on the RSVPselling.com website to create your Zenyth questions. Use your knowledge and skills to achieve the outcome you deserve. Treat Bill with kindness and respect. Regard the CEO as your equal. Work with your boss as a coach and a sounding board for every move you make but you must be the one to engage with David Thomas.

Damien Drost
RSVPselling™ Sales Master

Joshua felt daunted by the task ahead and apprehensive about telling Michael to back away and leave the CEO to him. He worked like he had never worked before, obsessively gathering further information on David Thomas and, to a lesser extent, Kirsten Slater. He knew it was time to step up in his professional life and it began with calling his boss.

"Hi Mike. I've done a lot of homework on the Zenyth situation. I think we can still win but we need to talk. Can we meet for breakfast tomorrow morning to discuss everything?"

Chapter Eight: Strategy of No Hope

Joshua knew the breakfast meeting would be challenging. He was certain that Michael would not be pleased with being relegated to a subordinate role. His engagement strategy denied Michael any initial access to Zenyth's CEO. Joshua would take complete control of this key relationship but the big question was whether Michael Blunt believed Joshua could execute at that level. He was relatively inexperienced and had no track record of credibly interacting at the CEO level. Regardless of Michael's opinion, Joshua knew he needed to be resolute.

Michael greeted Joshua warmly as they settled for breakfast. He was keen to find out what information Joshua had gathered and, more importantly, what Joshua would recommend as the right strategy to close the Zenyth deal despite the imminent demise of Bill Trench. Michael dispensed with small talk and leaned forward.

"So, Joshua, it sounds like you've been busy in the last few days. What do you think we should do about the Bill Trench situation?"

"We should treat him kindly – he's a good guy."

"Forget the sentimentality. How do we win the deal now that our key contact is leaving?"

Joshua placed pages of notes on the table. "There is real risk with Zenyth, but the good news is that we have enough accurate information to execute the right strategy and still win. We must get to their CEO, David Thomas, and fast. Let me take you through the main information on him and also Kirsten Slater. At some stage soon, she'll step into Bill's role. I've done a lot of homework on what they had in place at Mawson Industries before they both moved to Zenyth."

"What do you mean – they?"

"David brought Kirsten Slater into Zenyth just seven weeks after joining as CEO. She worked for him at Mawson as Client Services Director. Right now she is Director of Special Projects, whatever that means, but I'm sure it's just a place holder until they push Bill. The good news is that she attended the last presentation we did. I had no idea who she was at the time, she came in and sat at the back just after we started and she left before it was over."

"Who's in the power-base for making the decision?"

Joshua rummaged among his pile of paper and produced an organizational chart with hand written notes and his own color coding.

"This is what it looks like – the most important issue is their CIO. The IT department reports to finance but I think that will change. David ran a flat structure at Mawson and he was very focused on controlling costs and improving customer retention – I think this is our opening. I've also done my homework on their CFO and I think he's in the firing line just like Bill."

"None of this fills me with joy, Joshua. I was hoping you were going to tell me that the CIO was going to get the axe. According to Bill, he's the one selling against us internally."

"The last annual report for Zenyth highlights cost problems and I think this is why our deal has been held up for so long. The CFO won't approve the expenditure and the CIO is telling him it can be done cheaper internally. But I'm pretty sure the CIO will soon report directly to the CEO, rather than through finance. David will make all the management changes at once – that's what he did at Mawson."

For the next forty minutes Joshua went on to lay everything on the table for Michael. He provided supporting intelligence and methodically painted the picture for his boss. Michael was genuinely impressed and sat silently processing the information. Joshua now knew it was time to reveal his plan.

"Mike, the big issue here is what we do about all of this. I've thought long and hard and I'm not sure if you will agree but hear me out."

"Yes, it's obvious we need to get to the CEO and I've been giving it some thought."

Joshua did not want to lose the ascendancy. He lowered his voice. "Mike, we agree but let me finish. Although we are the preferred solution, we are well outside their budget. Right now, Zenyth is our deal to lose. The CEO wants to control costs and the CFO won't approve the business case. Kirsten won't want to inherit any of Bill's baggage. The CIO is a problem and he'll have direct access to David soon. We need to cover the CIO without becoming trapped again like we were with Bill. This is where you come in."

"I get it. I'm happy to step in with the CEO but – "

"Mike, I need you to cover the CIO, while I engage with David Thomas and also ask him to sponsor me down to Kirsten."

Michael was dumbfounded. The café was getting busy and two men in suits sat beside them. Michael spoke with hushed skepticism.

"You know, Joshua, I admire your confidence and willingness to have a go, but this deal is too important to risk your inexperience with their CEO. I'll engage with David Thomas and you work Kirsten and the CIO."

"No. I need to engage with David Thomas, and it needs to be a one-on-one meeting."

Michael was aghast. "You can make recommendations but I will decide how we play this. Let's take this upstairs to a meeting room where we can talk openly."

Joshua looked Michael directly in the eye and smiled cheekily. "Let's not – it's harder for you to yell at me in public."

"Joshua, I'm accountable to the senior executive team on this deal. Losing it is not an option for me or you. Surely you want the best and most experienced person from our side matched with their CEO?"

"The best person is me, I've done the homework and I understand what needs to happen – I can do this. You believed in me enough to offer me the promotion, now believe in me enough to get the job done with their CEO. I need you to cover their CIO. Let me run through the questions I plan to ask David Thomas."

The initial assault on Michael's ego was fading and he spoke in a matter-of-fact tone. "You understand the ramifications if you lose this deal – yes?"

Joshua resented the threat but nodded without saying a word.

"Joshua, I haven't agreed to anything yet, but show me the questions you plan to ask the CEO and explain where you think they'll take you?"

Joshua passed his list over and ran through them, one by one, explaining his strategy and rationale.

Michael finally nodded. "Let me think about it. Promise me you won't call the CEO without consulting me first."

"Absolutely, I won't do anything important in this deal without first consulting you. That's why we are having this conversation now. At the risk of annoying you again, I must ask one last thing. I also need you to have a difficult meeting with Bill."

Michael nodded. "You're right. He's a real risk for us and I have the best relationship with him. Does he know he is about to be fired?"

For the next twenty minutes, they discussed the delicate situation concerning Bill and agreed it would be a mistake to tell him what they knew. Michael would take Bill to lunch, just the two of them, to discuss the new CEO's agenda and ask if he knew why Kirsten had followed David over from Mawson Industries. Michael had developed a relationship of trust with Bill and, if he was savvy to what was really transpiring, he would surely open up and confess he was leaving. If that happened, then maybe Bill would tell Michael everything he knew about the current barriers to their proposal being approved. Michael would also seek insight into what the IT department was proposing.

Joshua had found the confrontation difficult. He was emotionally exhausted yet euphoric from dealing with his boss assertively. Michael, on the other hand, had reluctantly accepted Joshua's lead and left the meeting feeling uneasy. They had invested heavily in pre-sales resources and Zenyth was currently the largest deal in the forecast which gave it weekly visibility within the senior executive team. If they lost Zenyth it would damage Michael's career and force an unpleasant conversation with Joshua.

Joshua continued to work on his preparation for the various Zenyth meetings. He prepared a draft briefing paper for Michael's lunch with Bill and he also revisited his outdated account plan for Zenyth. He would leave nothing to chance. It was time to use his employer's strategic selling tools properly. He knew his briefing information in a call plan would be vitally important in preparing Michael to effectively execute. He also began preparing for his own meeting with David Thomas and there were several disturbing gaps in the information. Joshua liked the fact that at least he knew what he did not know. He would continue gathering information, validating intelligence, and then confirm his strategy with Michael and Damien before executing.

Joshua was leaving the office when Michael phoned. "I've been thinking about your proposal and although I'm not comfortable with you going it alone with their CEO, I'll let you try. I'll step in if he knocks you back."

"I won't let you down, we'll plan everything together."

"Okay, when do you want me to have lunch with Bill?"

"Tomorrow, if you can organize it. I've just e-mailed you a call plan. It includes what I think you should say to get the appointment as well as what to ask once you're with him. Just my thoughts, I've probably missed a few things."

Michael began scanning the dozens of new messages in his in-box. "I'm opening it as we speak. How about we discuss it now; do you have time?"

Joshua was approaching his car and flicked the remote, unlocking the doors. "I'm just about to get in my car to go and see the account manager from the systems integrator that owns the Mawson account. She's happy to talk if I buy lunch. Hopefully this will fill in some of the blanks with David and Kirsten."

"But doesn't the systems integrator see us as a competitor?"

Joshua was sitting in the driver's seat and hit the ignition. "Not at Mawson Industries. She has nothing to do with Zenyth. Her view is that we can coexist in accounts. I know we think that we do systems integration but, in reality, it's a very small part of our business. She thinks we just care about outsource services and network carriage, they don't do outsourcing. Anyway, I'm about to start driving and my phone will drop out in the usual spot. Do you mind reading the call plan and then phone me back so we can discuss it?"

"Sure. I'll read and you drive. I'll call you soon."

A few minutes later his phone rang. "It's Mike. Your document is great. I really don't have anything to add. I'll call Bill now."

"Thanks. There was one thing I forgot to ask you at breakfast this morning. We need a very senior person within our customer base who is willing to be a strong reference. Not just any customer, they need to specifically match some of Zenyth's attributes and they must be able to identify cost savings and tangible business benefits. Ideally, the person needs to be a CEO. Can you please look into who could do this for us?"

Michael agreed to do some research on their best reference customers, and he committed to message Joshua once the lunch meeting with Bill had been secured. Joshua drove to his own lunch meeting feeling empowered. He was acting strategically and knew that obsessively gathering information was the only way to minimize risk in his engagement with David Thomas.

Joshua's lunch went well and he gained the insight he needed. He then invested the rest of the afternoon in plotting and rehearsing his yet-to-be scheduled meeting with Zenyth's CEO. He knew what he planned to say to secure the appointment but he couldn't make the call until Michael had executed with Bill.

A text message from Michael confirmed that his lunch with Bill was on for the next day.

Joshua decided to write to his mentor.

Hi Damien,

Thank you so much for the guidance in your last e-mail! The V and P information has given me much to think about. I'm excited about applying what you've taught me in my planned interaction with Zenyth's CEO. I would appreciate a response to this e-mail overnight if possible, as time is of the essence. In the interest of brevity, I will get to the point.

Although I was very nervous when telling my boss that I would run the CEO relationship, it went quite well. Michael meets with Bill tomorrow for lunch. Attached is the call planner I did and it details the direction I want him to take the conversation in and the key information we need. I think Bill will tell Michael that he is actually leaving. Surely he knows, but Michael absolutely agreed that we should not be the ones to break any bad news. Michael will adopt a line of questioning focused on the new CEO's agenda and rumors concerning why he brought Kirsten over from Mawson Industries. If all goes well, Michael will secure Bill's support for our strategy. What do you think of our approach?

The other attachments are the draft account plan and call plan for my appointment with their CEO. I am still gathering information, and both are still very much in a draft state. I've really tried to apply the information in your last few e-mails to this situation. Any feedback is appreciated but the urgent thing I need now is your validation, or otherwise, of the plan for Bill Trench tomorrow.

By the way, I've been doing my homework on Mawson and I met with the account manager from the current systems integrator. The good news is that their technical environment is completely different from Zenyth's. Better still, the telecommunications and information technology supplier relationships at Mawson were fairly strained. Their IT Manager is apparently quite difficult and there is tension between the IT Department, business units, and suppliers. It is almost certain that David and Kirsten have not brought any competitive relationships over with them. The other piece of interesting information is that the Mawson IT Manager described David as 'Doubting Thomas'. I hope this means that the internal threat at Zenyth from the IT Department is minimal. Bill Trench is convinced there is no way the IT Department can deliver what we can for Zenyth. Hopefully we are still well positioned, despite Bill's demise, but I will validate all of this with David and Kirsten directly as soon as I can meet with them.

I have not forgotten the issue of The Joshua Principle but I need to focus on Zenyth right now. Looking forward to your overnight reply please.

Your student
Joshua

Joshua went to bed fairly early. He wanted to get a head start the following day by being at work around 7:30. He hoped Damien would respond overnight and that he could adjust the Bill Trench strategy with Michael if necessary. Joshua checked his e-mail after breakfast, Damien had replied.

Hello Joshua,

Your life is becoming busy and I sense this is a good thing. You seem energized, rather than stressed, with the pace of the Zenyth situation. Ensure, however, that you engage with their CEO only when you are fully prepared. Continue to gather information and ensure that every step is the right one. Act with understanding and ask questions of Zenyth executives only when you know where they will lead.

Well done with your call plan for Michael with Bill Trench. The strategy and planned questions are good. If Michael has the positive relationship with Bill you have described, then raising the Kirsten rumor may indeed cause Bill to admit he is leaving, if he actually knows. It is good that Michael is covering Bill so you can remain disentangled for your encounter with the CEO.

Hopefully Michael will secure Bill's support for your strategy and also obtain the additional information you need. Ensure, however, that you check the accuracy of anything he tells Michael. Concerning your other two documents; the strategy is excellent and you are on the right track with your approach to the CEO. You have correctly identified additional information needed before making contact. I am also pleased with the fact that you are thinking about what you may not yet know. You are, therefore, seeking to take ignorance out of the risk equation but there are a few things that require discussion and consideration.

You suspect that Zenyth's IT department is your biggest threat. You may be correct but never forget the potential option for them to simply do nothing. They have operated for a long time without your solution and, unless you do your job well, they may decide that a few more years of status quo will be tolerable. You allude to this risk in your account plan but it needs to become the very strong focus of your interaction with the CEO. Once you truly understand their drivers and the implications of resolving, or failing to resolve, their specific issues, then you can set yourself apart by aligning with the required business outcomes.

There is something important that is missing in your planning. What mode of business is Zenyth in right now? Are they experiencing high growth or are they in crisis; or are they in business-as-usual mode? Please go back and study my previous e-mails where I discussed this topic. The answer to this question may not be obvious but it will largely determine their level of motivation for investing in your solution. I cannot stress enough how important it is for you to understand their desired outcomes to which you must align. You need to know whether your solution must increase profit, improve efficiency, minimize risk, reduce costs, or improve cash flow. If David Thomas is seeking to maintain the status quo, even just temporarily, then it is unlikely he will buy your solution. He will just appoint his own person and wait for recommendations and a supporting business case. Your initial telephone call with the CEO must align to the right agenda. Your current draft documents do not address this and you must not go to the meeting with hope concerning alignment, you need genuine positive insight.

Let me know the outcome of Michael's meeting with Bill. I look forward to seeing your Zenyth planning documents again once you have all the necessary information, and with the full list of your planned questions. Avoid asking questions that may take you down an undesired path. Again, and most importantly, what mode of business is driving the agenda of David Thomas. How will you secure the appointment and establish credibility?

You are doing well but be patient as you work with purpose. Insight will be critically important if you are to interact effectively at the CEO level.

Damien Drost
RSVPselling™ Sales Master

Joshua continued to work all morning on documenting his new account plan and refining the questions he would ask David Thomas. He could only go so far, however, before the vexing issue of Zenyth's business drivers prevented him from continuing. Their annual report and other information did not paint a clear picture – or maybe it was his inability to analyze the data. He considered who could best help him, either at work or within his network. An e-mail exchange with Damien was not an option. He instead needed a real conversation, and one name kept coming to the top of his list but he was reluctant to make the call to his father.

Mark Peters was a renowned business leader who possessed both finance and selling qualifications; a rare and highly valued combination of skills. Joshua knew he was long overdue to reach out to his father but rationalized that he didn't want to become further indebted or lapse into conflict again. He debated the idea and, in the end, knew it was time to truly face the most damaged area of his personal life. He sent an e-mail to test the water. Within a few minutes, Joshua's phone rang.

"Hi Josh. I just received your e-mail, how can I help?"

"I know you're busy. It's about a deal I'm working on but it can wait until after work."

Mark feigned nonchalance as he didn't want to appear too eager. His son's contact was, however, a watershed moment. "I have a clear schedule today, what's the problem?"

"It's Zenyth Corporation. I need to understand their balance sheet and P&L."

Mark knew his son could have approached someone else to help and was glad to be asked. "I can download their latest financials and annual report now. Why don't you come over for dinner and we can have a good look at it then. I'll do some research beforehand."

Joshua was surprised by the ease of the conversation and accepted the invitation. He gave Mark some background before thanking him for investing his time. He then phoned his mother to let her know he was coming to dinner to talk business with his father.

"It's wonderful that you're asking your father for help."

"I have an important meeting with a CEO and I need to know how he thinks. Dad runs a corporation, so I think he can help me analyze their annual report."

He called Michael next; they had a twenty minute discussion reinforcing the strategy for his meeting with Bill. Joshua emphasized the need to understand the real drivers and politics within Zenyth but he also asked Michael to press Bill again for what really initiated the project. Was it supported only by a marginal business case or was there something more compelling? Joshua respected Michael's ability and he felt confident that the lunch meeting would go as well as it could.

The next few hours dragged by as Joshua worried about how Michael's lunch with Bill was going. It was nearly 3:00 before Michael called and it had gone better than expected. Bill knew exactly what was going on and was actively looking for another job. After Bill left the restaurant, Michael had sat for twenty minutes documenting the two and a half hour conversation. There was much to discuss and Michael asked Joshua to meet him in the boardroom at 3:30 for a formal debrief rather than fragments of ad-hoc information over the phone while he was driving.

For nearly an hour the two men were locked away, absorbed in enthusiastic dialogue concerning their strategy and what information needed to be validated before forming part of their arsenal of intelligence. Joshua emerged from the boardroom with his laptop, power supply, files and notes, all precariously piled in his arms as he made a bee-line for his desk. He now had most of the necessary information to finalize his strategy and initiate contact with David Thomas. If his father could deliver for him tonight, he would be ready to validate things with Damien and then sit down with Michael to lock-in the plan of execution. Bill had agreed to support their plan and Joshua anticipated contacting David the following week.

Joshua went straight from work to the family home and arrived before Mark. Clare was happy to have some time alone with her son. They talked casually until she asked the burning question.

"How is the relationship with your father?"

"I called him today – that's progress, we'll eventually sort things out."

"But when will you resolve the past?"

"I'll make sure tonight doesn't end in an argument."

"That's not what I asked. He loves you more than you know. The breakdown cut him very deeply."

"Things will be fine when he stops criticizing and lecturing me."

Clare smiled. "Ah – conditional love, the devil's rule for relationships."

"Not tonight, please. I'm doing the best I can."

Clare's voice wavered. "Life is too short to hold a grudge."

Joshua was taken aback by the depth of emotion in his mother's voice. They were both saved by the sound of the automatic garage door. Clare changed the topic. "I know you're making an effort. How about you carve the roast, but not in caveman chunks, remember to cut with the grain."

Clare disappeared and Joshua mulled over his mother's words as he carved. He focused on the fact that he really had not forgiven his father – or himself. He had spent years pretending there was no need, but it was time to finally let go of the heaviest baggage he carried from of the past.

Mark appeared in the kitchen. Joshua wanted to hug him but had almost forgotten how. Instead, he smiled warmly. "Hi Dad. Thanks for helping with this tonight."

Clare looked at her roast in horror. "Usually meat is butchered before it is cooked, not afterward."

Mark and Joshua laughed. The conversation during dinner flowed easily. It was a dialogue without defensiveness. Finally, there were no egg shells to avoid. They even discussed the television incident and Joshua was glad to be able to explain the rationale behind his actions.

After dinner, the two men retired to discuss business. Mark was clearly happy to have been asked to assist. "I figured this was the only time you'd want my help while you're being mentored by Damien, so I've tried to do my best for you here. I assume you'll tell him what I think, so hopefully I won't embarrass myself with wrong conclusions."

"Dad, I'm not an accountant and I'm pretty sure neither is Damien. I don't tell him everything and he really wants me to make the decisions, he's just the sounding board."

Mark raised his eyebrows. "I thought he was coaching you through everything so you learn every little element of his sales techniques?"

"He's mentoring me, not coaching. He's focusing on the strategy and thought process behind my actions. He's given me a framework within which to run the sales process. Anyway, there's a lot to talk about with Zenyth. This meeting with their CEO is going to be critical. Do their financials reveal anything concerning what's really driving their decisions?"

Mark opened a folder he had brought in with him. "It's actually quite interesting. If I was on their board, I would ask the CEO what they're doing about all the cash on their balance sheet."

"Isn't cash a good thing?"

"Not necessarily. Too much cash on your balance sheet can make you a hostile acquisition target because the cash can fund financing costs. Cash is also an underperforming asset; it means you don't know what to invest in for growth."

"I guess Zenyth is conservative."

"It's not about being conservative. Too much cash on the balance sheet is a wasted resource. I'm pretty sure that the new CEO will be under pressure to look at acquisitions or some other plan for expansion. But they have a bigger problem; I've analyzed the last five years of numbers and had a look at recent analyst guidance – well, criticism really. Their sales costs, as a percentage of revenue, have been going up for the last three years in a row. Their margins are also being squeezed and I found an interview with the new CEO that pretty much reveals his hand."

"Thanks for doing this – you must have spent most of the afternoon on it. Is that the interview last month, written by Patricia Smith?"

Mark was impressed that his son had also tracked down and read the article. "Yes. David Thomas stated that client retention is his number one priority and that he wants delighted customers. I bet the reason they've been losing customers is that competitors are targeting them. When you have market dominance, you're a sitting duck for niche players to pick off your vulnerable customers."

"Thanks Dad. I hadn't made the connection with any of this. So would you say they were in growth, crisis or business-as-usual mode?"

"Why do you think it matters?"

Joshua explained the concepts Damien had shared with him concerning modes of business and the consequential motivation for decision-making. He fumbled with his own notes and showed Mark one of Damien's printed e-mails.

"This is what I'm trying to figure out – the mode they're in and how it translates to the things that are driving the CEO."

"If I think about their situation in those terms, I guess I would say they have a mild crisis – customer churn is consistently eroding profitability. If I was David Thomas, I would invest in things that help retain and grow his profitable customers. All businesses invest in strategies to drive top line revenue but many neglect the fact that it is far more cost effective to retain a customer than acquire a new one."

Joshua was busy taking notes as Mark continued in a measured tone. "The smart thing for David Thomas to do is invest money in limiting customer churn. That's where he will get the best return on investment. He can continue the pressure on his sales operation to keep delivering new clients but he will only fix his profitability problem by stopping the defection of valuable customers."

"Are you sure? How can you know all this from looking at their balance sheet?"

"All I know is that they have too much cash on their balance sheet and they're suffering from eroding profitability, which is positioned as a cost of sales problem. But one thing I've learned in business is that the problem is almost never the problem. Symptoms are not causes, and I think that if you get to have a genuine conversation with their CEO, he will admit that the real problem is customer churn rather than customer acquisition."

Joshua looked up from the notes he had been scribbling. "But how do I have that kind of conversation with a CEO? I'm just a salesman."

"You can have a conversation with your own CEO can't you? Look, David Thomas is just another person but he's under real pressure to deliver results. He needs to fix a problem he describes as a customer satisfaction challenge. His P&L describes it as a cost of sales problem. Their annual report describes it as eroding margins caused by competitors. They are a market leader defending their incumbent position. All you have to do is understand what keeps him awake at night – but don't ask it that way. I hate it when salesmen ask that question. I usually say; my wife – she snores rather loudly. They always laugh too but then I ask if they have any other inane questions."

Joshua stopped laughing as Mark continued. "The only thing a CEO dislikes more than amateurs who waste their time, is sales people who waste their time. Josh, you seem to have done your homework and I hope my input is useful, but you must have a business conversation with him. He'll open up once he sees that you have genuine insight."

Joshua rubbed his face with fingers combing back his hair revealing a pensive look. "I can't begin to tell you how far out of my depth I feel. If I botch this meeting with their CEO, I'll be finished with my boss."

"Son, even the most successful men have insecurities. We all secretly worry that we are going to get found out. I feel like I've been out of my depth most of my life; I really mean it. Maybe David Thomas feels out of his depth too and you're someone who can help to get one of his problems under control. If you succeed, it will make your career."

"Thanks. You've given me a perspective that Damien never could have provided. I can't talk to him and everything is via damned e-mail."

Mark sensed that his son wanted to say more and waited patiently for him to continue.

"Dad, I'm sorry I didn't stay in touch. I know we've never really resolved things between us but why don't we start playing chess every few weeks and have more conversations like this?"

Mark pondered Joshua's suggestion. "I've loved tonight. It's been a very long time since you wanted my advice but I don't think that's a good idea right now. Damien is working with you at the moment, and this could be perceived as interfering in some way. Let's do that once the mentorship is over. You're about half way through, yes?"

"Yes, six months to go. I'll tell Damien that we talked about Zenyth, he'll be okay with it. I really do appreciate tonight Dad."

Mark smiled warmly. "I do want to play chess regularly with you though. How about you come over for dinner next week and we can play then?"

"I would love to. I want our warring days to be over."

"Me too, let's confine our battles to the chess board." Mark put his hand on Joshua's shoulder as they wandered off to find Clare. "You know your mother will force us to all play Scrabble together, she thinks chess is anti-social."

"An occasional game of Scrabble is a small price to pay for a home cooked meal."

When they found her, Joshua hugged his mother and whispered. "Thank you. I think it's all going to be okay. See you next week."

Mark walked his son down to the driveway.

"Hey Dad, how are you going with your training for the Kokoda trip?"

"We've done some tough weekend walks in the mountains. I struggled a little but I've got a big medical check-up next week."

"Sorry I'm not doing it with you. How about we have a round of golf some-time?"

"I'd like that and you'll enjoy beating me. My swing hasn't improved since we last played, I think you were fourteen."

For the first time in years, they hugged – tentatively at first, and then without restraint.

"Good luck with Zenyth!"

Mark stood on the driveway long after the glow of Joshua's tail lights had disap-peared. His chest was tight from withholding the emotions that now trickled down his cheeks. *Thank God for Damien*, Mark thought as he wiped his face and climbed the stairs into the house.

Joshua drove home reflecting on the events of the evening. His decision to truly bury the past felt like it changed everything. The physical contact with his parents had stirred him and he called Mandy, leaving her a message saying he hoped she was well and that he wanted to catch-up, if she was willing. Joshua entered his empty home but wasn't lonely. He went to bed feeling loved and connected – something that had been absent for years.

The next morning, Joshua phoned Michael to let him know that he was finalizing the Zenyth strategy. He would e-mail the completed documents for review the follow-ing day. By early afternoon he had completed everything for Damien.

Hi Damien,

Things really are moving quickly. Attached are two draft documents I plan to send to my boss tomor-row. I have filled all the gaps in the account plan and I am comfortable with the strategy and next steps. The call plan for my meeting with David Thomas is also complete and this is the main docu-ment I would like you to focus on.

I had a great session with my dad last night to get his perspective on Zenyth's P&L and balance sheet. He was really helpful and a few of his ideas have made it into my planning documents. My dad described Zenyth as being in quiet crisis mode. I'm not sure if he's right but I reviewed Michael's notes from his lunch meeting with Bill Trench, and Bill repeatedly said that customer satisfaction was the driver for the project. Maybe that's why Bill is leaving? Maybe Bill is just a nice guy that doesn't get it – customer satisfaction is only a symptom! The real problem is inferior service caused by organizational structure and technology constraints. I know I need to link our solution to the cause of the problem when I meet with David Thomas. Anyway, that's what I've tried to capture in the two documents that I would like you to review.

As background, here is a summary of what Michael found out when he had lunch with Bill Trench. Bill is aware of what is happening and he was told directly by the CEO a few weeks ago. Apparently, David Thomas did not pull any punches. He told Bill that he wanted a new approach with a different person running the department. They have agreed to keep it all strictly between themselves while Bill finds another job. David has assured Bill that Kirsten will stay in the background until she moves into the role. Bill's main concern, when he met with Mike, was whether the rumor had come from within Zenyth. He is trying to negotiate full payment of his annual bonus rather than force the new CEO to manage him out. Bill thinks he has a strong negotiating position because his team is very loyal to him and anything negative will make it difficult for Kirsten when she takes over. Bill has rationalized that it's time for a change anyway, and he is in the market looking for a job. The investment Mike made in the relationship has paid off and Bill said he is happy to do anything he can to help us.

The disturbing thing, however, is that Bill still could not articulate the business case for the project. As I've written, he keeps saying that the driver is customer satisfaction but he cannot go beyond the surface. I will ask Michael to phone him tomorrow for the customer churn figures. Hopefully, this will give us the empirical validation for our angle with David Thomas. You will see from my call plan that my messaging is focused on this issue and, if it resonates with David, I will have earned the right to ask the questions as listed. Fortunately, this doesn't actually change our solution architecture much.

The biggest problems that their call centre people face are billing issues. Apparently, the finance department constantly screws-up invoicing and payment reconciliations. This experience has shown me something quite interesting. In the same way that sales people easily fall into the trap of thinking that features are benefits, customers easily fall into the trap of thinking that symptoms are causes, or problems. Back to Mike's meeting with Bill; the really good news is that Bill has agreed to say what we want if the CEO calls him following my request for an appointment. This is obviously a key part of the strategy. If David Thomas calls Bill to ask why I have requested a meeting, Bill will simply say that I had questions he could not answer and that we are seeking to align ourselves with their business case and commercial drivers.

The other piece of information that Bill gave Mike was in relation to their IT Department and the internal politics. Bill is not alone in being out of favor with the new CEO. The CIO is also under pressure but Bill doesn't know if he has had the 'go and find yourself another job' conversation with the CEO. Bill does not like the CIO and thinks it's ironic that they finally have something in common! The bottom line is that you were right. Bill Trench is not in the power-base at Zenyth.

I'll stop here as I really do need you to focus on the two documents attached, especially the call planner for getting the appointment and then my meeting with the CEO. Thanks again for all you are investing in me! I very much look forward to your reply.

Your student
Joshua

Damien's response came back within a few hours.

Hello Joshua,

Your documents are excellent. Well done on talking with your father. You can learn from him but do not make decisions based upon his uncertain assumptions. You need to validate the customer churn issue before you stake the game on it. I know Michael is going to seek confirmation but he runs the real risk of 'leading the witness' when he talks with Bill. Remember, Bill has not yet identified this of his own volition and he may end up telling Michael what he wants to hear, even if unintentionally. Have you ever met with their CFO? Maybe you should request a meeting and just ask the question directly.

You are fortunate that the CIO is also out of favor and your internal competitor, therefore, is not strong. However, never underestimate an adversary that appears weak. Wounded combatants do desperate things, and anything that appears to be cheap can be alluring to the inexperienced buyer. Your strategy of Michael developing a relationship with their CIO is a good one. If he does this skillfully, you may gain insight and awareness of the potential threat their IT department represents.

Here, again, is some advice for your meeting with the CEO. Be a business person rather than a salesman. Know Zenyth's industry and business drivers. Show insight into the real benefits in resolving Zenyth's problems. Talk David's language, which is delivering business outcomes with the lowest risk and best value. Convey to him that you seek to minimize his risk by you developing an intimate understanding of his environment and requirements so that you can potentially adopt a fixed price approach if possible (this may be a way of changing the rules on your competition). Have proof of the business benefits you claim and do this through reference customers. Never use F words – Features or Functions. Be punctual, efficient and direct. Let David be in total control and do not seek to manipulate him in any way. Finally, if he agrees the project is important and a high priority, insist on regular direct contact for updates and feedback, even if he wants to delegate everything to Kirsten Slater.

I suggest you send a one page fax or a letter to David prior to calling his Personal Assistant to set up the meeting. Do not send an e-mail. Invest an entire day, if you need to, in getting the wording exactly right. Explain factually why you seek the meeting and ensure that the reasons are expressed exclusively in terms of what is in it for him. Explain that although you are preferred vendor and that the project team has been doing a good job, they have been unable to articulate the business outcomes required or the drivers behind the initiative. You are committed to aligning to business value for Zenyth and need to understand David's vision and requirements for delivering successfully. Tell him that you have some ideas but first need to understand his requirements and framework for engaging at a more strategic level. Nominate an exact time that you will call the following day to book the appointment. The next day, phone his PA and ask for her by name. Ask her if she received your fax; do not ask if David received it. She is the door to the CEO's office and treating her with respect and assumed power will be of great assistance to you. If she likes your communiqué and the subsequent conversation, you will get into the CEO's calendar.

The words you write must be your own and they must not be clichéd in any way. Communicate as a fellow business person with insight, intent on fully understanding his vision, agenda and framework for delivering genuine business value. The feeling you need to convey is that although Bill is a nice guy, he does not operate at the same level as you and David. Do not project any level of arrogance but convey the message subtly nevertheless. Although I am happy to review your letter or fax, I think your boss is more than capable of doing this with you. If you write it well, it will set the agenda and take the pressure off the initial phone call, eliminating the risk of nervousness damaging your efforts.

Remember to treat David's PA like the second in command of the corporation. Check to see if she worked for him at Mawson by phoning their switch and asking for her by name. If they say she no longer works there, then you'll know she probably left with the CEO. Senior executives often bring their PAs with them, and routinely accept appointments they book into their calendar. Even if she puts you through to David, you will have an ally for life in his PA. If you do talk to David, simply refer to the fax and the need to meet with him to understand how you can align the project with his vision and understand how the business outcomes need to be delivered.

Memorise all this and make it second nature for the call. I know you will do well.

Damien Drost
RSVPselling™ Sales Master

The idea of sending a fax had never occurred to Joshua, but he instantly realized it was a good idea. A fax would end up on the CEO's desk if it was presented the right way. He knew that e-mails were the worst type of formal communication, with messages automatically filtered or simply lost in the sheer volume of a busy person's in-box. He also knew that the Personal Assistant to any CEO lived to protect their boss from sales people, junk mail and anything else that wasted precious time.

He struggled to fall asleep, thinking about the communiqué he would craft the following day.

The next morning he raced to work early and phoned Michael, but was instantly diverted to voicemail. He left a message inviting his boss to breakfast. Joshua read Damien's last e-mail several times and then began to work on the single page fax that would set the agenda and, ideally, secure the meeting with David Thomas. His phone rang loudly against the deathly quiet of the deserted office. He looked at the screen and saw Michael Blunt's name.

Half an hour later, the two men sat having raisin toast and coffee. Joshua had handed over his account plan and call planner. The documents were no longer in draft and Joshua felt proud of his work. Michael was busy skipping to various sections of the documents as they talked. He was pleased to see that the additional information he had obtained from the lunch with Bill had already been added. They discussed the draft fax Joshua was working on and Michael agreed with the bullet-point messages. Joshua asked him to make a call to Bill during the day – one last attempt to see if Bill could validate that customer loss, rather than customer dissatisfaction, was the real trigger within Zenyth. In the meantime, Joshua would seek confirmation from other sources, and he regretted not having met Zenyth's CFO during the sales process to date. They agreed to meet for a sandwich at lunch to review the final draft of the fax to David Thomas.

The fax was brief and to the point. Joshua stated his concern that the project lacked alignment to the business and was lost in technical minutiae. He carefully, yet provocatively, incorporated the key messages he had agreed with Damien. Joshua also provided proof they could deliver by mentioning specific tangible business benefits they had achieved for a similar client that was known to Zenyth. The one page communiqué finished with a request for a forty minute one-on-one meeting, the purpose of which was to gain insight into David's vision and priorities as new CEO, and discuss how to realign the struggling project. They made some final adjustments together. Joshua then sent the fax to the CEO's office at 4:50.

Two days later, Joshua asked to be put through to David's Personal Assistant.

"Hi Desray, my name is Joshua Peters and I just wanted to confirm you received my fax."

"Yes, I passed it on to Mr. Thomas yesterday but he's not in right now."

"That's okay. You've been with David for years at Mawson before coming over with Kirsten to Zenyth. The project is important so if you're okay with it could you slot me into his calendar for forty minutes later this week, just a one-to-one meeting?"

Desray didn't like the overly familiar approach. "But David has never met you – right?"

Joshua sensed he was in trouble. "Sorry, I don't mean to be presumptuous. It's just that the meeting is about a current project that's in trouble. I won't be wasting his time."

There was long pause. "It's okay but I can only give you thirty minutes. David has a slot on Friday but he must be out of the office by noon. How is eleven-thirty?"

"Eleven-thirty is great. Desray, this meeting is very important for both of our organizations. What's your advice to me for when I meet him?"

"Don't be late and get to the point."

"Thanks, I really appreciate your help. See you on Friday."

The next few days were surprisingly relaxed. Despite the important meeting that was looming, he knew he would be ready because he was working with accurate intelligence and had a solid plan that addressed the risks. It wasn't that he felt confident, he knew better than to be lulled into any false sense of security, it was just that he was prepared, ready to have a business discussion rather than do a sales call. He would be completely focused on discovering what it would take to deliver the outcomes David Thomas needed and, in doing so, also achieve what his own corporation needed – revenue and a new significant customer.

Joshua used the next few days to begin thinking about his future career. Whether he won Zenyth or not, he would resign and move to a more complex selling environment. He was thinking of enterprise software solutions but his thoughts were continually drawn back to the unresolved question posed by Damien weeks earlier – The Joshua Principle.

He began reviewing the months of correspondence and copied and pasted his mentor's words into a document, under subject headings. He also created a chronological record of their correspondence, meticulously ensuring the threads were maintained. For the next few evenings he sat at his dining-room table, the compass bearing silent witness to him leafing through dozens of printed pages. Joshua could see the maturing of his own thoughts and words over the months, and the evidence clearly showed that he had not fully engaged in the philosophical and personal aspects of success. He knew that he had denied himself valuable insights by pushing Damien to move on. The RSVP information itself was not that complicated but Damien had always said that mastery was not about mercurial secrets.

On a notepad beside the compass, Joshua's inadequate attempts at defining The Joshua Principle were scribbled. He was certain that the correct definition would feel instantly profound, but nothing he had written felt right. He held the compass in his left hand as he reviewed his notes, clicking the lid open and shut with metronome-like precision. It would have irritated anyone sitting with him but he was alone with his thoughts. The Joshua Principle needed to be his own revelation but he felt nowhere close to enlightenment. There was no rush though, and Joshua knew it, he still had months of access to Damien.

Friday morning arrived and Joshua wore his favorite shirt and tie. He had imagined that he would be nervous, but his preparation had eliminated any feelings of fear or dread. Rather than negative emotions, Joshua looked forward to what would unfold in the meeting. He knew what he would say, what he would ask, and what he needed from David Thomas. His meticulous preparation had created a feeling of optimistic anticipation. The drive to Zenyth was relaxed and he arrived at a nearby café one hour early and quietly reviewed his notes, mentally rehearsing his opening with David. He had role-played, with Michael, every imaginable scenario and potential aggressive or awkward question. He was ready for any eventuality – except a rain storm, and he did not have an umbrella!

Lightning flashed and thunder rattled the windows of the café. The Zenyth building was only a two minute walk away. He hurriedly made for the cashier and fidgeted impatiently as the two people in front of him dithered and chatted with the attendant. Joshua looked to his left, people outside were scurrying for cover as large drops began to pound onto the pavement. He slapped a twenty dollar note on the counter and made for the door. He ran toward Zenyth as the rain became steadily heavier. He was half way there when a flash of lightning and clap of thunder nearly took his breath away. The gap between the two was almost indiscernible; he could feel static in the air. The rain was becoming torrential and he held his leather compendium over his head in a vain attempt to shelter himself from the elements. He swung into Zenyth's revolving door, resembling a corporate drowned rat.

Outside, the downpour was now accompanied by a ferocious wind. He was soaked, but felt he had made the right decision in making a run for it. He registered with security and went to the men's room. Inside, he lurched around in front of the air-dryer before switching to paper towels. He dried his face and combed his hair back with his fingers. Joshua looked in the mirror and focused his thoughts. *Showtime.*

It was 11:15 when Desray came to reception. Joshua was immediately impressed. Although she was an attractive woman, she dressed for business and walked purposefully toward him. She knew how to deal with men on equal terms and shook Joshua's hand with firm confidence. Her voice was pleasant but professional.

"Hello Joshua, it's good to meet you. I hope that's not perspiration? David really isn't that intimidating once you get to know him."

Joshua laughed. "I may be a bit wet but at least I'm here on time. Thank you for organizing the meeting."

Desray showed him to the boardroom before leaving to let David know he was there. Joshua's heart began to pound and he walked to the window to watch the wild storm outside.

"Joshua, thanks for being on time in this atrocious weather."

Joshua turned around and smiled. "Thanks for meeting with me. I know you have been very busy since taking over here at Zenyth."

They shook hands and both momentarily looked outside as another flash of lightning lit up the sky. Joshua had deliberately placed his folder and keys at the end corner of the table. Not as a signal of power but to avoid them sitting squarely opposite each other. Joshua wanted the physical environment to mirror what he needed psychologically – cooperative discussion, rather than confrontation. David sat at the head and placed a plain manila folder on the table. He opened it, revealing a small stack of papers with Joshua's fax on top. A few of the words had been circled and some notes had been scribbled, but Joshua did not focus on any of that; he maintained eye contact with David.

David took his pen out of his suit pocket and placed it on top of Joshua's fax. "So, Joshua, I hope you're not here to try and sell me something."

"There was something I deliberately left out of my fax, and I suspect it's the single most important thing about the project. Both our organizations have made substantial investments to date but, if I was in your position, I would be considering deferring or cancelling the whole thing – unless this key issue is addressed."

David Thomas was a heavyweight executive and knew how to maintain a poker face. "That sounds a little dramatic."

Joshua leaned forward. "Bill Trench is a good guy and your project team is certainly capable but I'm worried that the focus is wrong. Bill just hasn't been able to articulate the real business problems or the drivers for how we need to deliver in line with your vision for Zenyth. Everyone involved seems stuck at the technical level."

David was unmoved and Joshua sensed he was impatient for the punch line. "Bill says the problem is customer satisfaction, but I've done my homework and I think customer retention is the real issue – and it's causing serious erosion to Zenyth's profitability. Your interview with Patricia Smith was clear – you said that incremental improvements are not enough."

David nodded thoughtfully but understood the intimidating power of silence.

Joshua knew the meeting was at a critical juncture and lowered his voice. "Are you withholding approval for the project because it's not yet aligned to the business outcomes that must be delivered?"

David rubbed his chin. "Possibly."

"David, I know this may seem a strange question, but you're very busy and have many demands on your time. Why did you agree to meet with me today?"

David was not convinced that Joshua was worthy of his trust. "Bill started this project before I arrived here at Zenyth. I find it rather strange that you've been working with us for months now, and have been selected as preferred vendor, yet you don't have an understanding of our business requirements."

"David, as far as I can tell, there's never been a senior executive sponsor for this project. I share your concern about lack of alignment – that's the reason I'm here. I need to understand how you define business value for this initiative. What needs to be achieved before you will regard it as successful?"

"Bill Trench is a member of the executive management team. Are you saying that you can't work with him?"

Joshua was beginning to feel worried but maintained his composure. "Not at all, Bill and our teams have been interacting extremely well together but limited to the technical issues. There's obviously a reason for why approval has been withheld – I want to understand what makes this project worthy of investment. We've helped other customers achieve serious improvements in this area, and I can introduce you to another CEO who will validate that we delivered to their bottom line with cost savings and operational improvements."

"Now you're trying to sell me something."

Joshua sat back and smiled cautiously. He talked in a more relaxed manner. "David, we are all selling something and I would like you to sell me on the real problems here at Zenyth. I want our project teams focused on the real issues, not symptoms, and come back to you with a proposal worthy of your approval – something that represents genuine business value with minimal risk. Maybe we can fix-price if I can have the necessary information that enables us to understand all the risks. Bill is a great guy, but for whatever reason, he has not been able to link the technical aspects to the business outcomes that need to be delivered. You're Bill's boss and you drive the culture and priorities here. I think you need to be the executive sponsor for the project."

"Why would I do that when I employ someone else who can be responsible?"

"This is too important. You're on record stating that customers need to become delighted advocates. I think that customer churn is a problem that has strong focus for you and the board. I think this project needs to be urgently realigned to customer retention strategies and tangible improvements in service levels."

David's body language became more open. He liked the fact that Joshua was not intimidated and had done his homework. He looked at Joshua's fax and circled something while he pondered the situation.

Joshua had not forgotten that David owed him an answer. "Enough of what I think – why did you agree to meet with me today?"

David decided to change the tone of the meeting with a rhetorical quip. "So, Joshua, are you a salesman or an analyst?"

"Neither. I'm a business person."

"You've obviously done your homework. Congratulations on joining the dots, I wish Bill was able to do the same thing."

Joshua knew better than to engage in a character assassination of Bill. "Me too, I like Bill but I really am committed to you getting the right outcome here."

"This conversation stays in this room – yes?"

Joshua nodded and closed his folder. "Absolutely."

"I haven't spoken with Bill since receiving your fax. Do you know why?"

"Yes, Bill is not part of Zenyth's future."

David leaned forward. "Did he tell you that?"

"No. Bill hasn't said anything to me. He's a complete professional. I formed this view after my own analysis and research, and the fact that you brought Kirsten Slater over from Mawson."

"Kirsten is on special projects."

"I think that customer service is a *very* special project, and I think you and I both have the same frustrations with Bill being unable to align investment to achieving the required outcomes. Kirsten, on the other hand, is an agent of change. She's proven that she can deliver for you – I would like the same opportunity."

David wasn't sure how to feel about the brash confidence of the young man in front of him. "Joshua, your comments are rather presumptuous, and if it wasn't for the fact that you're right, this meeting would not be going well."

"I'm sorry David. I don't mean to create that impression. It's just that I really do care about us delivering what the business needs, and I know you don't tolerate fools or time wasters. I want to work with you and Kirsten to deliver what's required."

Joshua had achieved his goal. The title on Joshua's business card was irrelevant. For the next fifteen minutes the two men had an open and candid dialogue. Joshua's demeanor was matter of fact, as if this was the kind of conversation he had every day, but inside he could barely contain himself.

Joshua glanced at his watch. "David, I'm sorry to interrupt but I promised Desray that we would be finished in time for you to make your next appointment. How should I prepare for the next meeting?"

David appreciated that Joshua had alerted him to the time. "You're right, I do need to go. Stay here for a moment while I get someone I want you to meet."

David reappeared a few minutes later with a relatively young woman, dressed business casual.

"Joshua, say hello to Kirsten Slater."

David shook his hand. "Joshua, it's been good meeting you. Tell Kirsten what you told me, and make a follow-up appointment through Desray for when I'm back from Europe."

David looked at Kirsten. "We all know that we need a different approach. Let's see the revised business case as soon as possible."

An hour later, Joshua was in his car heading for the office. He made the call to Michael.

"I hope you just left there Joshua. I had assumed you screwed it up and weren't man enough to call me."

"Sorry, it was a train wreck. I had to go to the pub and have a few drinks to recover. I'm on my way in with my resignation. You did say that I had no job if I lost another important deal."

The phone was silent for an agonizing moment. "You are kidding, right?"

Joshua erupted. "It was unbelievable! David was brutal. If we had not done all the preparation, he would have chewed me up and spat me out. I can't describe how awesome it was. Mike, the deal is ours if we play our cards right, and it can be bigger! He had to leave for another meeting but he introduced me to Kirsten and I spent over an hour with her. He absolutely pushed me to my limit but I did it! Thanks for trusting me."

"Calm down. Are you serious?"

"Mike, I'm on my way in now. Let's talk face-to-face, but it's all good. I suspect that, before today's meeting, he was just going to let the project die. Our real competitor was them doing nothing. Their IT Department is less of an issue than we thought. David and Kirsten gave me what we need to know to get this over the line. I'll run through everything when I see you in twenty minutes."

Joshua felt exhilarated but drove at an unhurried pace. Back at the office, he met with Michael and recounted the two meetings with gusto, but the fact that the appointment was a make or break event was not lost on either of them. They both knew that, despite doing everything possible to prepare, it could have easily gone the other way. Joshua had stepped up successfully and Michael felt deeply relieved. Joshua headed home early to adjust his account plan and expand his meeting notes.

Sitting at his dining-room table, he reflected on how the meeting with Kirsten had been far easier than the examination by David Thomas. She was a straight forward person and confirmed that the project was actually triggered by the loss of a major account a year earlier, before the arrival of David. Bill had been fiddling around the edges but it wasn't entirely his fault.

The previous CEO had only paid lip service to the issue of customer retention. He was far more comfortable in the sales and marketing realm, and had sought to drive new business revenue as a cure-all for their profitability issues. His lack of focus on their existing customer base was ultimately the cause of his demise. He failed to have a strategy, he failed to invest and he failed to lead. Bill had been doing his best but suffered from having neither the ability nor the support to drive change across the organization. Unfortunately, for Bill, he had also been tarred with the same brush as the now defunct CEO.

Kirsten had been working on a plan that was soon to be presented by David to the Zenyth board. It proposed a restructure, with her heading a newly formed department amalgamating three currently distinct entities of customer support, professional consulting and field services. The goal was to provide seamless continuity of service for Zenyth customers, ensuring the very best service levels, regardless of which part of the organization was in play. Joshua's corporation covered only one side of the equation. Zenyth's lines of demarcation were blurred between Information Technology, including voice and data telecommunications, and Information Systems which incorporated myriad customized software applications, including finance.

Kirsten's plan called for integration of business processes and software, but she wanted more than mere technical integration. Project systems, time sheets, support, customer relationship management, logistics, financial accounting – they all needed to come together. She demanded the ability for office and field staff to have instant access to all relevant information. Joshua's current proposal addressed one element only, and his challenge was to become a foundational part of the architecture for Zenyth's new customer support operation. Kirsten and David were obsessed with integration of information and processes delivered in a 'virtual office' for Zenyth staff working centrally or off-site. They saw this as the enabler for achieving their goal of customer intimacy which was dependent upon proactive account management and market leading service.

Over the next ten days, Joshua worked in a heightened state of motivation and awareness. He corresponded every few days with Damien, and validated his strategies with Michael. Joshua met regularly with Kirsten and they developed an excellent understanding of the requirements. Michael, in the meantime, had marshaled increased resources internally to meet the challenge of crafting a broader, yet more tailored, solution. More importantly, and as a result of Kirsten's guidance, they developed an alliance with two incumbent complementary technology providers. They invested in scoping an integrated architecture that would deliver the required business value for Zenyth. Teaming agreements were being drafted and Joshua was impressed with Michael's ability to navigate internal politics and facilitate the imposing task of securing agreement on the terms and conditions of the collaborative scope of work. Joshua had been careful to keep their piece of Zenyth's solution separate, and with clearly deliverable business benefits. They had crafted a solution that delivered early incremental benefits and fed into the bigger picture, delivering the required transformation over time.

Several weeks had passed since the initial meeting with David Thomas, and Joshua now sat in the reception area waiting to be ushered into David's office. Desray had greeted him warmly and showed Joshua through to the CEO's office. He felt as if he was entering Zenyth's inner sanctum. David and Joshua exchanged pleasantries and sat. A confidential report, authored by Kirsten, was on the table.

"Don't worry, Joshua, this meeting will not be like the last. Do you know what's in this report?"

"No, but I'm assuming our proposal is included?"

"Yes. It's one of the options."

"May I ask if the solution we've been working on with Kirsten is the recommended path forward?"

"You can ask, but you won't get an answer today."

David clearly wasn't going to say anything more. Joshua passed a five page document to David, just in case all of their information hadn't made it into Kirsten's internal report.

"I think you will be pleased with this. I've made sure that it meets Kirsten's requirements. She's familiar with the detail and numbers. It proposes a low risk incremental approach to delivering improved service levels but with an architecture that feeds into the twelve month plan for integration to your key software applications. I know this sounds clichéd but it's a low risk, evolutionary approach, rather than high risk revolution. The first phase can happen quickly and be delivering for you within ninety days. We've proposed firm pricing against comprehensive scoping and with checkpoints for measuring success."

David smiled. "Can I steal your line concerning evolution versus revolution?"

Joshua smiled. "Only if you buy something from me."

"There are no guarantees, and this level of investment will need board approval."

"Yes, Kirsten confirmed the approval process with me."

"Joshua, how can an evolutionary approach work? I cannot afford more of the same – evolution sounds rather slow."

"By evolution, I mean adapting and leveraging existing systems and infrastructure. Low risk doesn't mean low value, and we can implement quickly. We can deliver tangible improvements without you writing-off existing investments, and you'll be able to leverage what we are proposing within the long-term architecture."

"Yes, it's all in Kirsten's document and she already briefed me – which leads me to something I want to ask you. Why did you insist that this meeting be just with the two of us?"

"Kirsten and I have formed a very positive working relationship but it's essential that you and I have the ability to discuss any issues or opportunities directly."

"Why do you think a direct relationship with me must exclude Kirsten from being present?"

Joshua wasn't sure how to respond.

David continued. "Who do you think makes the decision on this?"

"I think she makes the recommendation but that it's your call."

David smiled and shook his head. "Not really. This is Kirsten's decision, but I *can* say no and so can the board."

"I guess I just didn't want this project or the corporate relationship to become ineffectually stuck in technical or project minutiae again. We never really got to have this part of the conversation in our last meeting, but I need to provide you with regular updates and talk directly if there is a serious problem."

"I understand. You don't want to be trapped in another Bill Trench scenario. I was in daily contact with Kirsten while I was overseas, and she said you are the first salesman she's worked with that truly listens. It's okay Joshua, work with Kirsten – I trust her. Feel free to call me directly but only if you really need to."

"That means a lot to me, thank you. Do I need to apologize to Kirsten?"

"She's fine, but how about you have the next meeting with her? Only invite me if both of you feel it's necessary."

"Fair enough, but you and I can talk directly if needed?"

David looked him in the eye. "You've earned it, Joshua. Yes."

Joshua had one last item on his agenda. "I have something important I need to ask, and it's the main reason I needed to meet with you today. Our teams have done thorough due diligence. That's how we are able to propose firm pricing. But what about your own IT department – what happens when they promise they can deliver a better solution for less money?"

"I am very skeptical when it comes to technical people delivering for the business. IT managers tend to act as if the 'i' stands for infrastructure when they should, instead, focus on innovation. Our IT Department doesn't get it, that's something else that needs to change."

"What about one of our low-end competitors that promises the world for a cheap price?"

"I'm no fool. I know that cheap is usually expensive in the long run. Value is far more important to me than price, but you're not our only option and what you propose is expensive."

"We are solving a serious problem together and it requires proper investment. David, what's our solution being compared with?"

"Nice try, but I would prefer you focused on reducing your price to us."

Joshua changed tack. "I think now is the right time to organize for you to meet another CEO where we've already delivered. They have a similar organizational profile and can provide evidence that we're low risk and best value."

David looked sideways at Joshua. "When I was with the last corporation, I hosted an achievers club trip for our top sales performers and their partners. It was a lavish affair and we did an exclusive dinner at an oceanarium. The tables were arrayed in front of a massive viewing window. Anyway, as often happens, a few people drank too much and the leading salesman ended up showing off by climbing on the railing above ground where people were smoking. Staff yelled at him to climb down and he slipped and fell into the water – all hell broke loose. We were all seated having dessert down below when, all of a sudden, there was all this commotion. We were horrified watching him thrash around as a shark began circling. It sensed his panic and went for his legs ..."

"What happened – was he attacked?"

"No. It darted away at the last second. There was no way it was going to bite him."

Joshua was hooked. "Why not?"

David leaned forward. "Professional courtesy."

The two men laughed before David continued. "I also tell that joke to every lawyer I meet. The only variation being that it's a lawyer who falls in. Please don't take it personally."

"No offence taken. Most salesman jokes use a snake as the metaphor, but I thought it was very funny. Next time we meet I will explain the difference between a software salesman and a software program. It has a comparable punch line that you can use to good effect. Our fifteen minutes is up, it's time for me to go."

The two men walked to reception and shook hands. "Thanks, Joshua, for coming to see me. What's the punch line of your joke?"

"You only have to punch information into the software once."

David smiled. "I know just the vendor to use that on."

"David, seriously, we can deliver but I need to lock-in the best people on our side. I know this project has urgency, so when do you think we'll know if we are going ahead together?"

"Always the salesman. Kirsten will get this on the agenda for the next board meeting, but there's no guarantee."

"Sure, but I think this all makes sense."

David raised his eyebrows. "We'll see. Your proposal is more than we budgeted."

Despite David's comments, Joshua left the meeting feeling positive. The engagement was solid and the solution was compelling. Zenyth needed what they were offering. *Surely David is just negotiating for a better price*, Joshua thought as he walked toward his car.

Chapter Nine: Firing and Hiring a Boss

Joshua had worked closely with Kirsten. Even before David's posturing on price, she had pushed hard for the numbers she needed to make the business case work. Joshua had done well in securing the best value his organization had to offer. The price was thirty percent higher than what had previously gone to Bill but offered far better value. The business benefits were compelling and Kirsten had confirmed the return on investment was within Zenyth's approval metrics. Yet, just as with David, she had been evasive concerning the presence of any real competition. The Zenyth team had played this particular card very close to their chests.

Damien had been right when he had advised Joshua to have proof when dealing with a CEO, and Michael had delivered the ideal executive customer reference for David Thomas. Bill had resigned and was not the only manager to leave Zenyth's ranks. The CIO was also moving on, and the CFO was rumored to be following. Joshua understood Zenyth's decision and procurement process as best he could and he was aligned politically at the right level. According to Kirsten, approval for the project was expected in seventeen days at the next board meeting.

Joshua's thoughts were now dominated by his correspondence with Damien. They had been exchanging e-mails several times a week, discussing the Zenyth situation and what he had learned. Frustratingly though, he was no closer to identifying

The Joshua Principle. He was beginning to wonder if he ever would. Rather than dwell on the elusive, he decided to turn his attention in earnest to the issue of his future career. He worried about the reaction to his resignation, not just from Michael, but also from David and Kirsten, to whom he had made personal commitments. He was concerned about the best way to handle things when the time came but for now he would focus on how to land the ideal role with the right corporation.

Hi Damien,

I've really enjoyed our communication over the last few weeks. After considering your comments and discussing it with my father, I have decided on a move into the software industry. I would really appreciate your thoughts as this is where you have a lot of successful experience. Attached is my CV for your review and please let me know how it can be improved. I would also appreciate tips for job interviews.

I am going to have mixed feelings when I resign. Michael is not a bad boss and I've learned some valuable things from him. He won't be happy but my biggest concern, if we win Zenyth, is resigning after making personal commitments to David Thomas. I'm just not sure how he will react. Do you have any thoughts? Kirsten validated the process for them raising the purchase order once the project receives board approval. They say that we are not their only option and I absolutely understand that the deal is not done until their money is in our bank account.

Finally, I know you want me to figure it out for myself but I still do not have a definition of The Joshua Principle. I feel like the more I focus on it the harder it is to define. You will be the first to know once I have a flash of enlightenment.

Your Student
Joshua

As much as Joshua valued Damien's input, he also continued to discuss various employment options with his father. The biggest concern Mark Peters had with his son's desire to move was that he had not stayed with any firm for a sustained period. This, combined with moving to an industry in which he had no direct experience, meant that it would take time and patience to secure the right role.

Mark and Joshua had discussed the barriers to changing career, but without any angst. Instead, there was calm empathy and an understanding of the challenges. Joshua agreed that any potential employer would have a bias against someone without a positive track record in their industry. Although the issues were not trivial, Joshua remained committed to a career move. Enterprise software seemed appropriate with the right organization, and so he continued his research.

Joshua had a sense of purpose like never before. He devoured books, and the habit of television had long been shelved by his new love of reading. He had also become addicted to cycling and the endorphin-inducing effects of climbing steep hills, and the thrill of descents fast enough to break the speed limit. He felt fit and alert. All of this contributed to his new sense of self-worth, not pride or arrogance, but a sense of privileged awareness.

In his personal life, there had been contact with Mandy. She had eventually returned his calls and agreed to meet – she wanted closure. Joshua, however, sought an opening – a new beginning was something he believed was possible. The first face-to-face conversation since she had visited to retrieve the remote control had been awkward. Mandy kept her emotional distance, while Joshua did his best to mend fences. She couldn't forget the erratic television episode, nor was she ready to forgive the events that caused the disintegration of their lives together. Yet she agreed to meet with him again. If Mandy was to allow Joshua back into her life, progress would be slow. Trust is always much harder to establish the second time around.

His relationship with Mark, on the other hand, was continuing to gather momentum. They'd played a few games of golf and regularly engaged in chess after evening visits home for family meals. They were interacting as never before. For Joshua, the tension he and his father had endured for more than a decade was very much in the past, and negative memories were fading away. He felt his father was finally beginning to respect him. For Mark, the relationship with his son was becoming one of advisor rather than paternal protagonist, and he reflected on the amazing impact the mentorship was having on his son. He felt Joshua was maturing and becoming thoughtfully enlightened.

Damien's latest reply had taken a few days to arrive but Joshua had learned to be patient.

Hello Joshua,

I am pleased that you remain committed to moving to a new level in your sales career, rather than progressing to management. The software industry is a challenging yet rewarding choice. I have no doubt you are equipped for success but you must choose your employer carefully. You cannot afford to make a mistake. Fifty percent of the success equation is you, and the other half is your environment. We can discuss potential employers later. For now, let's focus on your résumé. It needs a lot of work and I would like you to revise it with the following in mind.

The purpose of a résumé is to secure an interview rather than get the job. Potential employers use CVs to screen candidates rather than select them. Because they look for reasons to exclude people from the interview process, your résumé must provide evidence of performance – proof that you can do the job. Will your résumé earn you an interview? Just as with selling to a CEO, you need to provide proof of performance and suitability if you are to progress through their selection and hiring process.

The RSVP process can also be applied here. You are selling a product and the product is you. Think of RSVP as follows. **R**elationships are essential because the best jobs are not advertised. Relationships also provide references, and I believe you will need the support of both Michael Blunt and David Thomas if you are to secure the career move you seek. This is daunting I know, as it means you will need to tell them in advance of actually resigning. This is one of the reasons why **S**trategy is essential, but also necessary for proactively dealing with your problematic résumé which highlights deficiencies that I will cover shortly. Not the least of which, is the fact that you have had too many premature moves and have no software industry experience. Also, consider the unique **V**alue you offer through your skills, knowledge, experience, commitment, attitude, and contacts. Finally, Joshua, you must understand the employer's selection and hiring **P**rocess. I think you can see that RSVP is useful beyond a sales environment, or perhaps you now see that securing a new job is simply another selling situation?

Employers hire someone because they have a problem or an opportunity, but they worry greatly about hiring the wrong person. This is because it is one of the most expensive mistakes they can make. It is expensive from the point of view of money, time, credibility and emotional energy. Recruitment fees are significant, but lost time and effort is much more costly. They also worry about the risk to their business and reputation if they entrust their brand to someone who fails to deliver or damages relationships through incompetence or unethical behavior.

A few months ago, I stated to you that employers always have a range of candidates that appear to be equally qualified, but skills alone are not what make a sales employee successful. Skill is a prerequisite, rather than a differentiator. What the employer cares about most is the person's ability to influence and deliver results, while also being a good cultural fit within their environment. There are myriad qualified and knowledgeable employees that don't get promoted, because of poor attitude. The sad thing is that they often never know the reason they were passed over for promotion. No-one really cares about what you know, or your qualifications. They care, primarily, about themselves and what you can do for them. All employers, consciously or not, seek the three Cs in hiring someone: Competence, Commitment, and Character / Cultural fit.

The problem is that your résumé highlights that you do not have university qualifications and that you are inexperienced. It implies that you lack competence, and that you change jobs often, suggesting a lack of commitment. Sorry to be so brutal about this but please allow me to explain how the genera-tions prior to yours – Generation-X and Baby Boomer bosses – view your demographic. Gen-Y was initially described as the bubble-wrap generation or cotton wool generation. You have been raised within an education system intent on reinforcing self-esteem, which is an admirable goal in itself, but parenting and education should also be designed to prepare a person for a competitive adult world. Gen-Y employees can be perceived as casual, impatient, itinerant 'click and flick' technology buffs, not willing to serve an apprenticeship to diligently prove themselves before being rewarded with responsibility or promotion. We both know that you do not fall into this negative stereotype. Your challenge, nevertheless, is to create a document and a targeted approach that overcomes the very real prejudice to which you will be subjected. You need to create a CV that demonstrates proven competence and positions the rationale for why you are seeking a new employer. I think your strategy for securing the best possible employer must include obtaining the support of your boss, in advance, and will therefore require trust in order to execute.

You have much to consider with your résumé. We will discuss interviews when the time comes. I fully understand that resigning will be difficult, especially as you will need Michael's support before you have a letter of offer from your new employer. It is also right to consider your new customer, assuming you actually win the Zenyth deal, and honor the personal relationship and commitments made to their CEO. This can be managed by perhaps resigning only after delivering for Zenyth. I'm not sure how you feel about this delay but it would enable you to maintain your integrity by delivering on what you promised, therefore, earning the right to ask for his support in being a referee. It means that you need to be patient but I think you have the maturity to give this consideration.

There is no rush with resolving The Joshua Principle. We have months of time remaining, and it is best that it be your own definition. I am pleased with the progress you have made during our mentor-ship. You are becoming the person worthy of the success you seek. I look forward to seeing your revised CV along with a draft letter that will accompany it. Do not rush this work as it requires much thought and effort.

Damien Drost
RSVPselling™ Sales Master

Joshua had never thought of a résumé in the terms described by Damien. The e-mail was a revelation. Damien had also proposed a sensible solution to the problem with David Thomas. He did not want to resign until he had been paid for the contract anyway, and this approach enabled him to meet everyone's needs – except those of Michael Blunt. He wondered whether his boss would be supportive or bitterly disappointed.

During that week, Joshua re-worked and honed his résumé but he could not get away from the facts concerning his inexperience and itinerant employment history. The CV needed to remain a factual document, focused on competence and performance. The covering letter would address the issues of commitment and potential cultural fit, but it proved more difficult to write than he imagined.

The Zenyth decision was expected in two days. Joshua finally finished his draft résumé and a covering letter designed to be tailored to an individual potential employer. The e-mails he had exchanged with Damien had convinced Joshua that he must target potential employers, rather than respond to job advertisements or the disempowering process of recruitment consultants. On paper, Joshua knew he represented risk in any senior role. He needed to proactively approach the right people and use his documentation to support the process.

It was Thursday morning when Desray called. "Hello Joshua. David wants to see you, with your boss, if that's possible today. Can you both be here at 2:30?"

"Do you know whether the board approved the project?"

"Sorry, I can't say. It would be a mistake to assume the best. David is no coward when it comes to delivering bad news. He prefers to do it personally, rather than delegate."

"Is Kirsten going to be at the meeting?"

"Sorry, he asked me to call you just now. The meeting is not scheduled in his calendar so I can't tell if Kirsten is invited. You'll have to ask her. Can you confirm you'll be here for 2:30?"

"Sure. It will be me and Michael Blunt. I think he's available and I'll confirm with you via e-mail shortly. Thanks Desray – I would appreciate a clue if you can give me one."

"No clues, but it was a long board meeting."

Joshua immediately rang Kirsten but the call was diverted to voicemail. "Hi Kirsten, David has asked me to come in with my boss this afternoon for a meeting. I assume that you'll be there. Is there anything you can tell me? My boss really doesn't like surprises."

Michael called within seconds of Joshua hanging-up. He had just seen the Zenyth calendar invitation. "Well?"

"The board meeting was yesterday but his PA gave nothing away. Hopefully it will be okay but I really don't know. I just left a message for Kirsten and she might give us a heads-up. People don't usually deliver bad news face-to-face, right?"

"Whether it's good news or bad news, there's nothing we can do about it now. Come and collect me from my office in time for us to grab a coffee out there before the meeting."

Joshua decided to call Kirsten again at lunch time if she had not contacted him before then. Maybe they wanted a last minute concession or there had been a problem. Regardless, Joshua knew he had done everything possible to win the business and now they would have to wait and see what unfolded.

The morning dragged and there was no contact from Kirsten. He called again but did not leave a second message. At 1:30, Joshua appeared at Michael's door and the two men headed for the elevators. Michael was relaxed, and Joshua admired the circumspect attitude of his boss. On the way to Zenyth, they agreed what they would do if David demanded additional discounting or revised commercial terms. They would hold their ground and, beyond that, there was little preparation needed. They had worked diligently for a long time. Now they would simply see whether they would be rewarded or disappointed.

At 2:25, the receptionist ushered Joshua and Michael into the Zenyth boardroom. They were alone and the atmosphere was tense even before Desray entered and organized water. She reappeared a few minutes later and told them that David would be in shortly. Her demeanor gave nothing away. David and Kirsten entered the room at 2:34 and they looked serious. Joshua introduced Michael as they all shook hands.

After sitting, David looked directly at Michael. "There was a problem with your price."

Michael responded instantly. "I know. Our CEO had to approve the deep discounting. He wasn't happy about it."

David saw nothing humorous in Michael's comment. "Are you saying you can't move on what Joshua put in the proposal?"

"I'm saying that it represents exceptional value. Joshua lobbied very hard within our organization to secure this offer for Zenyth. Although our margins are low on this, we know we can deliver successfully for you."

There was a tortuously long period of silence. Everyone in the room knew that the next one to talk would come off second-best.

David finally spoke. "Then I have some bad news. You will have to deliver on the promises Joshua has been making on behalf of your corporation."

For the briefest of moments Joshua was confused but then David and Kirsten smiled. Michael simply stood and leaned over the table to shake their hands.

David looked at Joshua. "Congratulations, you did an exceptionally good job in pulling this together with Kirsten. We are looking forward to working with your team."

Joshua nodded as he also stood to shake hands. He looked David in the eye. "Thank you. We won't let you down."

David turned to Michael. "The reason I wanted you here was to let you know that this project was dead in the water until Joshua came to meet with me. Make sure you don't lose him."

Michael looked at Joshua and nodded. "I've had an offer of promotion in front of him for a while now but he seems to love being a salesman."

David signaled that the meeting was over by looking at his watch. "I would prefer that you do not move him anywhere until we've successfully implemented. I'm sorry, I have another meeting, but I really did want to congratulate you both in person. Kirsten can stay and run through the commercial details and she has a letter for you confirming our commitment. It will take a week or so to finalize the contract and another twenty-four hours to generate the purchase order. We are committed, so let's schedule the resources on both sides as soon as possible. This project is very important, make sure you deliver."

"We will." They said it in unison.

David shook their hands again before leaving the room. The meeting with Kirsten lasted another twenty-five minutes and mainly consisted of organizing target dates for various activities. Michael skimmed the proposed contract amendments and assured Kirsten that there were no barriers to executing the paperwork. She showed them out to reception.

Joshua shook Kirsten's hand and grinned. "I haven't forgiven you for ignoring my calls today."

Kirsten was a little sheepish. "Desray and I were under strict orders. Dave likes theatre."

She turned her attention to Michael. "We did want to meet you and let you know what a good job Joshua has done for both our organizations. If your delivery and support people are as capable, then we'll be a very happy customer."

They left Zenyth with the letter of commitment and they felt ecstatic. This was an important new account and it was the biggest deal of Joshua's sales career. As they walked to the car, Michael turned to Joshua. "That was a relief – now I don't have to fire you!" They both laughed. "Seriously, that was the best sales campaign I've ever been part of. You called it exactly right. You had a strategy and you had the guts to step up with David Thomas. Well done. I think now is the time to reconsider that sales management role."

Joshua was clearly chuffed but ignored the promotion bait. "It was a team effort, and you played a big role. Thanks for letting me take control. You must have thought my plan was risky."

"No, the deal was dead. Most other sales people would have adopted hope as their strategy."

As he unlocked the car doors, Joshua did his best to play down his excitement. "Thanks, but if we did lose the deal would you have fired me just like you threatened to do?"

Michael waited to be seated in the car before answering. He let the moment build before looking sideways as Joshua hit the ignition. "You'll never know."

Joshua glanced across to see if Michael was serious.

Michael grinned. "My bark is worse than my bite. You should know that by now."

"I've always been scared of dogs. You really did piss me off when you threatened me with the sack."

"I thought I only said another loss would damage your career, but regardless, I apologize. This is an impressive win – well done!"

The two men recounted the pivotal events at Zenyth as they drove. They talked about Bill, and Michael resolved to give him a call to thank him and ask if he had started with a new employer. Back at the office, Michael summoned everyone he could find. He proudly announced the Zenyth win as the largest new contract in the division for the year and praised Joshua's strategy and leadership in securing the account. Joshua thanked the team, especially Michael. The impromptu gathering quickly wrapped-up with Michael announcing he was buying drinks at the local pub to celebrate. Joshua's euphoric state was tempered by the immense sense of gratitude he felt toward Damien, Michael, his father and all the others who had helped him.

He went back to his desk and sent a brief e-mail to Damien, advising him of the fact that they had won the Zenyth account. He also phoned his father to thank him for the analysis and advice in dealing with Zenyth's CEO. Mark was immensely happy for his son and they talked enthusiastically before Joshua accepted an invitation home for a celebration dinner.

A dozen or so people attended drinks. Everyone was genuinely happy for him and seemed impressed with how they had snatched victory from the jaws of defeat. He also received several SMS messages and calls from colleagues and management. He looked forward to sharing everything with his parents and bought an expensive bottle of port as an appreciation gift for his father.

Dinner was unexpectedly wonderful. Mark toasted his son's success and Joshua felt at home like never before, both physically and emotionally. The bond with his parents, and the relationship with his father, was restored. It had been stretched to breaking point for more than a decade but that was now in the past. After they cleared the table, Joshua detoured back from the bathroom to collect the chess set and headed for the veranda to set it up. It wasn't long before Mark appeared with a cheeky look of disappointment.

"Leave it set up but I promised your mother we would have a game of Scrabble before she went to bed. Come on, it won't take long, she'll probably slaughter us as usual."

Joshua was surprised by how much he actually enjoyed this particular game of Scrabble. He did, however, have his standard run of bad luck in pulling unwanted tiles from the bag. Mark was following Clare and she seemed to have the knack of occupying almost every position where Mark was poised to lay down a killer high scoring word. Clare won, and Joshua came last, but he didn't mind losing because he could blame bad luck. Chess was altogether another matter.

It was 10:30, Clare had gone to bed. Mark and Joshua sat on the veranda playing chess and sipping port. They discussed the Zenyth win and Mark was genuinely impressed with his son's strategy and courage in personally meeting with the CEO to salvage a lost situation. Mark knew that failure with Zenyth would have been a significant set-back. It would have been his second big loss, damaging to his confidence and willingness to persist in professional selling. But that wasn't the case, and he was proud of his son.

Mark looked across at Joshua who was contemplating his attacking options. "I've been secretive about Damien and I'm sorry if that's been a problem, but it was one of the conditions."

"It's okay. I guess I'll meet him once the twelve months is over. You'll be free to tell me everything then. I assume you worked together at some stage?"

"Yes, but we'd lost touch. You wouldn't believe how difficult it was to organize. Anyway, you're right. Let's both honor the agreement."

They talked easily while playing chess. Joshua asked about the Kokoda adventure but Mark played it down, saying there would be time for a father and son bonding trip in the future. It was not a late night; Mark had an early morning flight to catch for business.

The following day, Joshua wrote an e-mail to Damien recounting all that had happened at Zenyth. He described the tension of not knowing whether the meeting with the CEO was to hear good news or bad. He described the theatrics of David Thomas and the anticlimactic feelings of success after a long campaign. He also wrote about the genuine sense of gratitude he felt toward Damien and that his success was due to the support of others – his colleagues, Michael, and his father. But Joshua's e-mail took the relationship with his mentor to a new level. He also discussed his relationship with his father and how much he had enjoyed playing Scrabble, of all things, with his parents. It was a few days before Joshua received Damien's reply.

Hello Joshua,

Thank you for your e-mail. Please accept my heartfelt congratulations with your win at Zenyth! You truly earned this success. I am especially pleased with the humility you genuinely feel concerning how it was achieved. You are right to identify the other people who contributed to the outcome and, in doing so, you are well on the way to being the leader you aspire to be. The very best leaders share the credit for success and are fully accountable for failure. They also seek to understand and learn. Every time you win or lose a significant piece of business, always conduct a review with the customer. Ensure it is not done by you or anyone too closely involved in the sales process from your organization. The review should seek to discover how well you read the relationship power-base, the decision drivers, and how you were positioned in terms of comparative value. Obviously, you must identify who the competition was and why they selected one vendor or solution over another. Discuss this with

Michael once you have a signed contract and purchase order.

Now that you will not be moving until the Zenyth project has been delivered successfully, it's almost certain that David Thomas will actively support you. Michael, however, is more important in the process and his reference support will be essential if you are to secure the optimal role. You must plan your approach carefully and be ready for one final attempt at getting you to accept a sales management role, something you should steadfastly avoid. He may also suggest a move inside the organization to a more senior sales role, which is something you may wish to consider. Please let me know your thoughts in this regard, and how you are progressing with the list of target software companies. Knowing who you want to work for is important, because the very best opportunities are not always advertised. You will need to be patient.

I am very happy that our work together has resulted in positive outcomes professionally at work, and personally with your family. I am especially pleased with the way your relationship with your father has been transformed. Parents love their children but often struggle with knowing how to help, rather than interfere. Your father did well in recognizing that he was not the best placed person to work with you as a mentor. His efforts in linking us together have been rewarded.

I have always been an avid chess player myself and you clearly enjoy playing it with your father. I was amused by your disdain for Scrabble even though you did admit that you enjoyed playing it recently with your parents. You work in a profession that is all about words (questions, really) and strategy. Chess and Scrabble are therefore bedfellows. Both games are good for the mind of a professional sales person or leader. I must say, Joshua, I completely disagree with your assertion that success in Scrabble is mainly due to luck. If you consistently lose, it's because you have poor skills or are not paying attention to strategy and execution. I encourage you to take a fresh look at Scrabble and invest more of your leisure time with it.

I know you are struggling with defining The Joshua Principle but the answer will come to you in the compass. There is more to it than the difference between magnetic north and true north. If not a self-realization over the coming months, then it can be conferred upon you when we meet face-to-face. I am happy for this to be one of the final revelations of your mentorship.

Let me know when you secure the contract and purchase order, as that is the moment you will have achieved the sale. But you will only really have a customer once your solution is implemented and they are deriving business value.

Damien Drost,
RSVPselling™ Sales Master

The Joshua Principle remained an enigma and he regarded Damien's latest clues as mere rehashing of previous comments. *Who cares about the vagaries of magnetic north versus true north? It's a relic from the past. GPS can position you exactly and tell you how to get there, with or without moral values.* His thoughts turned to Damien's comments on Scrabble. The last thing he wanted was any pressure or accountability to engage regularly in what he regarded as the word game from hell. *What will be next; exhortations to engage in hours of tedium playing Monopoly as a pathway to capitalist enlightenment?* He knew he was being unfair in his thoughts but hoped Damien would leave the topic of Scrabble alone. He decided never to mention board games to Damien again.

Over the next few weeks, Joshua received the Zenyth contract and purchase order. It was Michael who did the win review with Kirsten, and the information was enlightening. There had been eleven competitors. The Zenyth team reviewed response documents using weighted selection criteria to rank functional compliance and ability to deliver. Once this was done, they compared price with the functional compliance scores for the purpose of a value for money assessment. This enabled them to reduce the number of potential vendors down to a manageable short-list of three. Joshua's corporation had only just made the cut and had been the most expensive. Reference sites were to be used to validate the preferred vendor only.

Zenyth's IT department had also been keen to build a solution internally using a combination of technologies from their existing suppliers. The cost was presented as being half that of Joshua's corporation but there were real doubts concerning the ability to deliver. The Zenyth IT department had a poor track record in terms of delivering on time or on budget. When David Thomas walked into Zenyth as the new CEO, Bill Trench and the CIO were openly hostile toward each other. David simply suspended the project until Kirsten was appointed. In the end, the decision came down to business alignment, ability to deliver, and value for money.

Kirsten emphasized several key points during the review. "Price was the least important consideration, once we had our short-list. We actually *bought* Joshua and your team. The truth was that there were several options, including starting the process again, but Joshua did what others could not do. He took the time and did the hard work of truly understanding our problems and what it would take to make this project a success."

Michael's win report also highlighted some other important information. For Joshua, it validated Damien's wisdom. Initially, when the project was being run by Bill, the competition was in the form of external vendors. But Bill's business case was vague and weak. The proposed budget fell short of the investment required. The negative politics internally also meant that the CIO was undermining Bill, and was vitriolic in his claims that they could build a solution internally, for far less cost, if only Bill could clearly articulate the requirements. The moment David Thomas arrived at Zenyth, Bill's project was in trouble. Damien had been exactly right in concluding regime change meant that they had to start selling again, and it had to be at the very top.

Joshua and Damien continued to communicate. Damien was pleased his protégé had received the Zenyth purchase order and that the win review had validated their strategy. They now focused on selecting the best potential employers and how to secure interviews with the right people. His résumé was the best it could be and focused on his achievements. His covering letter emphasized that he operated strategically and was seeking a long-term career move now that he had identified the software industry as his committed career path. His father had been utilizing his network of business contacts and had provided the names of some organizations that were growing and could potentially be suitable.

Joshua continued to deliver for Michael in building his pipeline and closing business. Nothing as spectacular as Zenyth but every deal was important. He was now well above quota and earning commission on maximum accelerators. They had secured their best resources for the Zenyth project and the implementation was well underway. The organization was determined to ensure Zenyth would be a lighthouse reference customer. Joshua knew the day was approaching for the difficult conversation concerning his plans to leave and his audacious request for Michael to be a referee, helping him in the process.

Joshua had invited his parents over to have dinner the night before his father's overseas adventure. Joshua knew there was no internet or phone coverage in the New Guinea highlands, and Mark would be gone for three weeks. Upon arrival back in Australia, his parent's would meet in a Cairns resort for a well earned holiday, before returning to Sydney.

Although he had a limited repertoire, Joshua enjoyed cooking for others, and it was a special occasion. He felt good hosting his parents and they treasured the time together as they talked and ate. Mark focused the conversation on Joshua's career rather than his overseas sojourn.

As Clare was helping to clear the table, she noticed what appeared to be a pocket watch on the sideboard. "I didn't know you owned one of those."

Joshua looked up from the sink. "It's a compass. Damien gave it to me."

Clare opened it and examined the face before handing it to her husband so she could dry the dishes that Joshua was washing.

Mark studied the compass as he spoke. "This is real quality, Joshua. It's old and was made in Germany."

Mark took it with him to the lounge-room while Clare and Joshua finished in the kitchen.

Later, they had tea and cake but it was an early night. Joshua hugged his parents warmly as they left. He reflected on how being out of touch with his father would not have bothered him nine months ago, but now he knew he would miss him. Mark promised to send an e-mail once he was able. But Joshua closed the door feeling slightly uneasy, something was not quite right, both Mark and Clare had seemed unusually distracted.

The next day, he e-mailed Damien a list of potential employers in the software industry. It was a targeted list and the result of many weeks of diligent research. He knew that the large multi-nationals with HR departments were risk-averse when hiring, and they would regard him as relatively inexperienced. Joshua had therefore focused on companies that were niche leaders in growing markets. All of the organizations had a leader who could make an independent decision to hire someone with real potential. Over the next week, while has father was overseas, Joshua and Damien corresponded daily, and a plan for approaching target employers was crystallized. The Zenyth project had been going well and would be live within a month, ahead of schedule and within budget. It was time to have the conversation with Michael, and Damien gave Joshua some final advice.

The following week, he sat nervously in Michael's office waiting for him to arrive. Joshua's mobile phone chirped with an incoming message, he thought it would be Michael letting him know that he was running late. Instead, it was a message from his father: *Back in civilization and will call when I get to Cairns. Love Dad.* Joshua put his phone back in his coat pocket just as Michael appeared.

"Hi Josh, sorry I'm late. What did you want to talk about?"

Michael seemed to be in a good mood and Joshua waited for him to settle behind his desk.

"Mike, you're not going to like this, and I need your support."

Joshua closed the door and sat down again.

"Let me guess. You've either screwed up or you're here to resign. I am guessing it's the latter."

Joshua was surprised by Michael's intuition. "Well, yes, not exactly."

"What's going on?"

Joshua composed himself and delivered the announcement exactly as he had rehearsed it in his mind. He finished by apologizing to Michael for his decision to leave the organization.

Michael Blunt was a good man, despite his overbearing style. He regarded Joshua as a valuable asset but he also genuinely wanted the best for him. He sincerely believed that it was in Joshua's best interests to stay and that it was the smart thing to do.

"Joshua, this is not the right decision. The Zenyth deal has made your career here. Surely you don't want to start from scratch somewhere else?"

"I've made up my mind – it's time to move on."

There was an intimidating silence before Michael spoke. "People leave their boss before they leave the corporation, so if I'm the problem, tell me. Why do you really want to go?"

"Mike, you've taught me a lot but there's nothing you can say or do to get me to stay. I need to move into higher value and more complex solution selling. Zenyth gave me a taste of selling at the highest level and in a way that creates real business value. I don't want to sell commodities and I don't want to sell to technical buyers anymore."

"I don't get it – you can continue to progress and succeed right here. If you don't want to move into management, then let's find you a more senior sales role here."

Joshua shook his head. "Sorry, I'm not going to change my mind."

"Are you going to a competitor?"

"I don't actually have another job yet. That's where I need your support."

"What? None of this makes sense. Why are you taking the risk of telling me you're leaving when you don't even have another job lined up?"

"Mike, I trust you. I want you to be a reference for me as I go through the process with companies I'm targeting. None of them is a competitor."

Michael said nothing for what seemed an eternity. He folded his arms and leaned on the desk, speaking slowly and deliberately. "You owe it to me and yourself to stay. You're making a big mistake. Let's pretend this conversation never happened; sleep on it and let's talk tomorrow."

Joshua's heart was pounding. "Mike, I owe it to you to be honest. My mind is definitely made up. I want to do this with your support and work to ensure I am productive right up until the day I leave. I also want to ensure a seamless hand-over."

That was not what Michael wanted to hear and he was becoming aggravated. "I have another meeting now. Have you told anyone here that you plan to leave?"

"No."

"Good – this can be salvaged. Promise me you will sleep on it?"

"I won't tell anyone here. We can talk again tomorrow about the transition."

Michael stood up and escorted him to the door. "You have a very big future here if you want it. I'll call you in the morning."

Joshua walked directly to his desk, packed-up his laptop and headed for the elevator. He was shaken and needed space to regain his composure. He had mixed feelings but was glad to have the most difficult conversation of his working life behind him. As he drove, he began to doubt the wisdom of what he had just done. Damien was complicit in going down this path and he wondered if it was the first piece of bad guidance from his mentor. He knew Damien would be expecting an update, as they had been corresponding every day lately, but he would wait to see how it played out with Michael. He toyed with the idea of calling his father now that Mark was back in communication, but decided instead to send a text message.

The meeting with Michael the next day was over coffee and it had a very different tone compared with the previous encounter. Joshua had not slept well, and he wearily said that he hadn't changed his mind. Michael, on the other hand, was surprisingly circumspect. He apologized for having put Joshua under pressure, and simply asked if there was anything he could do to convince him to stay. Joshua was unequivocal in his response but mustered all the empathy he could manage. Michael nodded thoughtfully and then accepted the situation. He agreed to act as a referee, provided that Joshua remained committed to the business and his customers while still employed. It was done.

He e-mailed his account of the saga to Damien, recounting the sleepless night filled with doubt and feelings of guilt so skillfully imbued by Michael. He arrived home in the early evening to be greeted by Damien's reply.

Hello Joshua,

I fully understand how difficult the conversation was with your boss. You did well to maintain your position and not be swayed. As much as Michael seemed to know why you were there, he must have also felt a little ambushed. Regardless, he obviously felt compelled to do everything possible to convince you to stay, including the use of guilt. You may have doubts right now but you will look back later and be glad with your course of action. Alerting Michael and gaining his support was not easy, but you will find the conversation with David less difficult.

I have been reviewing the websites of the companies you forwarded to me and the list is good. It is very important, however, that you remain focused on selecting a boss as well as an organization. The person who will manage and mentor you in the new environment needs to be a strategist; someone who can take you to the next level. My next e-mail will give you a framework for the interview process but, for now, consider the fact that you will be interviewing your potential boss just as much as he or she will be assessing you.

Well done on getting through a difficult few days. I will send you a follow-up e-mail tomorrow.

Damien Drost
RSVPselling™ Sales Master

Damien's insights concerning CVs had been most helpful. Joshua knew he would need every possible advantage when it came to interviews within an industry in which he had no track record. He had begun the process of firing his boss and now he would need to find a new one. Damien's next installment would be crucial. Joshua arrived home the following evening to be greeted by an e-mail.

Hello Joshua,

You've had a chance to sleep on my previous e-mail and now we will continue on the topic of job interviews. I have stated previously that success is a 50:50 proposition. By this I mean that you bring fifty percent of the potential for success, and your employer represents the other side of the equation. You know that companies look for the three Cs when hiring someone and you should also consider these same things in evaluating your potential employer: Competence, Commitment, and Character or Cultural fit.

In addition to the three Cs, you need them to discuss the three Ps. You should evaluate the potential for success within their organization based upon their response to the following topics: People, Proposition and Patch. Your employer has an obligation to provide an environment within which you can be successful. This means that they need to have people you are proud to work with (competent, committed and of good character), and a value proposition that is uniquely differentiated in the market; and a territory – patch – that is viable, with an achievable quota. During the interview process, you should explore all of these things. You should also gain an understanding of their expectations for the role, and the process for selecting and issuing a letter of offer to the successful candidate.

Joshua, here are some words to transform any job interview. 'I believe the most expensive mistake you can make in business is to hire the wrong person in this kind of role. But equally for me, I cannot afford to take a job with the wrong employer. This needs to be a long term career move for me, so rather than sell to each other, I would like to understand whether this is a good fit for both of us. I've done my homework for today, so may I also ask questions?'

Adjust the phrases to suit your own style. The important thing is to establish genuine empathy for their difficult task of evaluating candidates for the role. Experienced managers, however, often regard sales people's words in an interview as a façade. They can be cynical, so be prepared for what they may ask and be ready with your own insightful questions.

There are excellent resources in this regard on the RSVPselling™ website. Select the questions you will use and let me know which ones on the list appeal most to you. The key thing is to prepare for the interview by doing your homework. Treat it like a sales situation by creating empathy, rapport and genuine understanding. You must understand why they need to fill the role.

Damien Drost
RSVPselling™ Sales Master

Joshua knew that during job interviews it would be vitally important to ask questions without coming across as an upstart or arrogant in any way. He was looking at the RSVPselling.com website when the phone rang; it was his mother. She told him that she had just spoken with Mark and that she was flying to Cairns the next day to meet him. Later, Joshua also received a call from his father; it was good to hear his voice but Mark sounded tired.

While Mark had been away, Joshua had been corresponding daily with Damien. Joshua was pleased with the current state of the mentoring relationship. Damien had transitioned to simple coaching, instead of persisting with questions and philosophical machinations. Their correspondence now read like peer interaction, rather than a teacher lecturing and probing a student.

As the weeks passed by, Joshua became increasingly conscious of the fact that the mentorship was drawing to a close. He wanted to be prepared for his face-to-face meeting with Damien by having an appropriate gift to present, but he struggled to identify what that could be. It proved to be almost as frustrating as defining The Joshua Principle but eventually he settled on the best way to tangibly express his thanks. He would create a professionally bound anthology of his mentor's wisdom.

He began to plan what it would look like and started selecting content from Damien's correspondence. He also focused in earnest on securing a new role with the very best employer. He discussed his top choice, CEL Software Corporation, with his father and researched their market and customers.

The next few weeks flew by. Michael treated Joshua well and there were no discernable feelings of betrayal or animosity caused by his notice of resignation. Their relationship actually improved and Michael sought Joshua's input concerning the best internal candidate for taking over his accounts. They agreed that Tania could do the job. Within a month, the first phase of the Zenyth implementation went live and Joshua booked a meeting with David Thomas. He also mailed letters and résumés to six target corporations. His preferred potential employer was still CEL Software and their Sales Director, Janet Reynolds, had a solid reputation.

Before meeting with potential new employers, he needed to know that David was on side. Joshua worried his request could evoke a negative reaction but his concerns were ill-founded. Damien had been correct in predicting the outcome; David appreciated that Joshua had waited until the project had gone live, and he committed to being an enthusiastic referee when needed. He left Zenyth relieved and focused on how he would secure an appointment with Janet Reynolds. His strategy was to use referees in an unconventional manner but he knew he needed to execute perfectly for that to work.

The telephone call with Janet was tough but she agreed to meet later the following week. He was determined to gain as much insight as possible beforehand and secured two informal meetings with CEL customers. One of them knew Janet well. Both meetings were invaluable in providing a perspective of CEL's strengths and weaknesses in the market but one also provided personal insight into his potential new boss. Joshua did not stop there. One of Damien's e-mails had suggested meeting with one of Janet's current employees for the purpose of understanding the corporation's culture and her operating style. He simply telephoned the switch and explained his situation to the receptionist, asking for the name and mobile phone number of the best sales person in her team. It had worked. Professional empathy made sales people the easiest to sell to; the conversation he had over lunch was enlightening.

Joshua sat with Janet Reynolds in the CEL boardroom. She possessed a disarming manner that masked a laser-like ability to get to the truth. She had granted him an interview because she liked his direct approach and evidence-based validation of performance and capability. It didn't take long for Janet to get down to business.

"On paper, you don't make the grade for this job but you sold me on giving you an interview. Why should I take the risk of hiring you?"

"I know that hiring the wrong person for this role is the most expensive mistake you can make. It will cost you time, energy and revenue. Worse than that, it could damage your reputation and brand. Equally for me, I can't afford to take a job with the wrong employer. I'm looking for a long term successful career move. Rather than sit here and sell to you, I would like to explore whether there is genuinely a good fit for us to work together. Is that an approach that works for you?"

"Sure, but you haven't answered my question."

"You see me as a risk because I don't have specific industry experience or a CV that shows stability and long term performance. Are these your main concerns?"

"Let's come back to all that later. You're right in saying the biggest mistake I can make as a manager is hiring the wrong person, but what's the biggest mistake most sales people make?"

Joshua paused before answering. "The two big mistakes are pursuing business that cannot be won and selling to people who cannot buy."

"So how do you avoid wasting time and resources?"

"I qualify properly. I then invest with people at the right levels to set an agenda that creates value and an advantage."

Janet was skeptical but Joshua leaned forward. "Janet, I know this all sounds cliché but I've done my research. CEL is who I want to work for. I've done more than visit your website and read analyst commentary. I've met with some of your customers. I believe I can learn from you in selling real solutions to serious business problems for large organizations."

"That's all very well, but how does this overcome your lack of experience in our industry?"

"All risk comes from not knowing what we don't know. In the case of hiring me for this role, the issues are whether I'm competent, will I be committed and will I fit culturally. Employers usually hire based on skills, yet have to fire based on poor fit or performance. I would like you to get to the truth of who I am and what I offer by talking with the most qualified people."

Janet said nothing.

"I know that what I'm about to suggest may seem unconventional but I would like you to meet with the CEO of my biggest and most recent customer, and also with my current boss. I know that references are usually used to validate the decision at the end of the process but, in my case, I would like the reference phase to occur early. Is that something you would be willing to do?"

Janet sat back and a wry smile appeared as she spoke. "I am intrigued as to why your current boss would be willing to act a reference. Is he trying to manage you out?"

"Actually, it's the opposite. He wants me to take a promotion to sales management but maybe that's the first question you should ask him when you meet."

There was a period of silence before Janet finally spoke. "Let's come back to that at the end of this meeting. For now, I would like to focus on your approach to selling. Do you regard yourself as transactional or are you strategic in how you sell?"

Janet had unwittingly, or instinctively, set the scene for Joshua to talk about RSVP. "Both are important and require good relationships and effective tactics but it's also essential to offer unique value and have complete understanding of their buying process. Relationships need to be managed strategically which means positioning early, starting at the top, understanding the power-base within the organization and then aligning with winning agendas. But more than that, I know we have to become part of a compelling business case."

Joshua continued, focusing on strategy and changing the rules on competitors. The conversation demonstrated real substance in Joshua's knowledge and maturity. Janet was impressed with what she heard and progressively became more open. Joshua knew he needed to sell through asking questions and, more importantly, he needed to understand Janet's process for evaluating and hiring the successful candidate. He changed the direction of the conversation.

"Janet, what happened here at CEL to create the opening for this role?"

"To be candid, we hired the wrong person, they didn't perform. It was as you described – they appeared to be qualified for the role but they were not a good fit."

Joshua already knew this from meeting with one of their sales people. He was glad she had answered honestly. Janet had passed the first test and he seized the opportunity to begin to understand her selection criteria.

"What will make the right person successful in this role? What defines a good fit?"

Their meeting lasted ninety minutes and Janet agreed to speak with Michael Blunt and David Thomas as the next step. Joshua would brief both men concerning what he needed them to cover in their conversations with Janet. His adaptation of Damien's interview phrases had worked. At the next interview, Joshua would do a lot more of the questioning and move on from the three Cs to the three Ps. He would focus on how CEL took a compelling, unique value Proposition to market, and also the caliber and style of the People with whom he would be working. Lastly, he would discuss his territory – Patch – to ensure he had a viable market within which to operate. He would hone the list of interview questions he had obtained from the RSVPselling.com website to assist in his preparation.

The following week, both Michael and David advised that they'd had their conversations with Janet, and that it was all positive. The twelve month mentorship was drawing to a close. Joshua would soon meet Damien face-to-face.

Hi Damien,

Michael and David both called in the last few days to say that their meetings went well with Janet, and Michael's conversation with her was much longer than expected. Michael keeps making jokes about trying to get me to change my mind but he has honored his word to support me in the process. Janet really does seem like an impressive person. Michael told me I could learn a lot from her, as she absolutely understands selling at the highest levels and is not a forecast jockey. I will phone her tomorrow and make an appointment for my next interview. I'm comfortable with my list of questions to ask and will focus on the three Ps. I want to ensure that my territory can yield the results needed. I also need to understand what support I will receive to create momentum quickly.

I have begun to review and summarize everything I've learned during our time together. It is quite interesting how some things appear contradictory but nevertheless valid. For example: I must engineer outcomes yet also allow C-level people to be in control. Anyway, I just wanted to drop you a quick note to let you know it looks good for my next meeting at CEL.

Your protégé
Joshua

The next day, Joshua called Janet and she was keen to meet. He e-mailed Damien with a final draft list of interview questions and the reply helped him validate his strategy. He was well prepared when he met her on the Friday, and the conversation was completely different from their first encounter. This time she was doing most of the selling. Within forty minutes, she had offered him the role. It took another thirty minutes for Joshua to accept, but only after they had discussed the three Ps. He phoned his father with the good news, Mark was delighted. He also e-mailed Damien but it was Sunday morning before he checked for the response.

Hello Joshua,

Congratulations on securing your new career with CEL! Janet appears to be well equipped to continue your development. I am pleased that you are summarizing the principles of success in your own way but, if you are seeking to distil all you have learned into a series of truisms, be cautious of oversimplification. Success is not a litany of clichés or formulas. Albert Einstein once said, "Everything should be made as simple as possible, but no simpler." Paradox should be embraced. An example of this in business is that 'numbers never lie' and 'numbers never tell the full story'. Another is 'to be optimistically paranoid'.

Our twelve months together is inexorably drawing to a close. In the first few weeks of our dialogue, I promised to discuss the subject of purpose and how it relates to the compass sent as a gift. In business, the concept of true north is values-based leadership, which is essential for sustained success. Values are also important in overcoming your fears, avarice and other defects of the human condition. Failure rarely occurs as a single event but usually results from slow misdirection away from the intended course.

Choose your values and world view carefully; everything is connected – personal, social, and business. Values drive behavior and create outcomes, intended or otherwise. Stand for something or you risk falling for anything. The compass is to remind you to hold your chosen course. Choice, rather than circumstance, is what determines success.

Damien Drost
RSVPselling™ Sales Master

It had been almost eleven months since the mysterious package had arrived from Germany. The lessons were coming full circle, back to earlier teachings. Joshua and Michael had parted company on positive terms, and he was settling into his new role with CEL Software. Janet Reynolds was someone who brought out the best in him – he was working hard, learning much and beginning to earn the respect of colleagues and the management team.

As Joshua reflected, it was not the transformation in his selling skills and career that he valued most, it was the change in his thinking, habits and personal life that he treasured. Damien had enabled him to let go of limiting beliefs, and unhealthy ego had been replaced with wisdom beyond his years. In Joshua's mind, Damien had become a friend and he hoped there would be an opportunity for the friendship to continue after the twelve month mentorship was complete.

In his personal life, Joshua marveled at how the relationship with his father had been transformed by the introduction of Damien. But he yearned to also be restored with Mandy. Their meetings had become more regular, and she had slowly become open to the possibility that Joshua really was a genuinely different person. Her guarded interactions were a thing of the past, and finally she had agreed to have dinner with him.

He stood on her front step feeling nervous. Mandy opened the door, appearing more beautiful than he could remember. Joshua stood mute, his gaze betraying his thoughts.

"How is my television terminator this evening?"

They drove with the roof down and the evening was clear and balmy. He had booked an intimate restaurant hoping that the atmosphere would help set the tone. As the night progressed, they moved from discussing families and careers to Joshua's mentorship, but finally they faced the issues of the past. Mandy opened the dialogue as the waiter walked away after presenting the dessert menu.

"Thanks for not doing your usual trick of drinking too much and then getting me to drive."

"I drink a lot less now."

"I noticed. Now you're going to tell me that all your past misdemeanors were caused by alcohol."

Joshua looked her directly in the eye. "No, my screw-ups were entirely my fault, and the result of my own choices."

They talked about the most painful episodes, and he acknowledged his betrayal of trust. Joshua was sincere and his words were heartfelt, but Mandy wasn't convinced.

"But when we were at home alone, you were more interested in sport on TV, than talking with me. How big is your new screen?"

"I don't have one. I'm hoping to one day watch ours again."

Mandy scoffed. "What if I said that the new Joshua Peters is just a sales persona. Usually, when men listen and say the right things, it's because they think there's the chance of money or sex at the end of the conversation."

Joshua smiled. "I guess it's obvious that I'm not after your money." Mandy looked away but Joshua continued. "Seriously, Mandy, this mentorship has taught me to give all of myself. I wasn't committed in the past, I was selfish and I let you down terribly."

He waited for eye contact. "I know that when I'm with you I need to be fully there. I truly love you. If you can forgive me..."

"I'm not ready for that." She stood and walked away, asking the waiter to finalize the bill as she went to the restroom.

The wind and the engine were the only sounds as they drove. There was a surreal atmosphere of sexual tension and pensive thought. Joshua hoped Mandy felt as he did, and he reached over to hold her hand. She accepted.

They approached the junction where he could turn right to take Mandy home, or left to go to his place. There was no traffic, he paused at the intersection. She was ready with her response if he asked. To her great surprise, he turned right without saying a word.

Mandy looked straight ahead. "You are full of surprises."

"I know it can't be like the past. I just want a chance to show you that the changes are for real. We don't have to rush things."

"I would have said, no."

"I wasn't going to ask."

Within a few minutes they were at Mandy's door.

"Thanks for tonight Josh. Maybe this is a new beginning, but I need more time."

"I know. You need to be sure that the television will be safe." They both laughed.

There was a brief hug and he kissed her on the forehead before returning to his car. He drove away feeling elated – everything seemed to be headed in the right direction.

Chapter Ten: Revealed in a Riddle

Even on the most difficult of journeys, you need never walk alone.

The mentoring relationship would finish exactly one year after it had begun, and the date was only a few weeks away. Joshua's sales career had been transformed; he was now competent and purposeful in both strategy and execution. His personal life was also completely different – he was committed in his relationships and at peace with himself. He had long ago relinquished the frustrations of not being able to speak with his mentor and instead had embraced the clarifying medium of written communication.

Joshua continued to work on his gift for Damien. The anthology he was creating would take his education full circle, evidencing the knowledge and wisdom he had gained during his tutelage. The words were the confluence of mentor and student, and he hoped it would demonstrate to Damien that he had truly learned the intended lessons. He believed that he had distilled his mentor's wisdom to summarize success in selling and life in general. It would be printed and professionally stitch-bound into a leather covered book befitting the investment Damien had made in him.

Yet there was something bothering Joshua. Although he had unlocked the mysteries within the compass, he remained frustrated concerning the elusive Joshua

Principle. He e-mailed Damien to ask about the venue for their dinner meeting and requested one last clue. The reply came the following day.

Hello Joshua,

The Joshua Principle has been with you for some time and there will be no additional clues. I look forward to revealing it when we meet. I have another question for you to consider between now and when we finally see each other face-to-face.

Two men are walking down a busy and noisy city street when one man stops and turns to the other.

"Can you hear that small cricket?"

"How can you possibly hear a tiny cricket above all this noise?"

The first man does not answer but simply reaches into his pocket and discretely drops a coin on the pavement. Several people stop and look down.

Joshua, what does this parable reveal?

I have booked a private dining-room at The Sky Loft in the city for 8:00pm. I would like to include your father if you are agreeable. He invested much effort in establishing our relationship and I believe we will benefit from his presence. Please let me know your thoughts. There is no problem if you prefer it just be the two of us, as I can meet with your father separately.

Damien Drost
RSVPselling™ Sales Master

Joshua was happy for his father to attend the dinner. After all, it had been Mark Peters who made the introduction and Joshua had always been skeptical concerning the assertion that the mentorship was free. He suspected that his father had paid for the whole thing behind the scenes. He concluded that this was the real reason Damien thought it appropriate that Mark should attend. Joshua regarded the anniversary meeting as a form of graduation and, regardless of the motives, he wanted his father to be there.

Hi Damien,

Yes, I would love to have my father present. Thanks for inviting him.

Your last question seems straight forward yet profound. We hear what we listen for – the sounds to which we are attuned. We also see what we look for and receive what we expect. The last year together has enabled me to filter distractions and focus on what is important. Thank you.

Your protégé
Joshua

The dinner meeting was looming and Joshua counted down the days. He had collected his gift for Damien. The words, The Wisdom of Damien Drost, were embossed in gold letters on the cover and spine. A graphic artist had taken the various texts, arranged by subject, and professionally printed the pages within. A message to Damien appeared on the first page, along with a dedication to his father. It had cost Joshua a substantial sum but the expense was trivial compared with the investment that had been made in him. He had included several dozen blank lined pages in the back for Damien's own use.

He received an e-mail from Damien two days before their fateful appointment. He didn't know it at the time, but it was to be their last correspondence.

Hello Joshua,

You have done so very well during our time together. Here are some final thoughts for you to ponder concerning professional selling:

- You will always be delegated to people you sound like
- People are best convinced by reasons they themselves discover
- Only the customer can quantify the value or call it a solution
- Lead and serve rather than manipulate or push

Humans are uniquely endowed with the ability to laugh and weep. Emotion and stories help us to remember lessons; something you can apply to the process of selling. All the great leaders throughout the ages were masterful story tellers, and you can change your world if you also learn to tell powerful true stories.

All will be revealed in two days, including the rest of this sentence: 'Behind every successful person is ...' The answer is not, a very surprised mother-in-law!

Seriously, do you remember, early in our correspondence, where I discussed the issue of accountability for the investment made in you? The rest of the sentence relates to this very point. You are already successful because you are committed to making a difference. You have been enlightened and empowered, but what will you do beyond achieving personal prosperity? Soon you will have The Joshua Principle, together with the rest of the sentence: Behind the success of Joshua Peters, is ...

I have discharged my debt and you will soon understand your obligation. Do not reply. Our next communication will be face-to-face. Dress for dinner is formal and please bring the compass.

Damien Drost
RSVPselling™ Sales Master

Joshua laughed but was disturbed by the ominous tone at the end of Damien's e-mail. He then realized that he did not own a tuxedo.

The limousine arrived with Mark at 7:00pm. Joshua wasn't sure whether he was excited or anxious as he settled into the back with his father. The wrapped gift lay between them on the seat, and Joshua soon became absorbed in his own thoughts. Mark also sat silently considering the evening ahead, until his son retrieved the compass from his pocket and began repeatedly opening and closing the lid.

"That clicking is driving me crazy."

"Sorry Dad. He asked me to bring the compass tonight. Damien's last e-mail was a bit strange."

"I'm sure it will be okay. You should feel proud of what you've achieved in the last twelve months."

"Thanks. Do you want to know what the gift is for Damien?"

"I'm happy to be surprised along with him. I'll be watching when it's opened and I'll take some pictures."

"Hey, thanks! I hadn't even thought about bringing a camera."

There had been an accident on the main road into the city and the driver took back streets so they would arrive at the restaurant on time. Mark broke the silence.

"I don't mean to pry but I promised your mother I would ask you tonight. How are things with you and Mandy?"

"We are doing great. Dating again is actually better the second time around."

"I'm glad, in what way?"

"I now understand the importance of giving yourself and being fully there when you're with someone. The law of reciprocity takes care of the rest."

Mark nodded before looking out the window. They each lapsed into solitary thought for the remainder of the journey. The limousine parked out front of the city high-rise and Mark told the driver he would call when they were ready to go home.

The lift doors opened on the top floor and an elegantly dressed lady stood at reception finishing a phone call. Joshua took the lead when she replaced the handset.

"Hi, party of three in the name of Drost."

"You have excellent timing Mr. Peters. That was Mr. Drost on the phone just now. He's on his way but has been delayed in traffic. Please follow me."

They walked past an impressive wine cellar, accentuated by wrought iron and dark timber. At the end of the walkway she opened a pair of intimidating doors, revealing a spectacular private dining-room. She took their drinks order before leaving, closing the doors behind her. The room was dimly lit with tall candle stands flickering soft ambient light from each corner. The stunning view from the floor-to-ceiling windows was accentuated by the setting sun. They could see the ocean horizon over the eastern suburbs. In the harbor below were Australian war ships berthed at Garden Island Naval Base, dwarfed by a US aircraft carrier. It was a spectacular scene but their eyes were drawn to the single table in the middle of the room.

Joshua laughed. "Surely not."

There were three dinner settings and, in the middle, a Scrabble board with what appeared to be a game in progress. There were letters in play and tiles on racks in front of each chair. There was also a beautiful wooden box and Joshua recognized the artisan's work immediately. It was the same style as the one that contained the invitation and compass a year earlier. Joshua carefully held it and studied his own name burned into the lid just as before. He suspected what was inside and reverently opened the box. He took various chess pieces out, studying the exquisite craftsmanship. Mark sensed his son's emotion and maintained his distance – this was a moment between mentor and student.

Joshua spoke in a hushed tone. "We should have waited at the bar rather than come in here without him."

"We still can – put it all back and let's go."

Joshua hesitated before changing his mind. "No. This is where I want to meet him."

He returned the hand-carved pieces and shut the lid, pausing to read the tiles on the Scrabble board. Mark moved forward and they looked together. RSVP across, and YES vertically above – S being the common letter.

Joshua turned to his father. "I made the mistake of complaining about Scrabble in one of my e-mails. Damien replied by telling me that winning actually had something to do with strategy. It was the first time I doubted his credibility."

Mark laughed and pointed to the rack of letters in front of him. "That's a novel idea."

Joshua studied the Scrabble letters used as name settings: JOSHUA PETERS, DAMIEN DROST, and MARK PETERS.

A waiter appeared with their drinks and Joshua replaced things as they were. They moved to the window to savor the view.

"Are you nervous?"

Joshua maintained his gaze on the fading horizon. "I was earlier, but I'm ready now."

He turned to his father and looked him in the eye. "Thanks so much for making this happen. I think this cost you more than just time and effort."

Mark ignored the implied question. He was touched by Joshua's appreciation but gave nothing away concerning the real cost. He was saved from any awkwardness as the hostess re-joined them.

"Gentlemen, Mr. Drost is still caught in traffic but will be here soon. He sends his sincere apologies for the delay."

Joshua shrugged. "I've waited a year. A few more minutes won't matter."

Mark went to his seat and Joshua soon joined him. Their conversation subsided as Joshua became consumed by his own thoughts. Mark, on the other hand, became interested in the Damien Drost name tiles and leaned over, rearranging the letters.

Joshua disapproved. "Don't do that."

Mark turned the two racks toward Joshua. "Look at this. The letters in his name can be rearranged to say, ID DAS MENTOR. It's German for, your psyche is mentor."

Joshua was a little annoyed. "Seriously, put his name back how it was, he'll be here soon."

Mark appeared suitably chastised and turned the letters back toward himself. He carefully rearranged the tiles and gazed at the eleven letters for a minute before again turning the two racks toward his son. He obscured Joshua's view by holding his hands in front of the letters.

Their eyes were inevitably drawn together and Joshua saw that his father was weeping.

"Son, I love you."

Mark removed his hands from the table and Joshua's eyes fell to Damien's tiles.

Joshua mouthed the words he read – Dad is Mentor.

He sat open mouthed and confused, slowly shaking his head as he looked back up. Mark moved his chair closer. Joshua was dumbfounded. There was no anger, no joy – just disbelief.

"But where is Damien?"

"I'm here son. Damien Drost is my avatar"

Joshua sat bewildered, scarcely comprehending what had been said – and then his eyes began to fill with tears.

Mark spoke with a trembling voice. "I love you so much son. Please forgive my deception. I had to find a way to help you. You have every right to be angry but please let me explain."

Joshua sat mute in what appeared to be anguished confusion.

Mark continued. "My father once said to me that all you need to get through life is someone who truly believes in you. That's the rest of the sentence. Behind every truly successful person is someone who believes in them. I believe in you, Joshua, and I'm so very proud of who you are."

Mark stood and Joshua followed his lead as they embraced, both sobbing amid raw emotion.

Mark took a sip of water as he sat and then took a deep breath to compose himself. Joshua rubbed his face and frowned as questions began to flood his mind. His words were choked with emotion.

"But how – you were in New Guinea with no internet?"

"I was actually in San Francisco. I really did plan to do The Kokoda Track, but something prevented me. I didn't tell you when my plans changed because I wanted you to believe that it couldn't be me sending you e-mails while you were corresponding with Damien. I was worried that you suspected what was really going on."

"Who called the restaurant just now?"

"It was the limo driver. I've known George for years."

"I thought you had paid Damien Drost. I had no idea that you were actually him. I still can't believe you pulled this off! What about Damien's profile on the German website? How did you organize the German Hotel? I rang them when I received the package."

"None of that matters right now. Are you angry with me for deceiving you?"

Joshua silently shook his head in disbelief.

"Son, I used to tell you that there's always a price to be paid for success. I came to see that mine had been paid by those closest to me, especially you. I needed to set things right. Can you forgive me?"

Joshua nodded slowly. "I'm not angry. I can't think of anyone in the world who would have gone to so much trouble to help their son. I'm annoyed with myself at falling for the whole thing! I still cannot believe the amount of effort this must have taken. Did Mom know?"

Mark was immensely relieved that Joshua was not upset and decided to answer before moving on as planned. "Your mother knew nothing until the day we argued over you smashing my old television. She was very upset and thought you had fallen under the spell of some new-age success cult. I told her the truth after you left that day. She was the only other person who knew."

Joshua shook his head and smiled at his father. "Unbelievable."

Mark explained how he felt, looking back at his children's teenage years. It was a period when his career really accelerated but promotion meant working long hours, lots of pressure, and endless travel. He shared his regrets and apologized to his son before continuing.

"Teenagers never really listen to their parents. I never did with my father, until it was nearly too late. To cut a long story short, someone I respect said something profound to me a few years ago. He said that no-one on their death-bed ever wishes they'd spent more time at the office. I realized that you and Annie are the real legacy I will leave behind. Nothing else I could achieve has the power to change the world like each of you. Work, career, possessions – they count for nothing in the end. The greatest gift I received in my life has been the privilege of being your father. I had so much I wanted to impart to you but I needed a way to become someone you would listen to. That's why I invented Damien."

Mark asked for the compass and tipped all the Scrabble tiles onto the centre of the table. "There are more messages in the compass than you imagined." Mark rummaged through the tiles placing them all face up. "Help me form, true north od das veils." After a minute it was laid out in front of them. "Do you remember when Damien wrote to you saying that the compass could reveal the answer to the question that had been nagging at you right from the beginning?"

Joshua nodded; he was intrigued.

Mark continued enthusiastically. "The nagging question was: Who is Damien Drost? The compass had the answer. You had the clues right from the beginning."

Joshua looked unconvinced but Mark began rearranging the letters in front of them. Within a minute, TRUE NORTH OD DAS VEILS had morphed into TRUE NORTH IS DADS LOVE.

Joshua was in awe as Mark continued. "If you had discovered that, OD DAS VEILS was an anagram for, IS DADS LOVE, then you might have wondered if Damien's name was also an anagram."

"What about the second inscription, MARK TRUE NORTH? Is that also an anagram?"

"No, but you once wrote to Damien stating that the compass will be an heirloom – it already is. My father gave the compass to me with both inscriptions inside. That's a story for another time though, not tonight."

"So the compass belonged to your father?"

"Yes. Now it's yours. He gave it to me to teach a similar lesson – a lesson I almost forgot until it was too late."

Mark produced a miniature screw driver from his pocket. He picked up the compass, popped the secret compartment, and retrieved the folded piece of paper.

"Go ahead and read it."

"There's no point. I never did finish the statement."

Mark smiled. "I know, but read it now."

Joshua carefully unfolded the sheet and nodded as he read. "The Joshua Principle: Who we become is the true measure of everything we do."

"Joshua, this is how you maintain your course – alignment of values with direction. It's how you ensure balance in your life, by constantly assessing who you are becoming as you pursue what you think you want."

Joshua was completely blown away. "But how..."

"I made the switch on the night your mother and I came for dinner, before I went overseas. Remember the last clue? *The answer is already with you, think true north.* All you had to do in the last few months was look inside the compartment again."

Joshua thought back to all the times he had handled the compass, opening and closing the lid, rotating the body to align the heading with the needle. It had never occurred to him to open the secret compartment again and check the piece of paper.

Mark continued. "The real value of everything we do is determined by who we become."

Joshua heard the words as if they came from Damien rather than his father. The two personas had coalesced before his very eyes.

"I had another clue. I think there was a quote you e-mailed to me."

"Yes, it was John Ruskin. He once said that the highest reward for a person's toil is not what they get for it but who they become by it. Who we become, not what we achieve, is the real measure for determining the worth of anything we do. You may not believe me but the past year has changed me just as much as it has transformed you."

Mark knew Joshua's mind was reeling and he needed to give his son time to process everything before moving on. "Son, there is one last important topic for us to discuss tonight but let's leave it until after we've eaten. For now, you can ask me anything concerning the logistics of making the last twelve months happen."

"What about the profile of Damien and the photograph on the German website?"

"All manufactured. The social networking profile was the easiest thing to organize. I pulled the photo from an Argentinian business networking site."

Mark explained how he had selected the hotel in Germany and the other complex elements within the veil of intrigue, all designed to throw Joshua off the scent. He also told him how it had taken months of effort and planning to organize, and that he had his doubts concerning the ethical nature of his deception. Mark explained that Clare had serious reservations when she became aware of what was going on, and it had taken weeks for her to reluctantly accept it.

They discussed much and after they finished their meal Joshua presented his father with the gift that he had meticulously created for Damien. Mark removed the wrapping and stared at the cover of the book.

The Wisdom of Damien Drost

A Protégé's Anthology by
Joshua Peters

Mark marveled at the surreal experience of leafing through pages containing his own wisdom. He found it humbling and overwhelming. He hugged his son as he struggled to gather himself. Mark knew it was time to give his final impartation and his eyes were still glazed with emotion when he spoke.

"Do you remember, at the very beginning, when I wrote to you explaining the role of a mentor? Back then, I told you that I would be called upon to give account of my investment in you, and that you would perhaps meet this person when our time together was complete."

"Yes, but that person is you – right?"

Mark picked up the compass again. "This was a talisman to me. The inscription, OD DAS VEILS, also means, God that is hidden. Doubt is the necessary companion to faith, but God is hidden only to those who choose not to seek. Personal faith is about relationship, not religion. That's my true north, and – "

"Dad, I'm not sure where you're going with this but – "

"It's okay son, we can discuss faith later – there is something else." There was an excruciating silence as Mark struggled to continue. "There's no easy way to tell you this. The reason I went to San Francisco was to see a specialist. I have advanced pancreatic cancer. I'm dying – I will soon meet my Mentor."

Joshua shook his head slowly in disbelief. "No. No!"

Mark motioned for his son to stop. "Life is short but, in you, I have discharged my debt. You have a great obligation. Promise me you'll live a life worthy of all that has been gifted and entrusted to you."

Joshua barely registered his father's words. Mark repeated them, adding one last exhortation.

"Promise me you'll make a difference."

Joshua could not speak but responded unequivocally. He embraced his father as never before. They said nothing, their relationship transcended mere words.

––––––––––––––––––––

It was raining heavily outside and the rhythmic din distracted Joshua's thoughts. He turned around to see the church was full. People were spilling out into the foyer and they were from all walks of life. Mark had obviously impacted more people than just those in the business world. Coming through the crowd was the face he had been searching for – it was Mandy. She had sent him a text message earlier, letting him know that she was having difficulty in finding somewhere to park.

Joshua went back amidst countless awkward smiles. He hugged Mandy and they held hands as they walked forward, sitting together in the front row beside Clare and Annie. Joshua stared at the casket. There was a floral wreath on top with six photos selected by family. He focused on the one he had chosen with its damaged frame; father and son in a small fishing boat. He closed his eyes, praying for the memory to usurp the ghostly images seared into his mind shortly before Mark's battle was over.

Mandy gently squeezed his hand as the minister walked to the lectern. He was Mark's friend as well as his pastor, and he celebrated the life and achievements of a man he loved and respected. Joshua became aware of how much he had missed during their years of estrangement.

Before long, it was time for him to deliver the eulogy. Joshua walked slowly to the lectern and looked to the front row where the three women he loved were smiling at him stoically. He breathed deeply and focused toward the back of the church, on those with whom there was the least connection. It was his strategy for keeping himself together.

"I first knew him as my dad, then as my father, and for a while we endured conflict. But I grew up and he became my mentor and then my best friend. Mark Peters was the person I loved and respected more than any other man in the world. No one gets to select their father but if by some miracle I had been able to choose mine, it would have been him above all other men."

Joshua paused. "Dad's favorite music artist was Keith Urban and he especially liked the track, Song For Dad. A line in the chorus goes something like: If someone says they wish they'd met my dad, I just smile and say – you already have." He blinked back tears as his voice quavered. "So much of him lives in Annie and me."

There was another long pause before he changed the tone. "Dad cared most about who he was, far more than the roles he played or the things he achieved. He lived the example of an authentic father, husband and leader. He made a difference in all of our lives here today. Dad taught me so much and, above everything else, he showed me the redemptive power of love, the importance of saying sorry and the freedom that resides in forgiveness."

Everyone wept as Joshua's speech continued. He finished with a quote from Mark's favorite philosopher, William Penn. "I shall pass through this life but once. Any good or kindness therefore that I can do, I shall do it now, without delay or neglect, for I shall not pass this way again."

The eulogy was the most difficult thing he had ever done – until now. He braced himself for the ordeal of carrying his father's casket. He marched, staring straight ahead, avoiding the faces that dimly mirrored his grief. He moved slowly, with anguished purpose, staying strong for just a little longer. Joshua had held his family together over the past few weeks. He had resolutely carried out his father's wishes, made innumerable phone calls, liaised with the church and funeral home, and prepared the eulogy. He delivered his father's casket to the hearse, seemingly without emotion.

Now he sat in the back of the limousine with Clare and Annie, the darkened windows shielding them from the outside world. His pain seemed overwhelming, and he collapsed emotionally in his mother's arms. As he recomposed himself during the slow journey, he gradually and strangely felt grateful. His father had loved him unconditionally, believed in him powerfully, and had imparted the ability to successfully make his own way through life. By the time they arrived at the cemetery, he felt a peace he could not rationally understand.

The rain had stopped and only the very closest of family and friends were there. The stark finality of the open grave was confronting, but they had all said their good-byes while Mark was alive and lucid. Before the morphine had dulled his senses, he had told his son the dramatic story of how his own father had intervened many years earlier, well before Joshua was even born. Joshua held the compass that was a talisman in changing three generations of fathers and sons. He gently closed the lid and slipped the treasured object away. A final prayer was offered and the casket lowered.

The minister and Mandy waited at a respectful distance as everyone else returned to their vehicles. Only Clare, Annie and Joshua remained at the graveside. Joshua reached into his coat pocket and retrieved a copy of the headstone message they had agreed on together the previous night. He read the words out loud as their final goodbye. It included The Joshua Principle, just as Mark had requested.

Mark John Peters
Husband — Father — Mentor
Loved his family and made a difference
"Who we become is the real measure of everything we do"
Loved and treasured always by Clare, Annie and Joshua

Annie and Clare reluctantly sprinkled dirt into the grave and Joshua released the sheet of paper and watched it flutter down like an autumn leaf to the lid of the casket. They held hands as they labored up the hill, each silently reflecting on the man they loved so deeply and differently. Mandy met them and they all hugged and wept. Joshua walked with her before returning to his mother and sister in their limousine.

He sat in the front passenger seat and closed the door. Joshua saw that Annie was reading a letter, tears rolling down her cheeks. The driver turned to him and spoke in a soft dignified voice.

"Your father also instructed us to give you an envelope."

Joshua looked to his mother in the back – she nodded and smiled, blinking back tears. He faced the front, opened it and then unfolded the single sheet of paper within. He slowly read his father's hand written letter. It finished with the question that Mark had wanted to ask on the night at the restaurant when he revealed everything. Joshua opened the door and stood outside alone.

Grief and gratefulness; the paradox of love, he thought. The storm clouds were retreating and the sun was breaking through.

He looked up and whispered. "RSVP – yes." Joshua would never walk alone. The Mentor was pleased.

— The End —

Epilogue: Truth within the Tale and Free Resources

Joshua's personal and professional development was intensely condensed, and your journey will be different. All progress is nevertheless the result of an individual's decision to alter attitudes and actions. Things tend to change, for the better, only when we do. Make a difference by changing your own life to become the person worthy of the success you seek. The life changing story of Joshua Peters can become your own. His gift to his mentor is in the Appendix which follows.

This book is not autobiographical. The story and all characters are fictional, but the lessons draw on proven truths and real life experience. A complete epilogue is available on the RSVPselling.com website, where you can get to know Tony Hughes and discover how his definitions of two words helped him survive a plane crash. Read also how he overcame personal tragedy and adversity in pursuing a successful career in professional selling.

As an owner of this book, you have free access to the Sales Aptitude Test for Professional Selling. It is available on the website which also contains a bibliography (recommended reading) and summary information of the RSVP principles. The Opportunity Qualification Tool is also available on the website at no charge, along with other valuable aids for sales people and sales managers. Go to rsvpselling.com and explore.

It is a condition of purchase that you observe copyright and do not lend your book nor divulge website passwords. Live the law of reciprocity; if you feel that this book can help others then buy them a copy as a gift or direct them to the website so they can make the purchase themselves. Books are easy to order and can be personally addressed and mailed to anyone you choose; simply go to RSVPselling.com and follow the links.

Appendix: Sales Mastery

Success in Professional Selling

We all need to sell our ideas and positively influence others. Selling is, therefore, a form of communication and a fundamental life skill. The ability to sell is especially important in leadership and business. Failure to sell creates the most severe problem an enterprise can face – lack of revenue. Almost every commercial problem is manageable, except terminally low revenue. Cost-cutting initiatives inevitably move an enterprise into negative momentum, and sustained lack of revenue is always fatal. Sales people are therefore essential in driving the health of most organizations by providing the revenue needed to employ those in manufacturing, logistics, services, support, finance and administration.

Success in professional selling is dependent on operating in viable markets and being able to offer uniquely differentiated value. There can be no success without these two mandatory elements. On this foundation the sales person can succeed only if they build good relationships providing accurate understanding of the customer's requirements and the competitive landscape. The next step is developing strategy for aligning with the political power-base, creating genuine customer value, and dealing with the competition. Finally, the sales person must understand and align to the customer's selection and buying process.

Whether selling products, services or solutions, all professional sales people must be competent in developing and managing relationships. Beyond this, however, the sales person's value is defined by the level at which they operate. The three categories are: transactional/relationship, transactional/tactical or genuinely strategic. This is highlighted on the Value Quadrant for Professional Sales Agents© on the RSVPselling.com website. Relationship sellers usually regard themselves as responsive and service orientated but their behavior often manifests as 'professional visitor', often with 'sir-lunch-a-lot' entertainment expenses. At the low end of this category they are usually trapped in ineffective relationships and function as market messengers reactively responding to existing demand. Tactical sellers operate effectively in competing against the opposition, and they are sometimes characterized as hunters or warriors. Transactional sales people, regardless of whether they have a relationship or tactical bias, are rarely strategic in how they operate.

Strategic sales people, on the other hand, are driven to create value for both customer and seller. They identify significant problems and opportunities, and engineer genuine business value by engaging early at the highest levels within an organization. Strategic sales people leverage strong relationships by aligning to winning agendas and political power. They ask insightful questions and avoid talking too much. Strategic sales people are best characterized as engineers, working with the customer to create a mutually beneficial bias in the requirements. They also ensure they have a balanced pipeline of medium sized short-term deals and large strategic opportunities.

The best sales professionals prioritize activities so as to be effective and avoid the busy fool syndrome by understanding the difference between what is urgent versus the truly important. They are tactically excellent in execution and strategically effective in their positioning and creation of differentiating value. Good strategy is always dependent upon positive relationships for execution. Understanding people and managing their unique needs is, therefore, essential for selling at the most basic level. For this reason, the first principle of RSVPselling™ is focused on how to powerfully interact with others.

RSVPselling™ – be fully there, pay attention and execute with excellence!

No strategy can succeed without competent execution. Success demands that you pay attention and be fully engaged. Decide to be there now, and somewhere else later. Don't allow your mind to leave a meeting while your body is present. The seller must be fully there and focused exclusively on the buyer's needs and preferred method of communication. When you RSVP, you are committing to being there for them, completely focused on their concerns, agendas, problems, and opportunities. Be masterful at building rapport, developing trust and gaining accurate understanding. Execute well and be fully committed in all that you do.

Understanding Difference

Building rapport despite difference is essential because people buy from those they like and trust. Understanding the sources of difference and how they manifest in communication variables is essential, but this knowledge must never be used to manipulate. In addition to self-image and world view derived from upbringing and culture, every individual embodies a unique blend of variables determined by their personality and brain wiring. These factors need to be addressed, and potential barriers to communication eliminated, in order to effectively and rapidly connect with different people.

Personality types: The four primary personality traits were identified by Hippocrates in approximately 400BC. Although there have been dozens of derivations, his insights have remained valid over the past 2,500 years. We are all a variable combination of choleric (driver), melancholy (analytic), sanguine (expressive), and phlegmatic (amiable). Every person's unique blend of these traits can have both positive and negative aspects. A person's personality is most easily identified when they are stressed or threatened.

Personalities in Business – Summary

Positive Indicators			
Driver	**Analytic**	**Expressive**	**Amiable**
Competitive, forceful, tenacious, decisive, confident, outspoken leader, efficient, risk-taker, optimistic, positive	Considerate, loyal, deep, respectful, sensitive, thoughtful, detailed, organized, punctual, idealistic	Passionate, playful, extroverted, animated, party, fun, popular, talker, bouncy, lively, social, spontaneous	Conservative, shy, friendly, mediator, balanced, listener, controlled, tolerant, flexible, diplomatic
Negative Indicators			
Driver	**Analytic**	**Expressive**	**Amiable**
Impatient, bossy, rude, stubborn, offensive, unsympathetic, pushy, intolerant, domineering, rash, short-tempered, argumentative, bully	Skeptical, superior, brooding, pessimistic, withdrawn, loner, unforgiving, fussy, judgmental, moody, manipulative, arrogant	Self-absorbed, loud, contradictory, messy, attention-seeking, naive, forgetful, late, unorganized, scattered, temperamental	Hesitant, lazy, slow, unmotivated, fearful, pessimistic, aimless, doubtful, indifferent, delays, indecisive, resentful, victim

Brain dominance: Left brain or right brain dominance may be associated with personality traits but regardless, the following functions are predominantly managed and executed by the alternate hemispheres of the brain.

Left Brain Functions	Right Brain Functions
Logic, reasoning, speech, language, sequencing, organization, practical, details, concrete concepts	Imagination, spatial, feelings, emotions, concepts, intuition, non-verbal, shapes and patterns, abstract concepts

Men perform the functions of language and speech almost exclusively on the left side of their brain and their emotions are managed by the right side. Women, on the other hand, tend to deal with words and emotions equally on both sides of the brain.

Learning and communication preference: In addition to personality traits, every person has a preferred mode of learning and communication. The three designations are visual, auditory, or kinesthetic (tactile). Everyone absorbs and retains information best through either seeing, hearing, or engaging in tactile interactions. Utilizing combinations of the senses is best for ensuring effective learning.

Values and cultural difference: These are determined from family, social, cultural or religious background. Good manners vary according to culture but are nonetheless the prerequisite for bridging a cultural divide. Politeness must be immediately followed by a genuine desire for understanding through listening. Take the time to educate yourself and avoid cultural gaffs. The use of tissues versus handkerchiefs, chewing and table manners, the practice of spitting, the treatment of a business card; these are all examples of obvious potential difference. Choose to suspend judgment and focus on understanding and developing areas of commonality. See the Sales Mastery tab in member's section of the RSVPselling.com website for tips on bridging cultural gaps.

Other factors: Gender differences should also be considered. See the RSVPselling.com website for further information.

Rapid Rapport and Removing Communication Barriers

It is essential to communicate in the preferred mode of the other person, avoiding behaviors that create points of difference. All of the variables can be daunting, yet those who have mastered the science and art of professional selling adapt to their environment after rapidly identifying what others need from them. Regardless of the hidden complexities of human interaction and the combination of variables at play, there are simple behaviors enabling you to avoid communication barriers and instead rapidly build rapport. All of the following should become standard intuitive practice for any sales professional or leader.

Behavior	Purpose
Have a firm, warm and friendly handshake with positive eye contact (friendly, not intense)	Meets the needs of leaders, amiable and kinesthetic (touchy-feely) people
Smile and ensure congruent body language, painting word pictures through examples	Meets the needs of right brain, expressive, and visual people
Use accurate and thoughtful language while talking at an appropriate pace and tone (for most people, this means talking lower and slower)	Meets the needs of left brain, analytic, and auditory people. Helps when the other person has a culturally and linguistically diverse/different background
Listen to understand and ask insightful questions. Focus completely on them and their needs, and exhibit good manners	Meets the needs of drivers, and those from a culturally and linguistically diverse/different background (English as a second language)
Dress like them, and avoid distracting jewelry or inappropriate clothing. For women, no short skirts or gaping cleavage	Enables them to focus on the value you offer, rather than being distracted by the way you dress or appear

Behaviors must be motivated by a genuine desire to meet the other person's communication needs, without any form of manipulation. All of the above should be manifest, at all times, if you are to eliminate the risk of offence and, instead, successfully create rapport when first meeting.

Another way of subconsciously connecting is simply to mirror the other person in their language, intensity, and body language, but do so with caution as, if detected, it can be perceived negatively.

Once people get to know each other, and trust and understanding have been established, difference can then become something that is valued. In addition to all of this, individuals have agendas that also need to be understood.

Understanding Personal Agendas

Every organization is a collective of uniquely different people who have their own personal needs, priorities and agendas. Ideally, these should be aligned with the organization, but this is not always the case. Internal politics, restructuring, takeovers, retrenchments and career changes are common. Honoring the law of self-interest is important. A person in the buying centre or power-base of an organization may be in either a negative/conservative mode or a positive/ambitious mode. The motivations of individuals in either of these positive or negative modes are as follows:

Negative or Conservative Agenda		Positive or Ambitious Agenda
Protect their position or reputation	or	Look good. Be a leader or hero
Avoid mistakes and maintain control	or	Receive recognition or promotion
Avoid conflict	or	Be an agent of change
Save money or reduce costs	or	Improve revenues or productivity

An individual does not function in a vacuum. They are part of an organization that will have certain business drivers that influence all decisions. Success in strategic selling demands understanding of personal agendas and corporate drivers.

Aligning with Business Drivers

Every commercial enterprise is driven by a need to increase profit, and most government organizations are driven by a desire to improve service through efficiency and effectiveness. Ideally, these outcomes are achieved without increasing costs or exposure to unacceptable risk. In essence, there is a universal desire to achieve more with less and any proposal or business-case should focus on greater output (or more revenue) from existing resources (achieving greater productivity), or less cost or effort (resulting in better efficiency).

The pace of business (decision urgency and priority) is determined by the organization's operating mode, and it is vitally important to understand which mode is in operation when seeking to influence a purchasing decision. When a business is in growth or survival mode, decisions are made rapidly. When in maintenance mode (even keel or business-as-usual), decisions are usually made slowly. A business in maintenance mode will typically make slow decisions based upon incremental improvements in productivity and profit while also reducing costs. When dealing with a business in maintenance mode it can be difficult to identify specific drivers and obtain decisions. By contrast, a business in growth mode will make decisions rapidly, and the business drivers will usually be productivity and profit. A business in survival mode has its own unique requirements and although it also makes fast decisions, the business drivers are to reduce direct variable costs and improve cash flow (not to be confused with profit).

The mix of variables can be quite complex as individual differences and agendas combine with corporate drivers and modes of operation. But there is another element of complexity – politics operate in every organization.

Working with Organizational Politics

Human beings are political by nature and politics pervades every organization in the form of an invisible power structure not apparent in an organizational chart. It is impossible to avoid politics when dealing with a group of people with competing agendas or differing opinions. Political tensions are the result of individual needs and agendas being misaligned with organizational structures and business drivers. Although political factors are an unavoidable reality, they should be embraced in a positive and thoughtful manner by aligning with the right people and winning agendas.

When seeking to influence the decision process within an organization, you must first understand the political power structure as it overlays on the formal organization chart. The first group of people to consider may be described as 'The Buying Centre', the group of people that make recommendations for a purchasing decision. Everyone in the buying centre needs to be covered during the sales process, but a recommendation can be stymied or vetoed by the economic decision maker or senior person in the power-base. The power-base is highly political in nature, transcending the boundaries of the organizational chart and not fully visible to outsiders. There is almost always a senior person within the power-base, operating in the background as the 'puppet master'. This person can be difficult to identify within an organization and resists engaging directly with sales people. They often, but not always, have a predetermined outcome in mind when running a procurement process.

Government entities are particularly risk-averse and influenced by politics as individuals seek to manage perceptions of success and performance while delivering outcomes in complex, consensus-driven environments. Whether dealing with corporate or government entities, the very best sales people do their research and take the necessary time and effort to understand human agendas and political power in planning sales strategies. All of this can be addressed and leveraged with integrity. Manipulation and subterfuge have no place in modern professional selling. The best way to avoid relationship errors or political misalignment during a sales campaign is to start at the very top and then be sponsored and coached by the leader as you work down in the organization.

Trust: The First Transaction in Every Sale

Individuals make purchasing decisions, and they buy from those they like and trust. Trust must therefore be the first transaction in every sale. Trust goes beyond mere rapport and is built on genuine understanding and common values. The sales person must invest time and energy in gaining, and then demonstrating, an understanding of the customer's environment and needs. Failing to do the necessary homework before a meeting is a guaranteed way to damage trust and rapport. Recognized capability and positive reputation are also essential in earning the right to ask insightful questions which is the most powerful form of influence.

$$T = (U + SV) \times (C + R)$$

Trust = (Understanding + Shared Values) x (Capability + Reputation)

Leading sales professionals focus on gaining understanding and insight rather than pushing features and benefits. They frame what they have to say as thoughtful open questions. They are committed to working the sales process in the best interests of all concerned, and avoid trust-destroying rhetorical questions which are usually perceived as manipulative or redundant. Importantly, we learn nothing while talking, and a sales person's verbosity actually damages the process of gaining understanding and building trust. Strive to talk no more than one-third of the time when engaging with a senior executive.

Belief and Integrity

At the most basic level, selling is the transference of belief. Enduring success in the sales profession is built on belief in yourself, your solution and the corporation you represent. Without sincere belief and integrity in the sales process, trust cannot be established and maintained with the buyer. Sales process integrity means being committed to a methodology for truly understanding what will make the buyer completely satisfied, and establishing whether there is mutual benefit in doing business together. In this paradigm, the sales person never asks for the business prematurely or makes wrong assumptions concerning the real value of features or functions.

High achievers project sincere belief in what they offer, yet they focus almost exclusively on the customer. Although they are self-aware, they are not self-absorbed. They understand the maxim that 'nobody cares how much you know until they know how much you care'. They genuinely convey that they are not there to sell (talk and push) but to fully understand the problems and needs of the prospective client. They want to hear what the client has to say. They want to know what's going on in the client's world. They want to understand the client's issues and how to best deliver specific business value for them. They achieve results through a values-based approach to building trust and solving problems. Clients are attracted to them because they earn trust and create value.

Opening

Initial interaction sets an agenda and is far more important than the closing phase. It is vitally important to establish a relationship of trust and value, as rapidly as possible, and articulate the business value on offer in a succinct manner. The sales person should therefore communicate positive intent and establish credibility through relevant evidenced-based examples that earn the right to ask insightful questions. The RSVPselling.com website contains examples.

When engaging with senior people, always be slightly early and show respect for their time. Provide context before detail and demonstrate insightful knowledge of the customer and their industry (domain expertise). Senior executives are always busy and easily distracted, so you only have a limited amount of time to engage effectively. Focus, therefore, on evidencing that you have done your homework and then get to the point. Mentioning features or functions of your product, service or solution will immediately brand you as a low level sales person. Instead, focus on the business outcomes that need to be delivered, understand the problems and implications, and act as a subject matter expert. Methodically ask intelligent questions designed to create understanding of the customer's operational environment, business drivers, required outcomes, power-base and decision-making processes.

Qualification

You cannot sell to someone who is unable to buy. As self-evident as that may be, many sales people waste precious time with people who cannot make buying decisions. Qualification is the process of establishing whether it is possible to conduct mutually beneficial business and whether there is a high probability of winning if you choose to invest in a sales process. It is essential to focus on fewer well qualified opportunities where there is a high likelihood of success through The New ROI ©.

Successful sales people actually disqualify prospective buyers based on whether there is a serious or compelling problem (or opportunity) that has the necessary funding for resolution (or realization), and with the seller's product or service being an ideal fit. The best sales people understand that there is no shortage of qualified prospects, there is just a shortage of time and available resources to invest in the right opportunities. They operate efficiently and do not waste their time, energy or resources on people or organizations they cannot genuinely help or where they cannot reasonably expect to win. They accept that not everyone is a prospect.

Poor qualification of prospective business is the most common, and most expensive, mistake made by sales organizations. Invest only where you have a high likelihood of success through differentiating influence with the customer. To be strategic you usually have to be there first. Qualification questions and a free RSVP Opportunity Qualification Tool © can be found on the RSVPselling.com website.

Objections and Closing

An objection is an indication of resistance or misunderstanding. In modern enterprise solution selling, objections are evidence of mistakes by the sales person. They are caused by attempting to close the sale prematurely or by positioning features that are not linked to genuine business value. Positioning features and benefits without aligning them to specific acknowledged business needs creates price concerns or the perception that what you offer is over-engineered.

In modern professional selling, the concept of 'closing' occurs right from initial contact. Closing is not an event at the end of the sales cycle, it's the process of negotiating mutual commitments at every stage of the customer's evaluation and buying process. Success is achieved through developing real trust, understanding, and then the buyer's attraction to genuine value. 'Closing' is therefore best redefined as 'confirming'. The best professional sales people are not interested in pushing or applying pressure, because it creates distrust and unproductive resistance. Instead, they concentrate on how they can offer the highest value and lowest risk, and they focus on securing agreement – confirmation – concerning the next steps in making a decision, and at the right time then finalizing the commercial arrangements.

Professional selling can be defined as the process of helping someone to make a buying decision that is in the best interests of all concerned. This paradigm of selling demands cooperation, understanding, trust, and alignment with the buyer's needs and processes. In this environment, the old-school concept of 'closing' is redundant. Concluding business becomes a natural next step rather than a point of risk for the sales person. Focus on understanding their requirements and processes rather than applying unproductive pressure.

Momentum and Discipline

Positive momentum is precious – it's difficult to create and easy to lose. Negative momentum, on the other hand, seems to happen all on its own but is actually the result of not paying attention or not methodically executing the necessary inputs required for consistent results.

To maintain momentum and avoid inconsistency in revenue performance, you must recognize that there is always a lag between inputs and results. Most sales people work very hard when their list of qualified prospects is thin or sales are sub-optimal, but as their pipeline improves and sales come in they then tend to neglect pipeline development. They usually justify this neglect by rationalizing that there is not enough

time to also work existing opportunities. But as sure as night follows day, poor revenue results follow low prospecting and pipeline development activity. The people who
suffer from these ups and downs usually alternate between feelings of confidence and
panic throughout their sales year.

The key to consistent results is consistently engaging in prospecting and pipeline
development activities, regardless of the demands of current qualified opportunities.
Successful sales people measure these inputs and manage their activity levels accordingly. Every industry is unique yet there will be proven metrics for the required
rates of cold calling, referrals, appointments, presentations, proposals, and other key
activities. Understand the specific activity levels for your own industry and habitually
honor the law of momentum by having a disciplined work ethic.

It is essential to have a balanced pipeline of qualified prospects for short term, and
significant long term opportunities. There should be a minimum of three times quota
in qualified prospects, and achieving budget should not be dependent upon the largest deal alone. Continue with pipeline development activities regardless of how good
current sales appear to be, and despite how busy you are with current prospects.
An abundant pipeline provides the luxury of choice in where you invest your time and
resources.

Definitions for Sales Professionals

Benefit: Something that solves a specific and acknowledged customer problem; or
something that addresses a specific and acknowledged opportunity for the customer.
The features of your product, service or solution are not benefits. All benefits are
quantifiable in monetary or other terms. They save time or create tangible efficiency;
they reduce costs or create revenue and profit; or they create feelings of comfort and
reduce perceived risk.

Business Value = Benefit less Cost. $$BV = B - C$$

Confidence: The feeling you have before understanding the situation. Confidence is
the paradise of fools. Paranoid optimism is a preferred state.

Objection: Evidence of the seller's mistake in seeking to close prematurely, or wrongly positioning features as benefits.

Risk: 1) Not knowing what it is that you do not know. 2) Any potentially negative force outside your control. 3) Your boss or other senior executive who wants to meet your prospect but who has a big ego or does not listen. 4) Software or technology demonstrations. 5) Reference customers. 6) Desperate competitors.

Strategic Enterprise Selling: The process of engaging early at the most senior level, and aligning with political and economic power, in addressing the most serious problems or opportunities. Solutions are designed with unique compelling value while setting an agenda that disadvantages or eliminates competitors.

Transactional Relationship Selling: Building relationships of genuine rapport and trust for the purpose of gaining information and support for a buying decision that is in the best interests of all concerned. The sale is achieved through the transference of belief with emotion, and supported logically with facts and evidence.

Trust: Trust must be the first transaction in every sale.

$$T = (U + SV) \times (C + R)$$

Trust = (Understanding + Shared Values) x (Capability + Reputation)

Value For Money: Value is always defined by the customer.

$$VFM = \frac{FFP + LRP}{TCO}$$

Value For Money = Fit For Purpose + Lowest Risk Profile divided by Total Cost of Ownership.

The Seven Sins of Selling

The sales industry has historically promoted certain behaviors that in today's market can actually damage the chances of success. Assertiveness is often interpreted by prospective purchasers as unwanted aggression. Persistence can translate into being annoying. Positive questions from the seller are usually perceived as rhetorical and manipulative. Focusing on features, often triggers concerns with price or suggests that the seller is just not listening. The stark reality of selling is that pushing creates resistance, and aggression creates defensiveness. We all prefer to buy rather than being 'sold'.

Although most sales people intellectually accept these truths, defects nevertheless pervade most aspects of their engagement. Knowledge and beliefs do not always manifest in positive behaviors and actions. Here are the seven pitfalls of selling, to be avoided at all costs. Aspire to embody the antithesis of these seven sins.

1: 'Selling is the transference of information'. No. Selling is actually building trust and transferring belief. Information can easily be sourced by customers without the assistance of a sales person who should actually serve to filter and distil the mass of available data down to what is relevant and benefits the client. Facts merely serve to support an emotional decision to buy from someone they like and trust. Emotion creates more influence than information.

2: 'Talking is the best way to influence'. Only if your goal is to bore people into submission or negatively push them to your competitor. Words account for only 7% of received communication. People think at approximately 500 words per minute and you can only talk effectively at 125 per minute. You must engage the other person visually with positive and congruent body language or they will tune out. Effective communication means asking insightful questions and actively listening to clarify your understanding and get to the deeper meaning. Listening rather than talking is actually the best way to influence.

3: 'Features are benefits'. Not necessarily. Benefits must specifically solve acknowledged problems relating ultimately to time, money, comfort or risk. Prattling on about spurious features early in the sales process creates distracting noise and potential price concerns, preventing the buyer from focusing on the real value you offer in meeting their business needs.

4: 'Objections are opportunities'. Not so. Objections actually indicate that the sales person has sought to close prematurely or that they do not fully understand the needs of the buyer. Objections are not buying signals nor are they opportunities to close. Yes, objections need to be overcome when raised, but they are usually generated by amateurs. It is always better to avoid objections by first having them expressed by the client as problems before any attempt to close. Only seek commitment once you have complete understanding and the buyer's readiness to purchase has been confirmed.

5: 'The product is the product'. Not really. Selling the product, service or solution is the third and final sale in any engagement. The prospective client first needs to be sold on your worthiness (credibility) for investing their time and effort. The next thing they need to establish is trust in you and your organization. Can they actually trust you with the information you are requesting and can they trust you to competently and ethically make recommendations in their best interests? If the first two sales are made, then selling the product, service or solution becomes very achievable, once you have aligned with their buying criteria and their procurement process. The product is problem resolution, through the sales person, and the buyer will engage effectively once corporate credibility and personal trust has been established.

6: Skill and knowledge define value and success. Although these are important prerequisites, the real differentiator is positive attitude and ability to influence. Knowledge and qualifications can easily create alienating arrogance and pride. People don't care about what you know; they care about what you can do for them. This is why having a positive attitude and proven ability to deliver is crucial.

7: 'Success is just a numbers game'. Work ethic is important, and understanding the required activity levels for building and maintaining a sales funnel is essential, yet the mediocre focus on being efficient in the least important activities. Be effective and avoid the busy fool syndrome. This means doing the right things, with the right people, at the right time. Understand and honor the required activity levels for a healthy pipeline, but recognize that to progress a prospect to becoming a customer, it is not about numbers – it's all about people, process and strategy.

Ten Laws of Relationship Selling

1. People buy from those they like and trust. Corporations do not buy, rather, individuals do so from those they like and trust. Trust is built through shared values and genuine understanding. Do your homework and be a domain expert by truly understanding the customer's industry and your market. Applying unwanted pressure and closing prematurely is a mistake. Anything that damages trust and understanding is to be avoided.

2. People buy with their emotions and justify decisions with logic and facts. Selling is the transference of emotion and belief supported by logic and evidence. Factual information supports rather than drives the decision to buy.

3. Listening is the most powerful form of influence. You learn nothing while talking. Listen and ask insightful questions. Talk no more than one-third of the time. People are best convinced by reasons they themselves discover.

4. You cannot sell to someone who is unable to buy. Unless someone has a problem and the necessary money and the authority to commit, they are not a prospective customer. Your time is a precious finite resource; do not waste it.

5. People always act in their own best interests. Regardless of what a person tells you, trust only what is in their best interests. Thoughtfully validate and test commitments made to you or your corporation.

6. Features are not benefits. Product or service features will never win the deal but can eliminate you, often without you knowing. Features are only benefits if they solve the customer's specific acknowledged problems. Over-emphasis on features can create unnecessary objections and concerns with price or the complexity and risk of implementation and ownership. Avoid PPS – Premature Presentation Syndrome.

7. The product is not the product. The product is the outcome that is achieved when buying the product, service or solution. In addition to this, the sales person, their team, methodologies and ability to deliver are essential elements of any solution.

8. Problem solving comes before solution selling. The size of the problem determines the size of the opportunity, and price is only relevant if the customer wants what you are offering. Focus on creating value through delivering the best outcomes with the lowest risk. Never discuss price before agreeing value. Price should be no more than one-third of the equation in the buyer's mind rather than the predominant determining factor.

9. A sale is only a sale when you have irreversible commitment. Verbal commitments can easily evaporate and letters of intent are not binding. Signed contracts and purchase orders are good but it is only when you have a client's money in your bank account that a sale has been truly achieved. They are only a valid customer when they have realized the business benefits of your product, solution or service.

10. Attitude is everything. The selling profession is among the most difficult of careers. This is because it is highly demanding emotionally and intellectually. Success requires the solid foundation of positive attitude, self-belief, and adaptability; all combined with competence in execution and disciplined work ethic. Lasting success is always limited to the worthiness of the sales person as defined by their skill, values, habits and attitudes. Value for employer and customer is defined by your ability to positively influence and deliver results. Embrace challenges and difficulties because they create a barrier of entry to your sales competition, internally and externally. Scarcity creates value, and there are very few masterful sales professionals. If success in your environment was easy, it would not be as rewarding or lucrative.

Although these ten laws relate to tactical and relationship selling, they nevertheless also apply to strategic enterprise selling. There are however additional considerations as the complexity of the sale increases. The techniques and behaviors that work in simple relationship selling can actually damage the chances of success in large complex sales environments. Very senior relationships and dealing with complexity is what largely defines the need to be strategic. In large complex enterprise selling, having no strategy equates to having little chance of winning. Here are the additional laws of selling when seeking to operate strategically.

Ten Laws of Strategic Selling

1. Gather all necessary intelligence before formulating strategy. Never act without thinking and assessing all of the available accurate information. A strategy is only as good as the information that leads to it. Being an excellent climber is of no benefit if your ladder is leaning against the wrong wall.

2. Be first and set the agenda. Being strategic is best achieved by being there first and setting the agenda with the senior stakeholder. Truly understand the organizational dynamics and winning agendas aligned to the biggest problems or opportunities. Being there first enables you to influence the requirements toward your own unique value and disadvantage the competition.

3. Start high in the account and be a domain expert business person. You will always be delegated to people you sound like. Be a business person rather than a sales person by discussing their industry and business challenges and opportunities. Be equipped to discuss how your organization has helped others to overcome similar challenges or realize significant opportunities. Have proof of your claims. Avoid discussing features and functions of products, services or solutions.

4. Find and influence the 'puppet master'. This will be a senior person in the background who seeks to avoid meeting with sales people. They will only engage if they believe you have something of value to them personally. Initial influence or establishing credibility can often be achieved indirectly through third-parties.

5. Understand the informal power-base and politics. The organizational chart can be misleading and it is essential to understand the power-base and influence-dynamics that transcend the visible structure. Align your value with serious problems, important outcomes and winning agendas. Solutions must be embedded in the customer's business processes.

6. Align to serious problems, significant opportunities and winning agendas. The only person who can call it a solution is the customer. Problem solving must occur before solution selling, and the size of the customer's purchase order is directly linked to the size of the problem being solved or the opportunity being addressed. Understand the business case and real value of investing in your product, service or solution. Never discuss price before agreeing value. The buyer is the only person who can really quantify the value.

7. Think before acting and be patient and strategic. Tactical mistakes can usually be recovered but strategic errors are often fatal. Never be afraid of waiting and always be willing to invest in gathering additional information. Do not confuse laziness, inaction or procrastination with being strategically patient. Be humble and seek advice while thinking through the potential consequences of actions. Only birds are good at 'winging it'.

8. Identify and manage risk. Bad new early is good news. Risk resides in what you cannot control, especially from ignorance. In the software industry, 90% of risk is in demonstrations and the other 90% of risk is in reference sites (not a typo – think about it). Across all industries, risk also resides in people and competitors. Anyone on your team afflicted by arrogance or an inability to listen represents enormous risk. Beware therefore of your own executives who seek to interact with your prospect because they can easily say something damaging or introduce unwanted information. Existing customers are the greatest potential sales resource if they act as positive references but they can easily be a liability in highlighting your deficiencies and this is often the case the lower you interact in an organization.

9. Anticipate competitor moves and set traps. Know your competition and their methods of operation so that you can constantly change the rules. Do not allow them to use your weaknesses against you. Instead set traps for them and ensure you have set an agenda focused on your unique value. Ensure the customer publicizes your winning selection early and widely therefore making it difficult for competitors to interfere once they deduce they've lost.

10. Confidence is the paradise of fools. Confidence is usually the feeling you have before you understand the situation. Avoid arrogance and complacency. Be positively paranoid (competitively aware) yet not defensive or cynical. Take nothing for granted and validate any assumptions. Respect the customer and their power of choice at all times. Never underestimate the competition or the way in which circumstances can alter through changes in personnel, market conditions, acquisitions, and a myriad of other factors.

Say Hello to Seymour

In strategic enterprise selling, the people most willing to meet with you are almost always the least important in the sales process. Unfortunately these people can ultimately impede success. They love F words – Features and Functions – and the occasional advantage. They look for features and functions that have some alignment to their requirements. Often these see-more people (Seymour) do not understand that the purpose of analysis is to make a decision. They are information gatherers not decision makers, and continually need to see more before they can make a recommendation.

Evaluators and recommenders are an unavoidable and integral part of any organization's buying process. They are to be embraced, not despised, yet they represent a risk for the sales organization. This is because they can say 'no' but cannot say 'yes'. They can exclude you due to non-compliance to technical or functional requirements yet they are disconnected from real power and can mislead concerning budget, timing, authority and process. Strategic sales professionals engineer Seymour's satisfaction yet transcend their station within the buying organization to engage with those driving and directing Seymour's efforts and activities.

Say Goodbye to Seymour and Meet C-Levels

The equation is simple; C-level people – Chief Executive Officers, Chief Information Officers, Chief Financial Controllers, Chief Operating Officers, etc. – do not want to deal with sales people. They delegate to their managers and technical people (Seymours). But managers and technical people are not the real decision makers, and they rarely understand the prerequisite business drivers, politics, and funding complexities within the organization. To sell at the top, rather than being delegated to Seymour, you must achieve political alignment to real power by observing the following:
  · Be a business person rather than a sales person
  · Talk the language of 'business outcomes'
  · Know their industry and business drivers
  · Understand their problems and opportunities
  · Have proof of business benefits with relevant reference sites
  · Never raise the topic of features or functions
  · Let them be in control (never attempt to manipulate)

- Be punctual, efficient and direct
- Insist on regular direct contact with the ultimate outcome owner

Powerful Sales Questions

After you have earned the right to do so through demonstrating credibility and value, active listening combined with asking open questions is the most powerful form of influence. When dealing with senior executives never use any form of manipulation. Outdated hook and tie-down questions are to be avoided at all times. Examples of these credibility destroying behaviors include: 'If I could show you how to improve your bottom line, is that something you would be interested in?' or 'If I can demonstrate that we can meet that requirement, would you be willing to buy from us?' These types of questions are closed and manipulative. When dealing with C-level executives allow them to feel in control. Here are some generically powerful questions for C-level interactions:

- I've done a fair amount of research for our meeting today but there are some questions I think only you can answer. May we cover a few of these now?
- What is really driving the need to make this kind of investment? What has to be delivered in terms of business outcomes, and where do you see the risks?
- Who are the most senior people affected by this project? How will they be impacted and what is their role in selecting and implementing a solution?
- You are very busy and have many people seeking meetings with you, so why did you agree to meet with me today?
- What is your process and timing for making a decision and having a solution in place?
- If we do business together, it is important for me to understand exactly what will make you 100% satisfied. What needs to happen for this business relationship to be successful in your eyes?
- The meeting today has been very useful, what would you like me to do next?

RSVPselling™ Summary

"All men can see these tactics whereby I conquer, but what none
can see is the strategy out of which victory is evolved."
Sun Tzu

RSVPselling™ is next generation selling, and professional selling for the next generation. It's business strategy as a way of thinking and excellence in execution. It's also a low overhead framework for commercial strategy and opportunity management anywhere and at any time, and can be implemented in a boardroom within an account plan or in a coffee shop on the back of a napkin.

RSVPselling™ is especially relevant today because although there are many good sales process tools and methodologies, they tend to demand substantial time investment with high levels of process discipline and documentation. This overhead may be appropriate for large and complex sales if underpinned with strong disciplined sales management, but following a methodology, no matter how thorough, does not necessarily equate to operating strategically and effectively. RSVPselling™ is a practical way of thinking strategically for every sales engagement and can be layered on top of any existing sales process methodology. If these four elements are addressed, then sales success can be achieved:

Relationships

Strategy

Value

Process

Thinking RSVP need not replace current methodologies or sales tools and is simply designed to enhance the way you think and operate. The RSVPselling™ process simply requires that some important questions be asked of the sales person:

- Relationships: Do you have positive relationships with the right people and are you aligned with political and economic power? Do these relationships deliver real influence and differentiating information?
- Strategy: Do you have effective strategy for managing key relationships and obtaining all necessary information, and for defeating the competition, and engineering the customer's requirements and process?
- Value: Do you offer unique value embedded in a compelling business case?
- Process: Do you truly understand the customer's process for evaluation, selection and procurement, including all points of risk? Do you have process alignment?

RSVP – Relationships and the New ROI

"The trick of earning trust is to avoid all tricks."
Gerald Weinberg

Strive for relationships of integrity because trust is essential in all business dealings. Invest however with those who represent genuine power, more than mere influence or support. Beware of being caught at the level of Seymour. Powerful business relationships must provide differentiating insight and alignment with positive political and economic power.

Every buyer seeks Return On Investment (ROI) from a purchasing decision, but the seller also makes an investment in the sales process. In complex solution selling, the costs are substantial. The sales organization, therefore, needs their ROI but to obtain their return on the selling investment, they must first have Relationships Of Intelligence, Integrity and Influence within the buying entity – this is The New ROI ©. A Sales Master understands that ROI needs to be reciprocated with relationships of integrity with those who honor their word, and provide accurate, insightful, differentiating information.

Sales success at any level depends on positive relationships because customers buy from those they like and trust. Relationships with the right people can compensate for many short-comings, yet strategic sales people do not rely on relationships alone. Although a Seymour type of person may provide useful feed-back and coaching concerning how you need to position and price your product or service, do not rely on or be trapped with mid-level relationships. There is no substitute for starting at the highest level possible. Diligent research, planning and alignment with genuine political power is essential. When considering the issue of relationships, also ask yourself these questions:
 · Do I know all the people in the customer's power-base?
 · Who are the influencers, recommenders and decision makers?
 · Do I know the puppet master, the person pulling the strings in the background?
 · Do I know every person who has the power of veto?
 · Have I mapped my team to all the individuals in the buying-centre?
 · What relationships need to be established between my team and the customer's key people, and how are introductions and linkages best facilitated?

- Do I know every individual's buyer type: economic, technical or business?
- Do I understand every individual's dominant personality traits, communication preferences, political agendas, decision drivers, and risk versus opportunity mind-set?
- What relationships do my competitors have within the account?
- Who influences the customer externally in the form of analysts or consultants?
- What other companies are respected and watched by my customer and do these organizations use my competitors? If so, how successfully?
- What reference site relationships should be developed or prepared?

The best way to map and strategize an opportunity is to draw the organizational chart identifying the buying centre (all the people who have a say in the selection and recommendation process), and then overlay the power-base, which are the people with power of veto and who own the business outcome and funding. What recommendation from the evaluation team is most likely to be approved by the real decision makers? Who is really leading and engineering the selection outcome within the buying organization?

RSVP – Strategy

A strategy is only as good as the information that leads to it, and is of no use unless you can execute effectively. Much of the risk in developing strategy comes from not being aware of what you do not know. The hallmark of great strategy is the obsessive gathering of relevant information, then fully considering the probable consequences of any potential action.

Based upon accurate intelligence, strategy must be formulated for managing key relationships, positioning unique and compelling value, and defeating the competition. When considering strategy ask yourself these questions:

- Do I have all necessary information and do I truly understand the decision drivers and business case?
- What is my relationship strategy and am I personally aligned with the real power-base – those who have genuine political and economic power?
- How will I engineer the customer's focus on our unique value and prove capability and lowest risk?
- Where will I position price to leave room to negotiate?

- Who and what is the competition and how will I position against them?
- Does the customer have an internal option (IT Department, etc.)?
- Does the customer have other projects competing for funding?
- Which of my competitors is engaged with the customer?
- How will my competitors seek to position against us and what are our comparative strengths and weaknesses?

Tactical mistakes can usually be corrected but strategic errors are usually fatal. Ensure you have all the information and that you run the various scenarios through in your mind and with your team before initiating pivotal actions. What outcome do you expect? How will the customer respond? How will competitors react? Thinking, rather than talking, is the most important activity in professional selling.

There are specific engagement options for dealing with competitive threats. Jim Holden and Keith Eades are two authors who have previously linked military strategy to professional selling, and the following four strategies should be considered:
- Head-to-head: You have product or brand strength and market leadership
- Change the rules: You need to alter the agenda or selection criteria
- Incremental: Focus on a small piece of business or coexist with competition
- Containment: Engineer a non-decision so you can re-engage later

Head to head. This is a direct or frontal strategy that works only if you have unequivocal product, service or solution strength with acknowledged market leadership. You use it when you are not afraid of 'slugging it out' against the competition because you have best brand, solution offering and market presence. Most sales people adopt this mode of engagement, and the competition's price is often their main point of concern. This strategy is attractive because it is simple but demands superiority at every level. To be effective with this strategy you must have clear leadership with product and reputation, with a well established and positive customer base. This superiority must be validated from the customer's point of view. Be careful with smaller customers who often associate product strength or market dominance with unnecessary functionality or service levels and excessively high pricing. If you are not the industry giant or leading niche specialist, consider the following strategy.

Change the rules. This guerrilla, indirect or flanking strategy is essential when you do not have the leading solution or leadership market position. This strategy is an ideal default position because it necessitates the gathering of information and forces you to search for unique value that matches the client's specific requirements. This strategy should always be employed when nothing about your product, corporation or industry presence gives you a compelling edge. This strategy is essential when you cannot succeed based on the current engagement rules or selection criteria, typically because you were not there first. For this strategy to succeed you must have strong personal relationships with senior influential members of the buying centre and power-base. Beware of fighting the good fight only to have a mystery senior executive veto the recommendation for your product, service or solution. Seymour types will often falsely give the impression they are embracing your strategy only to revert back to their original criteria at the last minute to placate the real decision maker up the line.

Competitive Engagement Flowchart

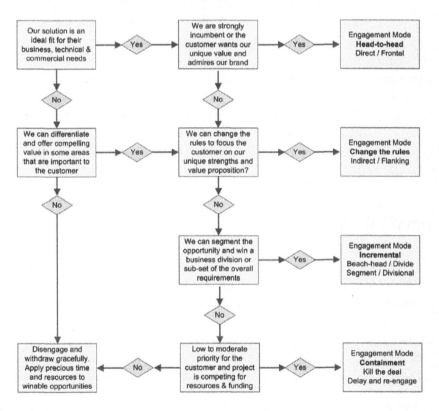

Incremental. This 'on the beach', divisional or departmental strategy can be part of changing the rules in a large opportunity. The goal is to establish a beach-head or divide and conquer the competition by securing a limited piece of business and support within the broader organization from which you can expand. This strategy should be employed when you cannot win the whole account but there is a worthwhile piece of business that will give you an internal reference and influence for larger decisions at a later time. It is also useful when you are not seeking to displace another vendor but rather enhance the customer site (or market) by providing a complementary solution or additional functionality not offered by the competitor. This strategy is also appropriate when you decide to coexist with the competition and temporarily share the account.

Containment. This kill the deal strategy is a valid option if you are certain you cannot win and your goal is to prevent someone else from taking the business. It is designed to delay the buyer so you can re-engage under new rules at a later time. Rather than seeking to change the basis for a buying decision, you work to have the decision itself postponed. This strategy is high risk and should be used with thoughtful caution because customers do not take kindly to anyone seeking to interfere with their procurement process. A containment strategy has two major problems: firstly, it can be perceived as negative interference; and secondly, it can force you to invest further in scoping studies, trials, pilots or other resource-intensive activities. This strategy needs positive senior relationships and time to execute. The focus needs to be on how deferring is in the buyer's best interests, and the message is ideally delivered by a credible third party.

RSVP – Value

Creating value is more important than articulating it. Value needs to pervade every aspect of your engagement with the buyer and be embedded within a strong business case. This ensures the necessary funding is secured without risk of competing projects diverting money or resources. Value creation, evidenced by a compelling business case, can only be achieved with intimate understanding of the customer's business through relationships at the right level that create, or uncover, value through solutions to serious problems or the ability to realize potential opportunities.

The goal of a professional sales person is therefore 'value creation' before 'value projection'. Once value is established, you can then focus on communicating your value proposition which must be unique and compelling. Understand, however, that value differentiation is what the seller needs to achieve but rarely what the buyer wants to hear about. Differentiation is nevertheless essential as the customer always has a choice of vendors from whom they can buy and who can do the job for them. Whether you are selling soap or semiconductors, widgets or ideas, products or services, bundled value or real solutions – your value proposition must be unique and compelling and seen by the competition as your unfair advantage. The solution must go beyond mere features of your product or service because the real problem is almost never uniquely solved by one particular product over another. Maybe the customer actually needs a reliable supply-chain, prompt service, effective change management, or something else. The product or service you sell is not a solution until it is fully aligned to addressing the real problems and delivering genuine business value.

Every product, service or solution is only worth what the market will pay for it. Your unique value proposition must therefore be focused on specific and tangible benefits for the customer, and directly linked to the resolution of their specific problems or opportunities – the bigger the better. Features do not necessarily equate to benefits or represent genuine value for the customer. The most powerful unique value propositions usually include your people and methodologies, not just your product and service. Government buyers assess value from a blend of functionality (fit for purpose) and perceived risk; price is then included in the equation to ultimately determine value for money.

Individuals and organizations universally seek best value and lowest risk. Apart from selling commodities, the cheapest product or solution is often perceived as higher risk and inferior value. Value is defined by the buyer, not the seller. Comparative perceptions are determinative. When seeking to identify and leverage your unique value, ask yourself the following:

- What do we offer that is of business value to the prospective customer, aligned to their specific needs and delivering tangible benefits?
- Is our product, service or solution part of a business case, and if so, what is it?
- How does the buyer prioritize projects, and are we aligned with the required return on investment, payback period or net present value calculation?
- Who and what is the competition, and what are our comparative strengths and weaknesses?
- What combination of our unique offering represents a compelling overall value

proposition compared with the competition?

· Product or service features enabling business benefits
· Service offerings that reduce risk and deliver business value
· Individual and team skills and proven domain expertise, industry knowledge and methodologies that assure successful delivery and cultural fit with the customer's organization
· Business model or geographic presence enabling lower risk or providing better efficiency

Strategic Pricing. Value is determined by the perceptions of the buyer, and price is only relevant if they actually want your product or service. A high price early in the process may disqualify you before you can sell value, and a low price may create perceptions of inferior quality. Early price positioning should therefore be high enough to reinforce your messages of quality but not so high that you could be eliminated prematurely. It is equally important to have a strategy for maximizing perceived value with relevant or unique features that make competing difficult for the competition. The amount of money available from the customer for purchasing a product or service is directly linked to the size of the problem or opportunity your solution addresses. You must solve big problems if you seek substantial purchase orders.

RSVP – Process

Rather than focusing on your sales process, understand the customer's timing and process for selection, negotiation, and procurement. It is usually unproductive and damaging to unnaturally seek to force the pace of business. Never assume that price or other incentives will change the customer's timing. Failure to fully understand the buying organization's processes automatically introduces serious risk and makes it almost impossible to forecast accurately.

Are you actually aligned to your customer's timing, decision drivers and processes for selection and procurement? The best approach is to understand the date that they need a solution implemented and then validate their commitment by asking what happens if the date slips or status quo prevails. Once you are certain the client is committed to a date for realizing benefits, identify everything that will need to occur to achieve the implementation deadline. Working backwards from this date, go through the list and create a time-line with critical dates for all milestones. Now you have a realistic date for when a purchase order or signed contract needs to be issued. Align to this timeframe rather than your own end of month, quarter or financial year-driven ambitions.

Work with your customer to understand and manage the risks, including whether they need to submit a business case or work through a convoluted process for approval and funding. They may need to adhere to an onerous procurement process. There may be critical reviews with steering committees, and there may be approvals required from senior management or at board level. There may also be interdependencies with other projects or initiatives. Once understanding of all this has been achieved, in partnership with your customer, then you are able to work with them to keep everything on track and adjust your strategy accordingly.

Every piece of business has a natural pace at which the selection and buying process needs to be fulfilled. Wise sales people ensure they have full understanding before forecasting when business will close. This means there are rarely surprises, just points of risk that can be managed with the customer. It avoids pressuring the buyer or creating unnecessary tension. Consider these questions when thinking about the customer's process:

- What happens if they do nothing and defer the decision?
- Is there a compelling event or a very strong driver for buying, and what is it?
- Are there external events that could impact the decision or timing?
- What are all the points of risk in securing a positive decision?
- What is the timeframe for delivery of outcomes, and what are the milestones?
- Concerning the selection criteria and weighting of various factors:
- Which features and functionality matters most to the buyer?
- What architecture and technology issues need to be considered?
- Where do they perceive the risks in the project or initiative?
- How important is brand and size in considering risk?
- How important to them is your experience and industry specialization?
- How is risk assessed and weighted, both commercial and technical?
- What role will demonstrations and references play and what will they look for?
- What is the required Return on Investment or payback period?
- Are they more focused on price or value?
- What are the preferences of the influencers and decision makers?
- What is their process for gaining approval to purchase, and who must sign-off?
- Who can say 'no'? Who has to say 'yes'? Who has power of veto?
- What is the process for handling negotiations?

- If a contract is required, whose paper and what advance information in needed?
- How do they generate a purchase order once the decision is made?

Process should always be aligned with strategy. The way a person thinks substantially determines their level of success, and in addition to strategy, personal leadership is what moves an individual from competence to greatness.

Personal Leadership

We are the way we are for reasons we never fully understand. Genes and our upbringing combine with our world view and beliefs to create our state of mind. We all have an innate and irrepressible need to protect our self-esteem, justifying our defects or limiting beliefs rather than engaging in the process of objective examination and beneficial change. As evidence of our inability to see the truth of our state, consider the fact that a camera captures a very different image compared with what we see in a mirror. We have all seen a video or photo of ourselves where we look grumpier or heavier than what we imagined. This is because the camera captures a third-party snapshot of how we really are rather than the filtered version we see in our own reflection.

The first step in overcoming any challenge is to face reality. In the context of leadership, we must first overcome the conundrum of the human condition which is prone to selfishness, short-sightedness, moral lapses and breathtaking stupidity. Beyond facing the awful truth, we also need to be intelligently self-aware (the dictum 'know thyself' is most often attributed to Socrates and embodies the concept of self-awareness which has today been enhanced within the concept of EQ – Emotional Quotient). Self-awareness combined with genuine humility is an essential part of being able to lead others and build teams that leverage strengths and compensate for weaknesses. Successful leaders value the opinions of others.

The very best leaders live by example and embody unbreakable determination in pursuing their cause, yet they do not bully or manipulate. Rather than create pressure they provide clarity, focus and energy for the people they lead. They focus on providing the right environment and ask the right questions rather than give answers. They are humbly self-aware, not self-absorbed, and they are honest, direct and accountable in their commitments and behavior. They understand that a good leader is first a good human being.

Much can be achieved when you don't care who gets the credit, and when you surrender the need to be constantly right. Leaders seek to understand before attempting to be understood. They understand that lasting motivation comes from within, and they therefore encourage their people to personally take ownership of outcomes. They build their people's self-esteem and promote their team's ideas by encouraging them to take calculated risks, stretching their capabilities. When things go wrong they provide support and do not lecture or punish. Neither do they rescue when the consequences are not catastrophic; instead they regard 'opportunities to fail' as useful. Later, without negative emotion, they facilitate reflection.

Great leaders are morally grounded in enduring values yet adopt purposeful pragmatism rather than judgmentally hold to narrow dogmas. They value difference, suspend judgment and accept diversity. Our ability to build other people in teams is more important than having all the ideas. Be counter-intuitive in your leadership style by humbly serving rather than grandstanding. Do what it takes rather than merely your best. You cannot lead from behind; pull people through rather than push. Accept the blame when things go wrong and learn the necessary lessons from criticism and failure so that you can adjust accordingly. Genuinely pass the credit onto others when things go well. Success is always a team effort.

Time is the only truly limited resource. Invest your time and treasure it, rather than spend it. There is no such thing as wasted time if you always have a good book with you when you travel. Do not allow the trivially urgent to prevent you from doing the important. Make time for what matters most. Set goals and priorities, and regularly measure your own progress.

Less is more – less talking creates more influence and more learning; less clutter and distracting noise creates more clarity; less information creates better cut-through in the message. The best way to improve something is to reduce it. Cut the unnecessary elements away rather than add complexity or overhead. The more we take the less we become; we only become greater when we give and contribute. We can become our very best when we let go of what we treasure and embrace the very things we fear. What does not kill us can make us stronger. Building character and developing emotional resilience is a valuable foundation for future success. Failure can educate, and with resolve to overcome, we can gain wisdom and prosper.

Happiness is a state of mind concerning how we perceive ourselves and our place in the world. Be grateful for what you have. Laugh as often as you can. Reject judgment, bitterness and revenge – they are self-destructive forces, devouring the host. Do not take yourself too seriously; instead have an optimistic attitude and positive sense of humor. Freely admit when you are wrong, and say 'sorry' and 'thank you' every chance you get. Forgive and move on. Be prepared to take risks but without foolhardy recklessness. Never be a victim; rather, be fully accountable for your own success and happiness. Do not blame others or bad luck for failure or set-backs. Believe in yourself and earn the right to ask for what you want. Never bully or manipulate and do not allow knowledge to manifest within you as arrogance. Do not allow success to make you egotistical; instead, learn genuine humility in acknowledging the contribution of others as well as good fortune or blessing.

Choose your friends and work environment wisely as both will change you through osmosis. Avoid those who are addicted to destructive gossip. Encouragement is far more effective than criticism – believe in the competent and help them become better. Expect the best of others and treat them with respect regardless of their station in life. Serve your employer and customers before your own interests – trust the law of reciprocity to reward your integrity and ability to create value. Show thoughtful initiative and a strong work ethic. We learn nothing while talking, and making a noise rarely makes a difference. Become a great listener, genuinely interested in others, asking insightful and powerful questions.

Success is living a life of purpose and achieving your goals, yet the passage of time is the only valid perspective for measuring achievement. There is no excuse for not being your best or failing to fulfill your potential. Barriers and difficulties are there to exclude average people, and for the purpose of ensuring the worthiness of those who achieve. Scarcity is what creates value. We all desire that our circumstances change but it is usually we who must change first. Become better rather than wish it were easier. Be the change you wish to see in the world – start with your own bedroom, garage, and backyard. You cannot manage an enterprise if you cannot manage yourself. Avoid gossip, criticism and judgment. There is genuine peace in not worrying about things that don't matter (inconsequential trivia) or are outside your control.

Knowledge and technical competence is not enough. Your value to your employer and customers is defined by your ability to positively influence and deliver results. Thinking strategically and executing masterfully is more important than adhering to methodologies. Think RSVP in every commercial endeavor and obsessively pay attention to excellence in execution.

Success or failure is the accumulated result of thousands of tiny decisions. Most people become disempowered through inner-corrosion rather than a catastrophic external event. Sustained success is the result of painful and diligent growth occurring below the surface, for the most part unseen by the outside world. Work on yourself rather than others. Self-awareness, self-discipline, self-leadership and positive attitude are what attract success beyond mere knowledge and skill.

Work is not different from the rest of life. Bring all of yourself to your work. Treat your sales career as a profession that creates value rather than being a competitive game. It has serious and profound lessons to teach if you are open to learning. Be the person worthy of the life you seek – success, failure, belief and doubt are all in the mirror if you can see beyond the façade.

Principles of Personal Success

Expectation: Every act and creative outcome begins as a thought. Although bad luck can occur, we generally receive in life what we expect. Expectations placed on another person can be an enormously positive or destructive influence. Expect the very best of yourself and others, and learn the lessons in every disappointment or challenge.

Focus: We see what we look for. We become and realize what we think about, whether good or bad. Setting goals creates awareness of opportunities when they present themselves. Choose what you focus upon deliberately and wisely. Have written goals with visual representations for creating emotional connections to what you want.

Reciprocity: Also known as the law of attraction. Be the difference you seek – change yourself to change your world and results. If you want better friends, you must first be a better friend. We attract what we radiate. Forgive others and don't keep score. Jealousy, envy, bitterness, and revenge all come back on us if we project these caustic emotions on to others. Work hard and be effective. Give and be generous with your time, energy and money. Be genuinely happy for others when they succeed.

Law of Diminishing Returns (Pareto Principle): 20% of activity yields 80% of the results. This immutable law was first articulated by Vilfredo Pareto and is often referred to as the 80:20 rule. It is to be observed by anyone seeking to operate efficiently and

effectively. Where should you focus your time, energy and resources for the greatest return? Be courageous in cutting away unproductive activities and relationships.

Law of Momentum: Positive momentum is difficult to create and easy to lose. Treasure it and pay attention to all the key metrics that ensure success. Be proactively consistent and avoid distractions.

Law of Self-interest: Regardless of what someone promises, people rarely act contrary to their own best interests. Understand their agendas and plan for them to act accordingly. Honor the law of self-interest when formulating strategy.

Law of Value: Scarcity creates value so embrace the difficult. Be unique in your ability to solve serious problems and achieve high value outcomes. Everything is worth what the market will pay, not what it costs plus a margin. Perceptions of value are defined by the buyer not the seller. Price is only one element of value and only matters if the buyer wants what you have to offer. Value = Benefit less Cost. Value for money is the buyer's weighted assessment of 'fit for purpose', risk and price.

The Journey

To be a good sales person, or to be a good manager, or to be a good leader –
first we must be a good human being, worthy of the success we seek. Read the
Desiderata by Max Ehrmann, written in the 1920s. A link is provided in the Epilogue
section of the RSVPselling.com website.

— End —

Acknowledgements

Successful writing and successful selling have much in common – you must transfer emotion rather than merely impart information. Thankyou to those who encouraged me to take a risk in telling a powerful story rather than to adopt an academic approach.

To my wife, Gail, who provided invaluable feedback and the freedom to invest time in this endeavor. Thank you so much for your love and support. To my father who believed in me and provided guidance, reflection and endless encouragement – I love you Dad.

Thanks to Matt Wills who coached me in writing and editing, teaching me to focus and cut away to create a business novel worthy of the reader's time and attention. To my editor, Catherine Bradshaw, a very special 'thank you' for your time, patience, creative energy and integrity in bringing out the best in the characters and story.

To the following people who contributed greatly to my journey throughout my professional life, I give you my sincere thanks. My father, Barry, for believing in me and providing the first opportunity to learn and succeed in the business world, nearly thirty years ago, and introducing me to the concept of mentoring. Joe Baker, for showing me the importance of the sales profession when I launched a business in the USA. John Lumb, for teaching me the value of a hard day's work. Keith Sutton, for teaching me about sales process and being a great sales manager when I first began in professional selling. Greg Newham, for teaching me about sales technique and positive attitude. John McInerney, for showing me how a leader creates the culture of an organization. Peter and Debbie Cox, for teaching me about myself and genuine leadership. David Thompson, for his insights on strategy. Anthony Howard, for being a great mentor through tough times. Richard Green and Brent Williams, for their inspiration and guidance in keeping me anchored to what really matters. Adrian Rudman for being so generous of spirit and assisting with bringing my dream to life on the internet. Thanks also to all those who extended their goodwill and invested their time, energy, wisdom and encouragement in working with me over the years.

Thanks also to my friends, family and associates who read this work during its evolution. Special thanks to Brian Periera and Anthony Howard for their valuable feedback and insightful analysis concerning the Value Quadrant for Professional Sales Agents.

Reading, more than anything else, has educated me and influenced my attitudes toward selling and leadership. The RSVPselling.com website has a bibliography of recommended authors and their work; but special mention to Neil Rackham, a pioneer and leader in applying science to the art of selling.

Most importantly, very special thanks to my wife Gail and my children who believe in me, love me unconditionally and constantly provide inspiration.